Julien Friedler

The Comedy Has Ended

Julien Friedler

È finita la Commedia

edited by Dominique Stella

SKIRA

Cover
Crucifixion, 2016

Design
Luigi Fiore

Editorial coordination
Eva Vanzella

Copy editor
Anna Albano

Layout
Fayçal Zaouali

Translations
Timothy Stroud for English
Silvia Denicolai for Italian

Photo credits
Vincent Everarts
Saverio Chiappalone
Emanuela Duranti

First published in Italy in 2022 by
Skira editore S.p.A.
Palazzo Casati Stampa
via Torino 61
20123 Milano
Italy
www.skira.net

© 2022 Julien Friedler for his texts
and images
© 2022 the authors for their texts
© 2022 Skira editore

Printed and bound in Italy.
First edition

ISBN: 978-88-572-4784-7

Distributed by Thames and Hudson
Ltd., 181A High Holborn, London
WC1V 7QX, United Kingdom.

Julien Friedler
È finita la Commedia

Venice, Church of San Samuele
23.04 – 25.09 2022

In conjunction with
59. Esposizione Internazionale d'Arte
Biennale di Venezia

Exhibition curated by
Dominique Stella

Production and organisation
CDStudio d'Arte, Padova: Carlo Silvestrin
www.cdstudiodarte.com

Architect
Carlo Della Mura

3D project
Mattia Fontanel

Communication and press release
Madagascar Communication:
Giada Chervatin, Anna Ferrarese

Transports
GIELLE Noleggio & Trasporti Srls
Berengo Mirko Trasporti

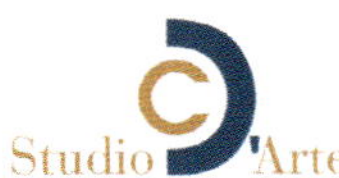

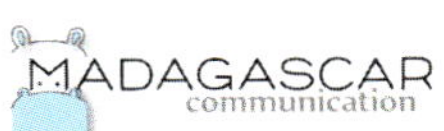

With the support of

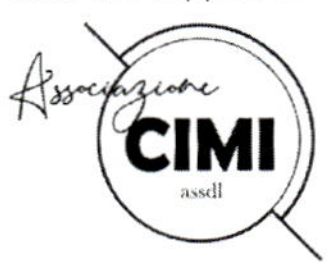

In collaboration with
Spirit of Boz

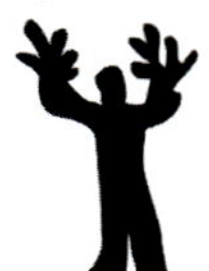

Contents

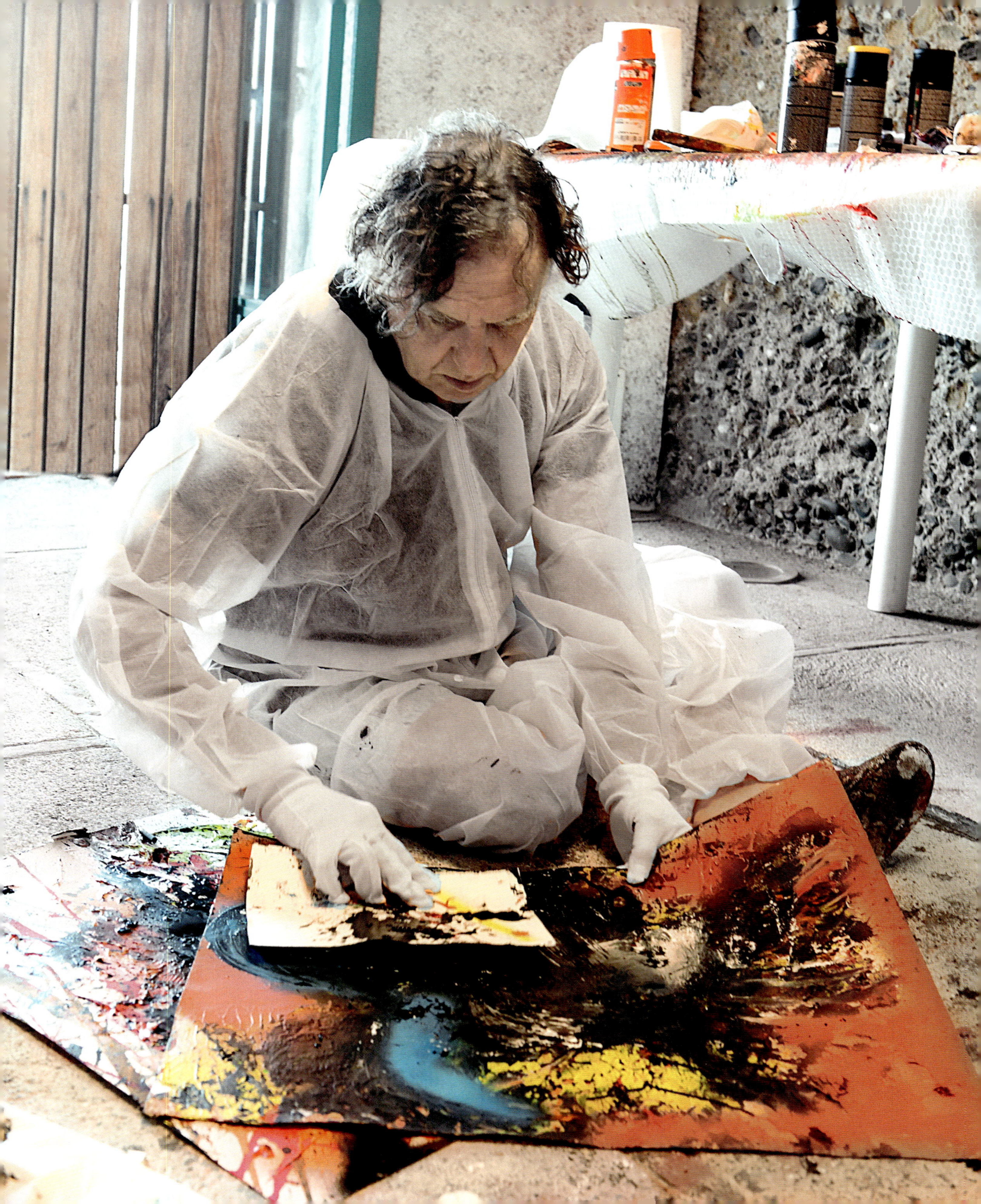

The Fundamentals – The Totalisation of the Sacred

Julien Friedler

It can never be said enough: the heart of *Spirit of Boz* will forever remain the inner life and its relationship to an enigmatic, elusive Creator, whose imaginary has been passed down through history. A Creator with many faces, who has existed since the origin, and who remains omnipresent in man's thought, in spite of His changes of form. From the age of cave-dwelling to the New Age, the same refrain has been repeated: an expression of the sacred — without this questioning — reworked, and put forward, so as to create a founding myth. Here, two conflicting views arise. One, a theological void, that never lets you go and condemns you to the abject, to be a piece of flesh abandoned in the Universe. The contrasting option assumes a subject, outside of matter, responsible for itself. A subject, modelled on the image of a hypothetical, but unavoidable Other. In this way, we can imagine a passing through to the other side of the mirror that takes the form of an encounter, a call, a feeling of strangeness, followed by an indefatigable search. For, in the end, how can we think of a modern spirituality that arises out of the present? On what basis can it be built? How can it be defined? As we have said to ourselves before, here there is a battle to be fought, and it will not always be a gentle one. In the end, our intuition is as follows: a massive return of the religious, sufficiently broad, powerful and all-pervading to overthrow our certainties and allow a completely new understanding to develop. With, as a horizon: a totalisation of the sacred, with a pacifying objective (pacifying because unified) and a globalisation of the spirit, open to all (not dogmatic, but rigorous). In this perspective, theological bridges will have to be built — consolidated by a sufficiently caustic, corrosive and hardened critique — to dust off the old reflexes. Other practices will have to be envisaged, in order to remedy the evil that is eating away at us (the self-hatred of the three monotheisms). In short, we will have to invent, create and imagine different approaches, other ways of thinking, surprising alternatives, in order to redraw a new and resolutely contemporary plan of 'spiritualities', one that is adapted to our lifestyles. From that moment on, it will be easier to understand our position. That of being a first draft, a test, a sketch for the future. Far removed from a pious wish or a utopia. Frightened by the fury of some, worried about the half-heartedness of others, our actions will have proceeded in fits and starts, with reversals and leaps forward, before slowing down so that we can refine our arguments. All this without ever losing sight of our goal: the inscription of the divine in a microcosm — *Spirit of Boz* — founded on universal principles. A microcosm conceived as a generator of ideas, a new way of seeing, feeling and acting. It is true that one can believe in doubt and have faith without knowing it. Reference will be made to a legend, an inspired quest, while the more refined among us will dream of an intangible Vision. A Vision of which we are the custodians. A Vision that will have dictated to us an atypical project, one that is destined to move, transform and metamorphose over time. We know its main resources: a book close to Judaism (*Le Livre du Boz*) and the *Forêt des âmes*, with Christian connotations (universality, egalitarianism, concern for our fellow human). Not to mention a forthcoming installation currently in progress: *La Vache rousse* (or *Djihad*). This will borrow its 'modus operandi' from Islam — in a gradual approach to the Eternal. And without forgetting a whole world of archaic and haunted images that suggest trance and its medium, the shaman. And without forgetting the goal of the entire operation: to generate a 'soul supplement' whose amplification, working-through and lived experience will aim at the only thing that is worthwhile: an inner soothing, by distancing ourselves from our passions. Our true ideal.

Julien Friedler in his studio, 2020

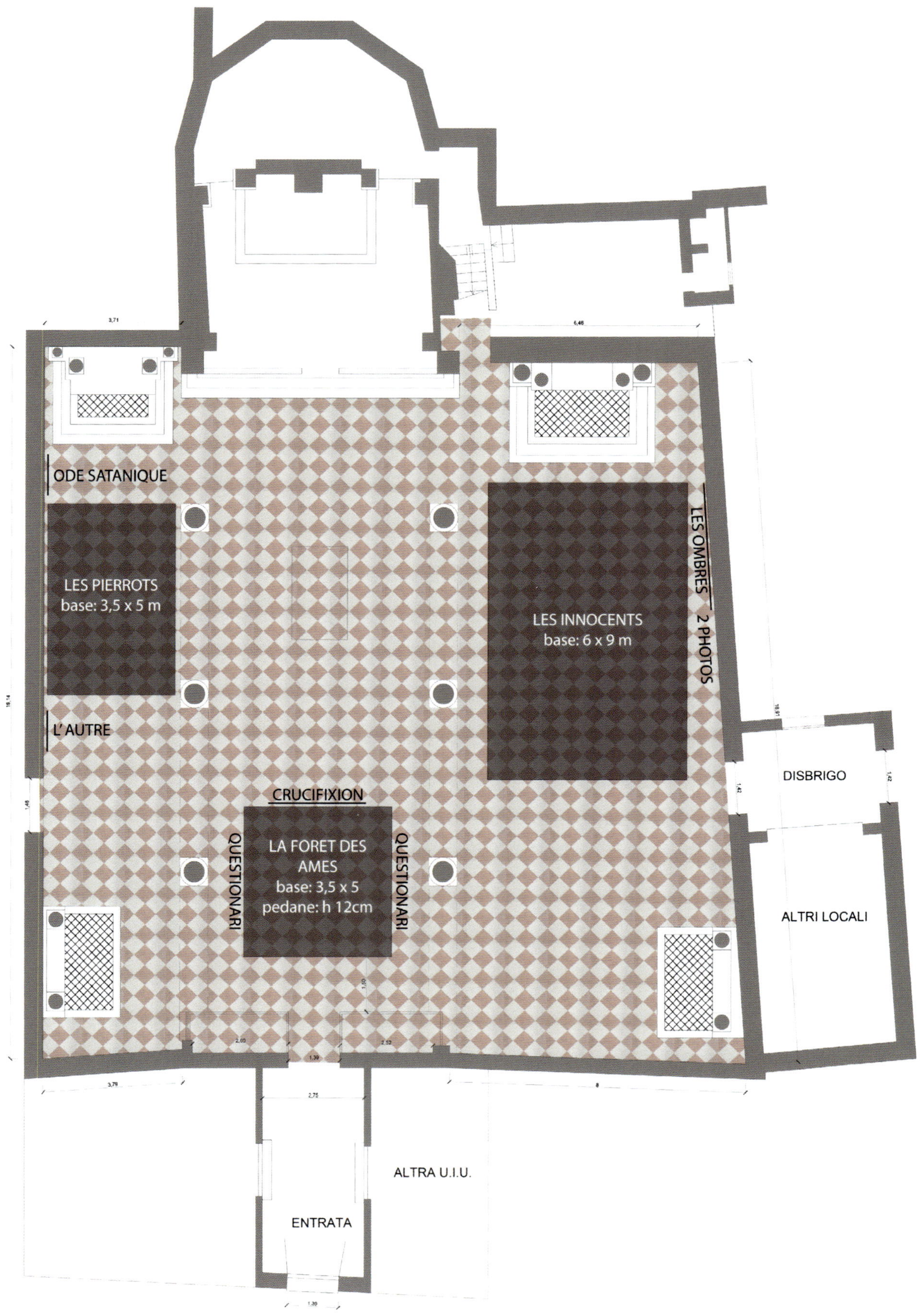

ODE SATANIQUE
LES PIERROTS
base: 3,5 x 5 m
L'AUTRE
LES INNOCENTS
base: 6 x 9 m
LES OMBRES
2 PHOTOS
DISBRIGO
CRUCIFIXION
QUESTIONARI
LA FORET DES AMES
base: 3,5 x 5
pedane: h 12cm
QUESTIONARI
ALTRI LOCALI
ALTRA U.I.U.
ENTRATA

È finita la Commedia

Dominique Stella

Titled *È finita la Commedia*, Julien Friedler's project takes as its subject the dramatic realities by which our lives are governed. He invites us to consider the human comedy in three acts, each represented by an installation, in an evocation rather than a critique of the world's pretences, the meanderings of history and the cynicism that together dominate our society. It is not by chance that his project is presented in the Church of San Samuele. The building is a place of meditation, prayer, gathering, celebration and mystery; it is also the place of an inner search, one that leads us to a higher questioning. Julien Friedler's works address all these themes in a search that invites each of us not just to discover ourselves, but also to become aware of the Other. Friedler wishes to touch people in their innermost being, and in their understanding of sacredness, the meaning of life and their belonging to the human community with their doubts, joys and sorrows, thereby connecting with certain teachings of the Church. It is for this reason that this sacred building is essential to the artist's project and a determining element. Entering San Samuele naturally induces meditative introspection, contemplation and spiritual elevation that are encouraged by the building's verticality and emphasised by the installation of the works around the church's spatial development. This presentation to harmonise with the structure of the place makes San Samuele an integral part of Julien Friedler's concept. The title of the project reflects the seriousness of the contemporary moment and invites us to resort to precepts that are more enduring than those endorsed by our time. A church is the ideal space to encourage us to reflect on our world, even without religious faith, but with the certainty that something must be saved, and Friedler accompanies us in this conviction through his works. *È finita la Commedia…*

Contemporary realities take form in an imaginary world that underlines the darkest aspects of the human soul without condemning it to damnation, but by questioning each of us, and inviting us to make use of contemplation and meditation to draw the strength necessary for regeneration. There is no levity in Friedler's works, as the title of the exhibition indicates: *È finita la Commedia*, no more laughing or singing, 'we're moving on to serious things', Friedler seems to be saying, 'let us consider our fate'.

It is this that lies at the heart of the artist's work: for him the primary concern is forever our 'inner life and its relationship with an expression of the sacred, with our enigmatic and many-faced Creator, that comes into being with our birth, and remains omnipresent in our thinking, despite our changes of form'. There is therefore a spiritual, almost mystical dimension in these works, but also a melancholic relationship with existence, and, in the three parts of the exhibition, Friedler confronts Man with the three experiences of life: Pain, Melancholy and Hope, sources that encourage reflection on the world. The three installations incite this meditation.

The layout of the exhibition is matched with the three major elements of the plan of the church: the nave, the aisles and the choir. Each of the installations' themes complements the other two, and the three of them together offer a meditative pause on the meaning of life, death and possible redemption.

First, violence, seen in the installation *Les Innocents*, illustrates the pain of spurned innocence, but also confinement, isolation and rebellion. The installation reminds us of the incomparable dignity of every child, even as the massacre of the Innocents is repeated every day. Their suffering assails

The project *È finita la Commedia* inside the Church of San Samuele, Venice, 2022

our insensitive, even anaesthetised consciences. The issue at heart is not of pity for them but of questioning ourselves and changing our attitude and involvement. The artist illustrates the notions of forced separation, division, fragility, and death in a symbolic form of desperate intensity, which, despite its radicality, is meant to be a source of reassurance and hope. The installation unites individual memory (the artist's own and his childhood memories) and collective memory, inviting us to reflect deeply on our culture, with its illusions and disenchantments, but also on the possibility of survival.

The Melancholy of the *Pierrots* corresponds to the Innocence of childhood. A naive and dreamy figure, Friedler presents him to us with the sad and nostalgic appearance of Verlaine's Pierrot:

> 'He is no longer the moonstruck dreamer of the song of yore
> Who mocked the ancestors in the over doors;
> His gaiety, like his candle, alas! is dead.
> And his spectre haunts us now, thin and clear.'

Both the poet and artist resurrect the originally cheerful and whimsical character — but in spectral form. This comedy figure with his traditional costume and lunar face that used to enchant both young and old, now looks sad. Friedler offers us the image of a gaunt creature, a revenant in the form of a robotic skeleton. All that remains of this lifeless body is a sad and disenchanted glint in his eyes that expresses regret for times past, a dream of happiness lost. This chilling evocation of our time suggests the mutation occurring in society, which affects our vision of the world and our own bodies, and that Friedler illustrates by the wandering of these disembodied souls on the fringes of Hades, like shadows in search of salvation. There is a multitude of them, all similar, a reduction of the human to a controlled and desensitised mass, not unlike Thomas Schütte's *Efficiency Men*.

La Forêt des âmes is an uplifting work that evokes the elevation of the spirit in which the artist offers a message of hope and renewal. Suggesting luminous souls that do not embody the Divine, but a positive-energy Consciousness that invites us all to experience a moment of meditation and reflection, this work attempts to convey what the artist calls 'a soul supplement', a moment of sharing and forgetting of the self so that we might become part of a collective process. Friedler describes this installation as being 'inspired by Christianity', as it conveys the principles of 'universality, egalitarianism and concern for one's neighbour'. His aim is to transcend the material and visual to elicit the most subtle and invisible connections, and thus conduct an inquiry of a psychic, philosophical and even religious nature.

The three installations belong to a single narrative somewhere between drama and salvation. Interspersed with paintings and photographs, the works fill the space of the church in three parts.

- Right aisle: *Les Innocents* (2000)
- Left aisle: *Les Pierrots* (2019)
- Nave: *La Forêt des âmes* (2009)

The paintings presented with the installations heighten the dramatic nature of the setting. These works are *L'Autre* (2018), *Ode Satanique* (2018) and *Crucifixion* (2016). In addition, there are two photographs titled *Les Ombres, barbelés* (2002), which are an integral part of the installation *Les Innocents*.

The three installations of *È finita la Commedia* reflect Julien Friedler's artistic universe and attest the diversity of his inspiration, yet they are linked by the creative philosophy that presides over his entire oeuvre, in which each production, whether installation, painting or performance, falls within the framework of a larger story, a 'legend', as Friedler calls it. This legend encompasses all the artistic actions he has completed and continues to perform — an expanding world that he calls *Spirit of Boz*. Friedler's world features such characters as Jack Balance and includes action programmes in which paintings, installations, performances and meetings are the elements that activate his imaginative universe. *Les Innocents* marked the beginnings of this teeming imaginary that strongly affects the spirit, *La Forêt des âmes* is its vehicle, which allows us to reach out to others, and the *Pierrots* are its melancholic image, a reflection on the fate of humanity.

This Belgian artist is permeated by a humanist vision that he defines through his works but also in a programme of sharing he directs as part of *Spirit of Boz*, an association founded with the purpose of establishing — through oral, literary, pictorial and creative expression in general — exchanges and links to create a community from different cultural backgrounds around the world, to which each member has contributed personal reflections and accounts of individual and collective realities. This programme is Friedler's response to the urgent need to reconcile action and thought with the goal of diffusing a humanistic and cathartic philosophy. His constantly evolving universe has contrasting facets, one based on collective inspiration (*La Forêt des âmes*), the other (the *Pierrots* and the paintings) on personal reflection.

Friedler's art provokes sensations, relationships and analyses and is conceived as an operation that brings together all forms of expression, whether stemming from his own experiences or those of others. His work is therefore multi-faceted and encompasses a variety of fields, from literature to philosophy, sociological analysis and the visual arts (painting, sculpture, installations). His pictorial production is generated by a creative need, the desire for spontaneous, instinctive transmission arising from the 'attempt to discover what constitutes the passionate essence of beings'. Friedler moves forward in an almost hypnotic manner, unconstrained by subject matter or materials, defining a rhythm, an informal mode of expression. His boundless energy stems from a capacity for dissociation and introspection that he applies to himself before turning his attention to others, to discover their most personal motivations: in short, it is a journey to discover the human soul in its atavistic and universal complexity.

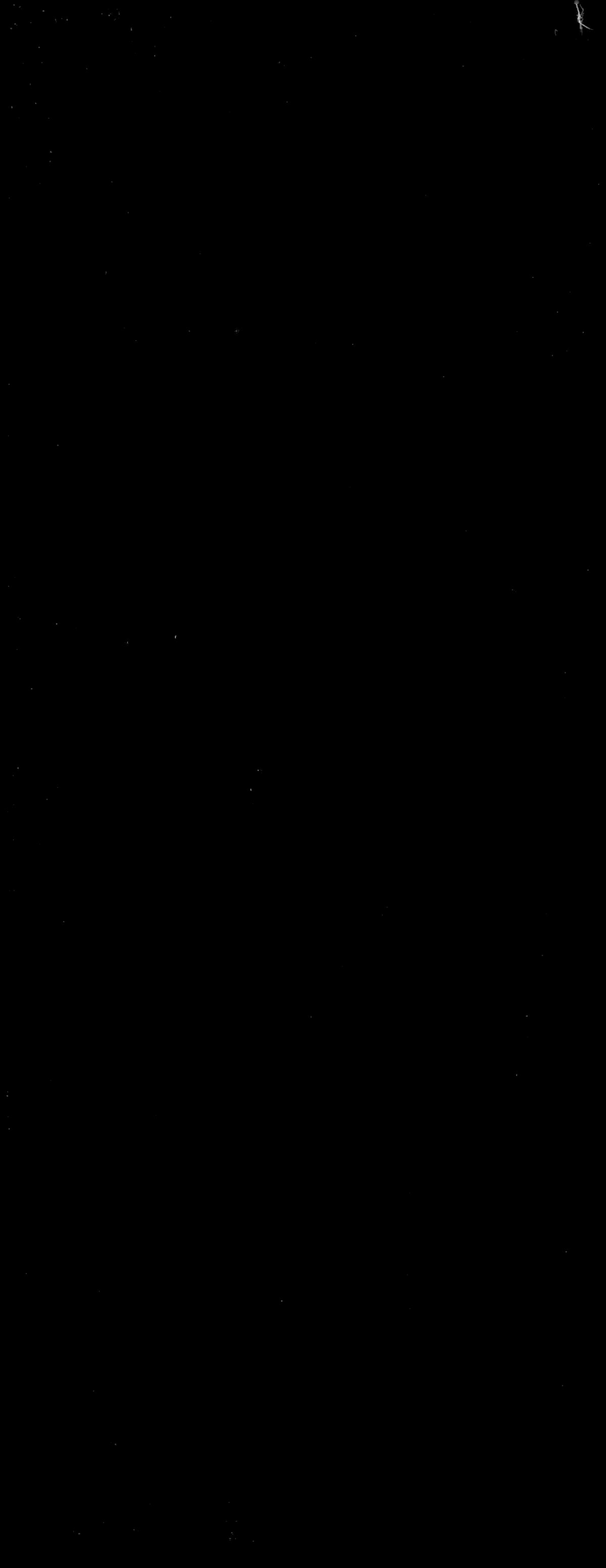

Works

Les Innocents, 2000

Barbed wire, stuffed toys, school benches and mixed media
original installation 9 x 11 m

The installation *Les Innocents* is a metaphorical representation of the intimate wound of the world, born of a constrained childhood, enclosed — as the philosopher Pierre Bourdieu describes it — in 'a terrible school of social realism, where everything is already present, through the necessities of the struggle for life: opportunism, servility, denunciation', and bearing witness to the bloody origin of life. In the course of its development, this monumental work took on the characteristics of a concentration camp, in which the symbol of a violated and abused childhood is combined with a reference to the martyrdom of the Jewish people. Unlike the paintings, which are the result of immediate, spontaneous expression, creation of the installation took place over several months, and thus involved greater awareness, and a more determined elaboration and creative will. However, Julien Friedler does not see in it the work of a conscious will, nor the desire to make a comment or remind us of the fate of the Jewish people… For him, it represents the universality of the suffering that has always been reproduced and repeated in the madness and violence of mankind. It is an expiatory gesture in which the artist invests his own powers of redemption.

'There's barbed wire, stuffed toys and school benches that together create a certainly tragic but also jocular scene. I have used a vocabulary of extremes, there's the Shoah, of course, but also a metaphor of an imprisoned childhood, of all those children in the world who are killed or injured in their innocence'. The installation *Les Innocents* is a powerful illustration of forms of suffering: pain, confinement, isolation, rebellion, experienced by the character Jack Balance. He — a special character in Friedler's universe — occupies the centre of the installation. He is like the artist's twin or duplicate, a symbol of the difficulty of being and of freeing oneself from human contingencies. Jack Balance is locked in a cage from which he escapes to travel the world. In order to exist, he has to constantly cheat, protest and rebel. The cage is illustrative of his personal situation but also has a universal symbolism. Jack Balance is a frustrated but humorous and cheeky clown whose regret is that he is a character and not a human being. He engages in a battle that the artist could not face without the fiction of this mask, yet the character's presence is virtual. His existence is given material form by a photograph. A chair, scattered stuffed toys, a plastic skeleton, and mobile phones that link him to his Creator are all invisible attachments that keep him in a state of addiction. A sign says: 'They call me Jack Balance'. It was around this character that the installation *Les Innocents* was developed.

The work also exemplifies the artist's personal journey, his own difficulty in living, his aspiration to go beyond the limits imposed by nature, and his fundamental questioning of the enigma of life and the divine. The work is also cathartic and emotionally purifying, a function that Friedler achieves by relating his own story and feelings, which he offers as the genesis of this universal work.

The artist's questioning of the world is omnipresent. As Friedler says in *La Vérité du Labyrinthe* (Text #22): 'A world often steeped in blood and hatred. The divine dissected, shattered, suffering. A war unceasingly taken up and replayed. For all the divines are in God, the ersatz of our dreams. None is better or more just. Or truer. Or more beautiful. Or more human. Or more powerful. At best, they will give us the idea of another man-made fresco to console ourselves with.

A fresco that converges, becomes reduced and concentrated in a single point. A point called upon to overcome itself. Had we not already evoked a pure Spirit, a beyond, an inconceivable void? In this case, aesthetics cannot fail to appeal to us. Perhaps this is a first clue? For such a display calls for an inhuman gaze that owes nothing to aliens or other extra-terrestrials. Besides, aren't they already caught in our nets: a legend of the divine created by our imaginations?'

Photographs: the installation's accompanying photographs are the shadows of this martyred humanity, everywhere and at all times.

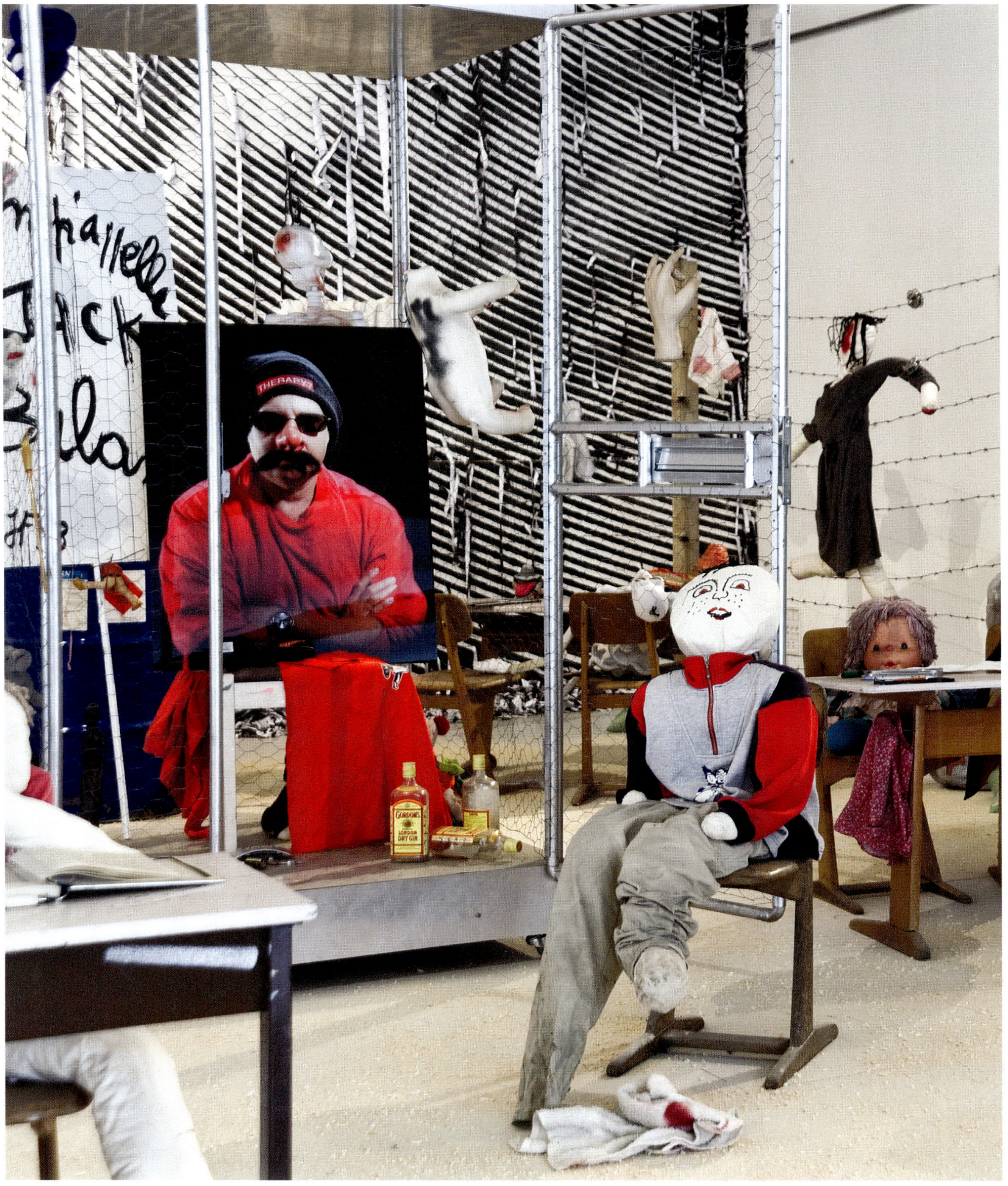

THERAPY?
GORDON'S
LONDON
DRY GIN
JACK

Les Innocents, 2000
Barbed wire, stuffed toys, school
benches and mixed media, original
installation 9 x 11 m

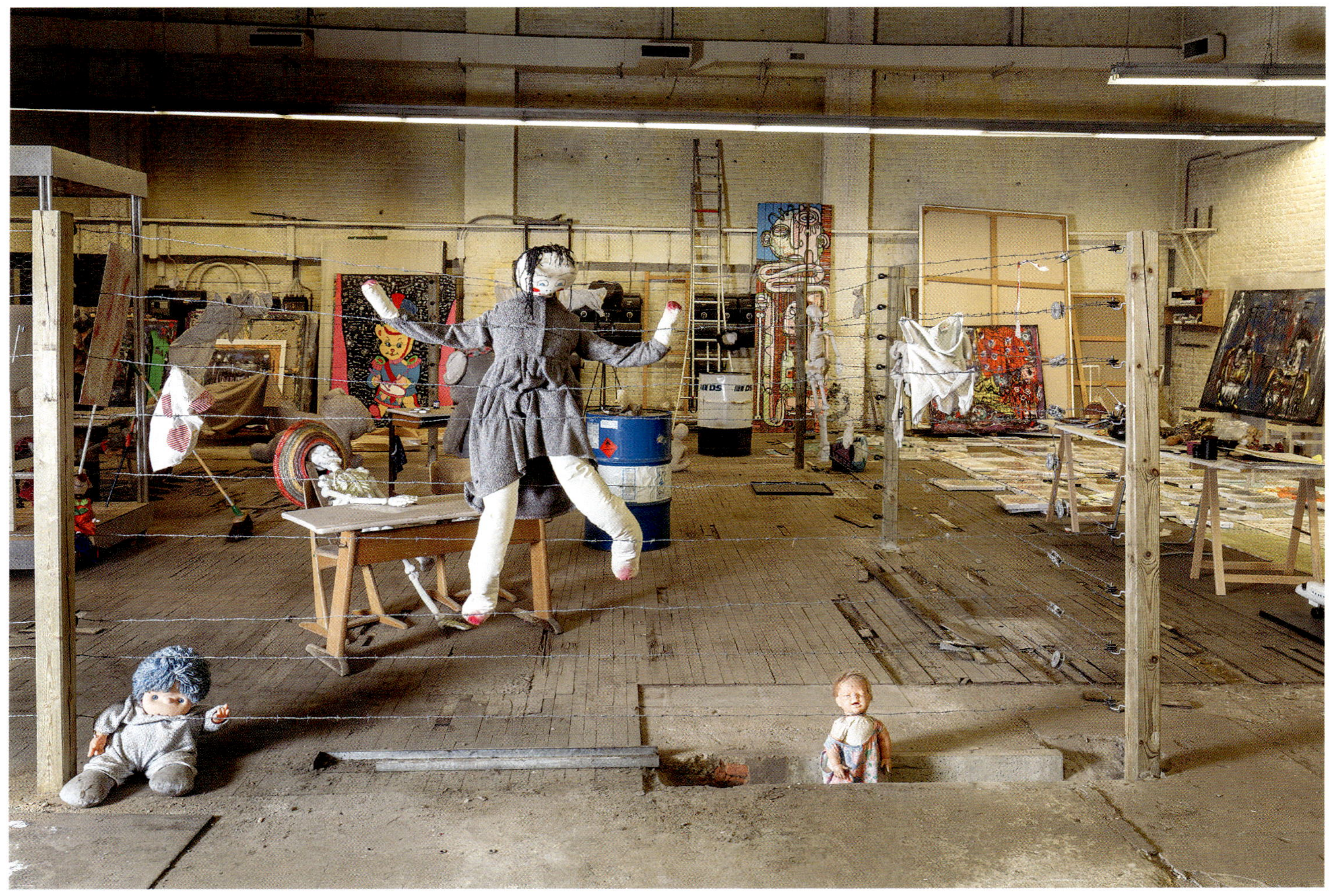

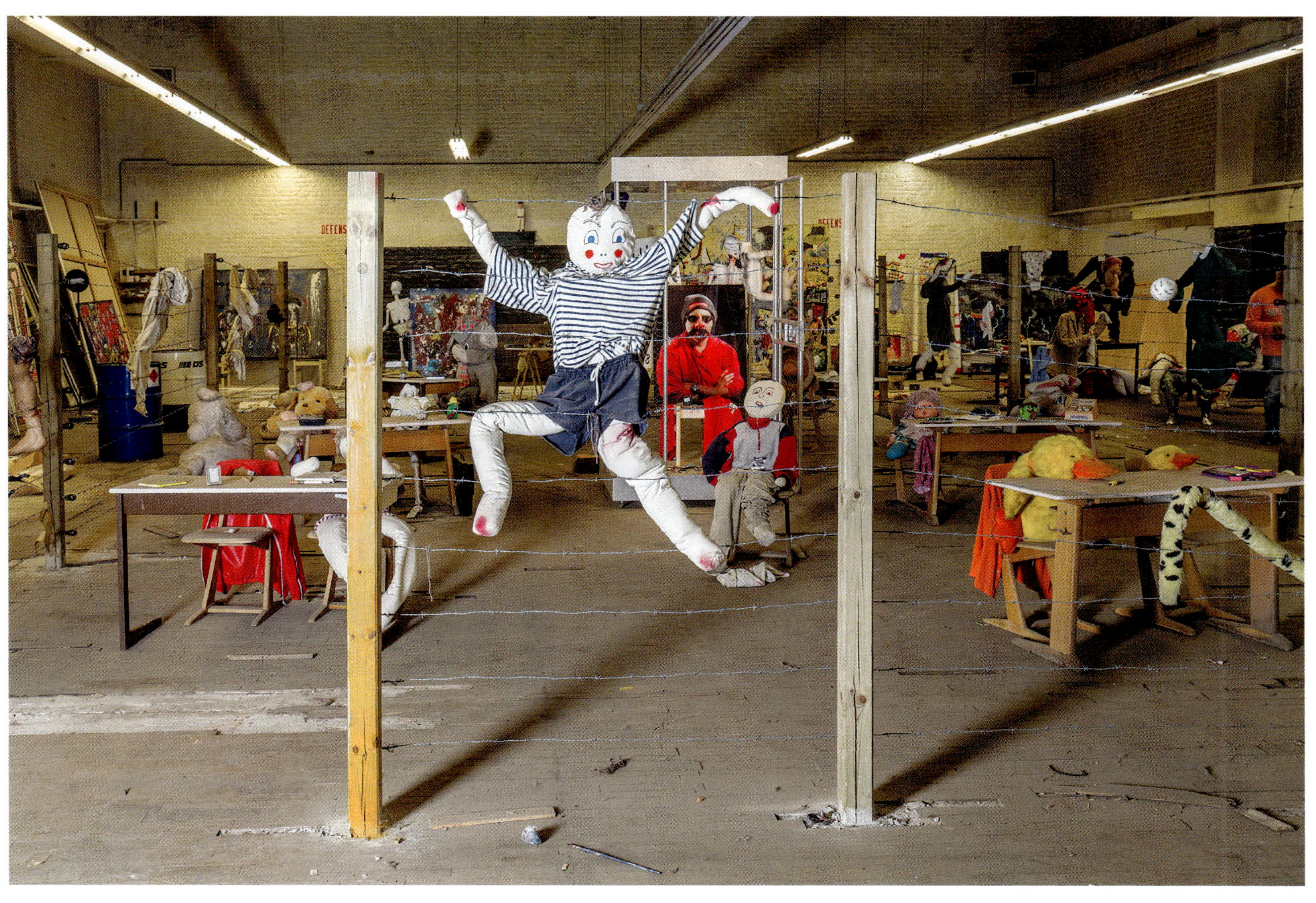

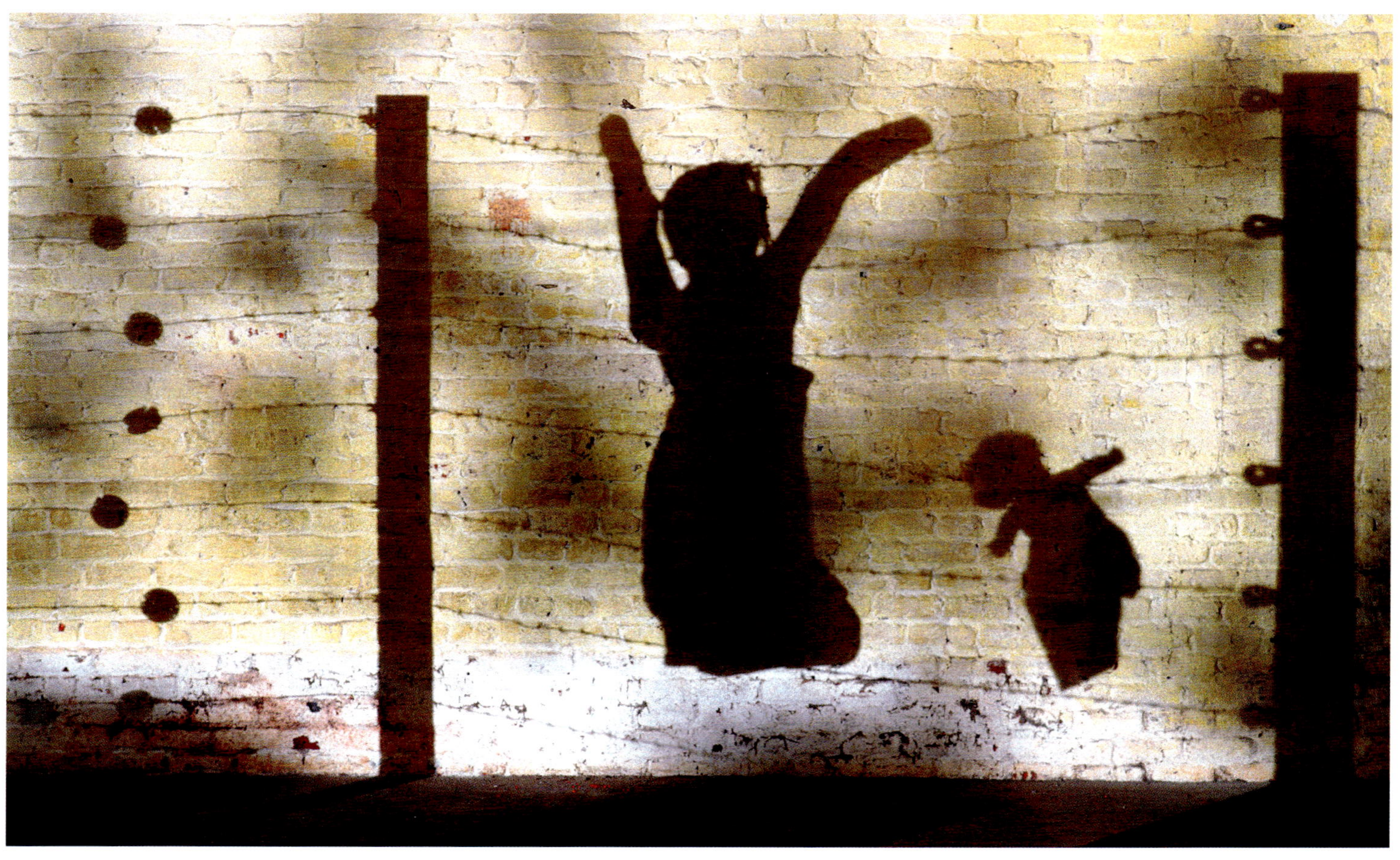

Les Ombres, barbelés, 2002
Photo on aluminium,
120 x 200 cm

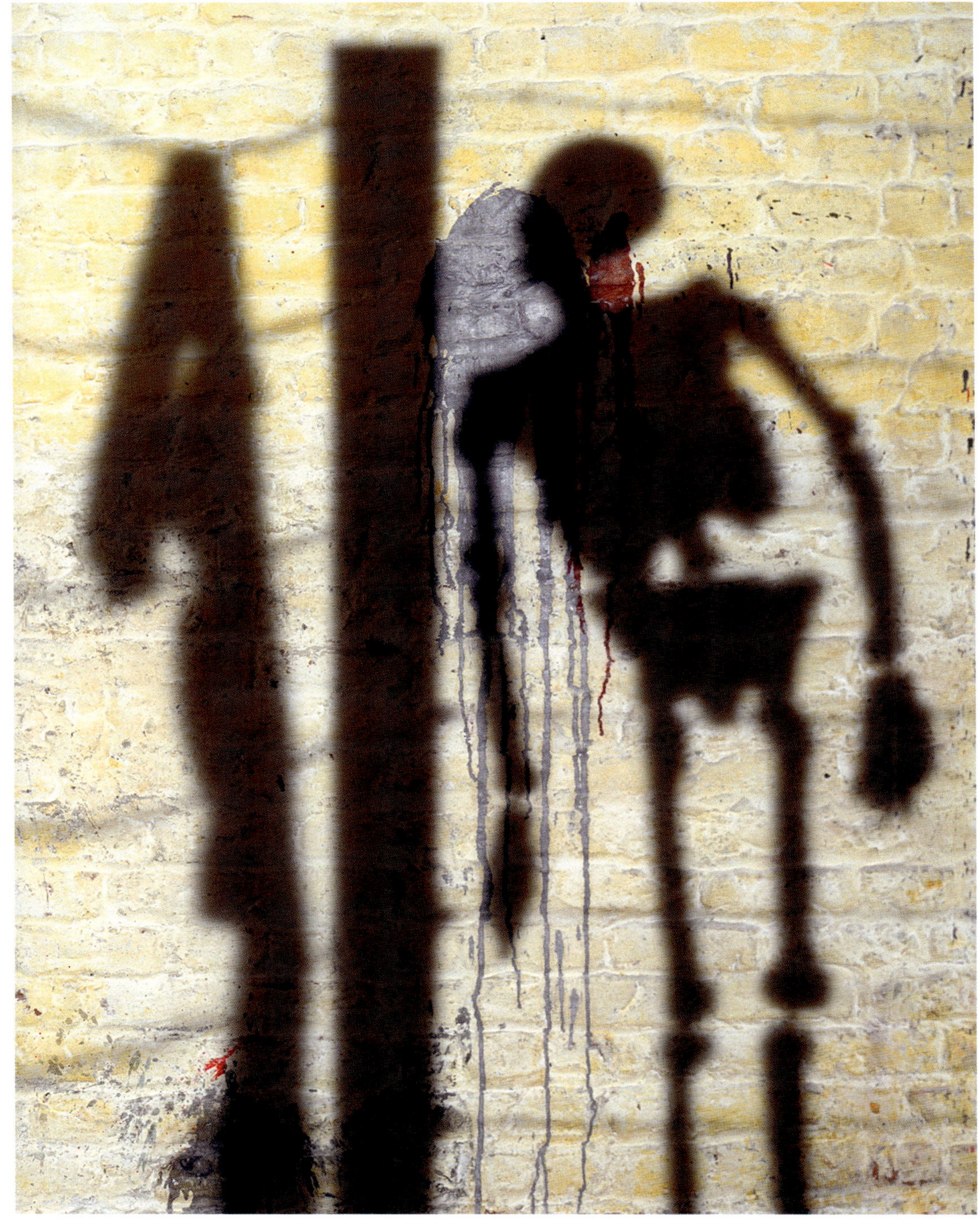

Les Ombres, barbelés, Squelette, 2002
Photo on aluminium,
150 x 120 cm

La Forêt des âmes, 2009

9 columns, wood, resin masks and LED lights
each column h c. 2 m

The light of hope and sharing of the universality of the
artistic message through the concept of *La Forêt des âmes*.

The association *Spirit of Boz – Julien Friedler* is the means
through which the artist intends to carry out an action for 80
years, a period that will outlast his own life. The association
oversees a programme called *Be Boz Be Art* that operates
using different forms of intervention and introduces new artistic
practices to areas of the world with the purpose of giving them
visibility. *La Forêt des âmes* is part of this programme. *Spirit of
Boz* is a vehicle for exchange and interaction for the benefit of all,
and has been well received in the remotest of communities. The
Be Boz Be Art project is based on three programmes that entail
multiple talents and daily realities very different from our own. The
discovery of and familiarisation with these realities — in mutual
respect — enrich the diversity of expression and transmission, and
thus engender opportunities for exchange.
Sometimes artistic awareness can be found in situations of
the greatest indigence and apparent ignorance, realised in the
expression of a few words of purest poetry, the drawing of a few
lines, or the mixing of colours, suggesting that art is a driving
force that leads to the revelation of possibilities. It is with this
awareness and conviction that the *Spirit of Boz* association
engages in participative actions that entail the involvement of
people from the most diverse social origins and most remote
geographical areas. These actions are based on the criteria set
out in the *Give up* programme, which has the aim of collecting
spontaneously created works during trips made by the *Boz*
team (Rwanda, Togo, Mexico, and so forth) to meet cultures and
traditions that are often unknown elsewhere. The team collects
objects of everyday use or original creations, often of a tribal
nature, from those people who wish to contribute to the project.
Through this project, Friedler's aim is to collect these signs
arising from the unconscious, which he likes to explore and
whose meanderings he follows by means of the third *Be Boz
Be Art* programme, called *La Forêt des âmes*. This programme is
based on a printed questionnaire, to which the answers, which
are carefully collected and preserved, form the substance of
the work. The questionnaires with their answers will be packed
in boxes that will themselves be stacked in columns, with each
column representing a tree. The growing number of trees will in
turn create a forest — a forest of souls. This forest of souls is first
and foremost a movement, a motion towards the Other as well
as towards the Self, a work of art that develops, in the course
of the exchanges, into a true concentration of convergence.
The installation of nine columns is the precursor of this forest.

Questionnaire of *La Forêt des âmes* - *Le Tour du Boz en 80 ans*
La Forêt des âmes asks for answers to six questions

1. Does God exist?
2. How would you describe this epoch?
3. How do you see the future?
4. Are you happy?
5. Is sexuality important?
6. Who am I?

The questions may appear banal but they all lie at the heart of
our social construction and form the core of existential issues
that determine how our cultures develop. The *Spirit of Boz* team
travels to the four corners of the world to distribute and collect
these questionnaires. From Togo to the Amazon, the United
States, Indonesia, Rwanda, Argentina, Belgium, Indonesia and
Tibet, *La Forêt des âmes* is marked by unexpected encounters
and discoveries. Begun in 2006, the project is due to run over
a period that contradicts our current conception of time: the
Tour du Boz is planned to continue for 80 years. The purpose
of the questionnaire is to encourage encounters. More than
75,000 questionnaires have already been collected, and at each
presentation of the installation, the public is invited to fill one in.

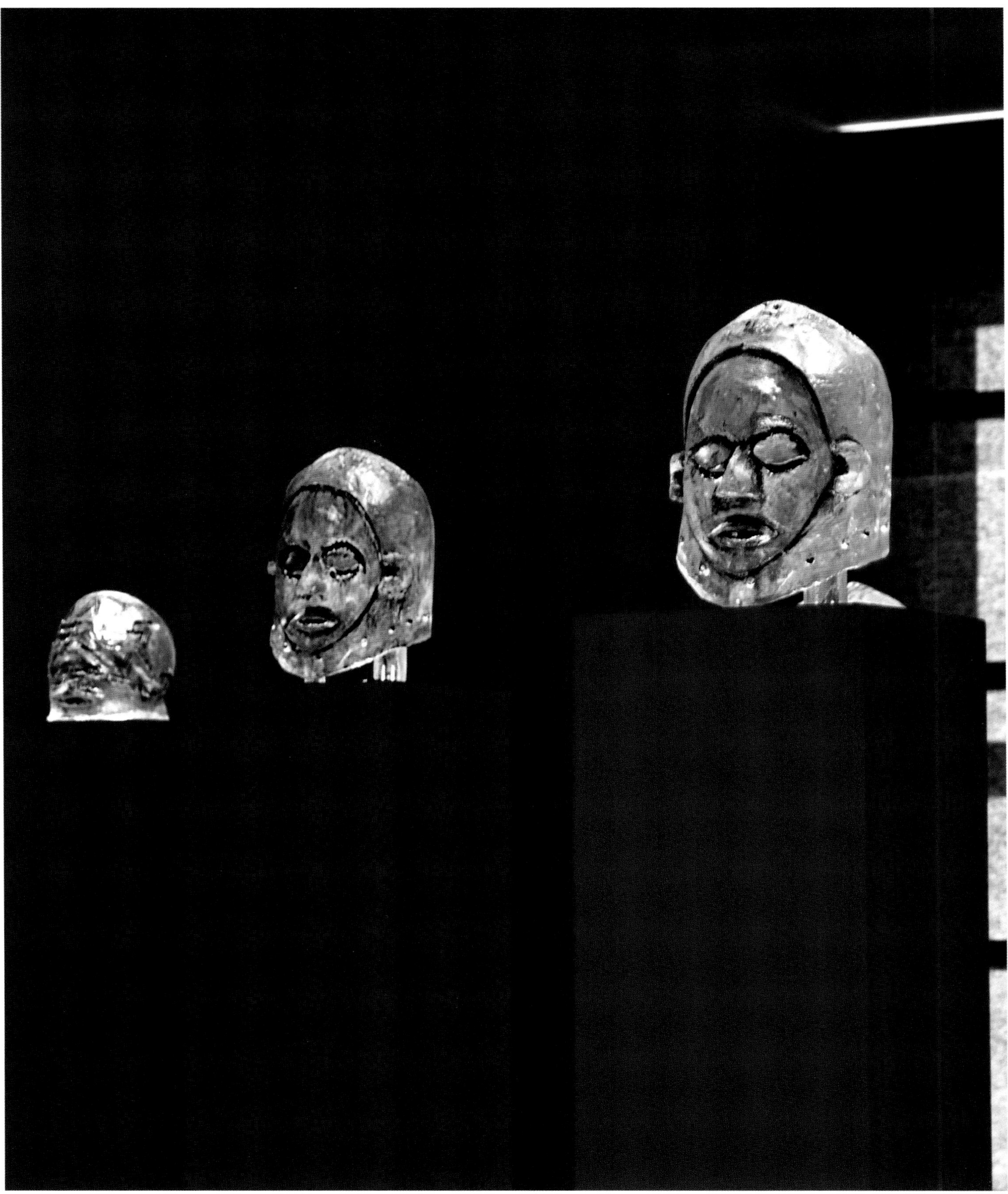

La Forêt des âmes, 2009
9 columns, wood, resin masks
and LED lights,
each column h c. 2 m

The installation La Forêt des âmes,
2009, in the Belfry of the
Saint-Germain l'Auxerrois
church, Paris, 2020

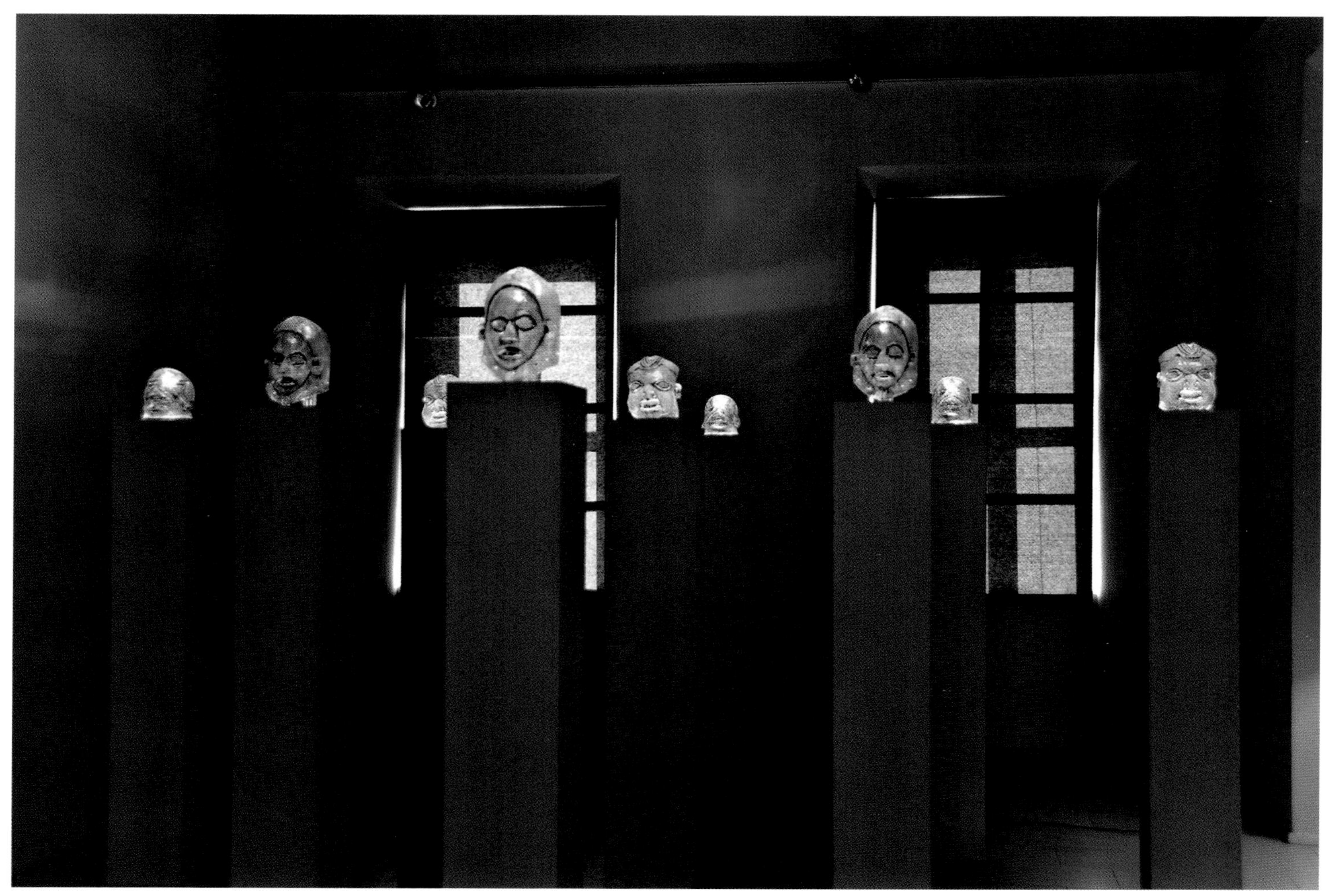

pp. 26–27
Questionnaires of La Forêt
des âmes - Le Tour du Boz en 80
ans
Mixed media on paper,
c. 21 x 27.7 cm

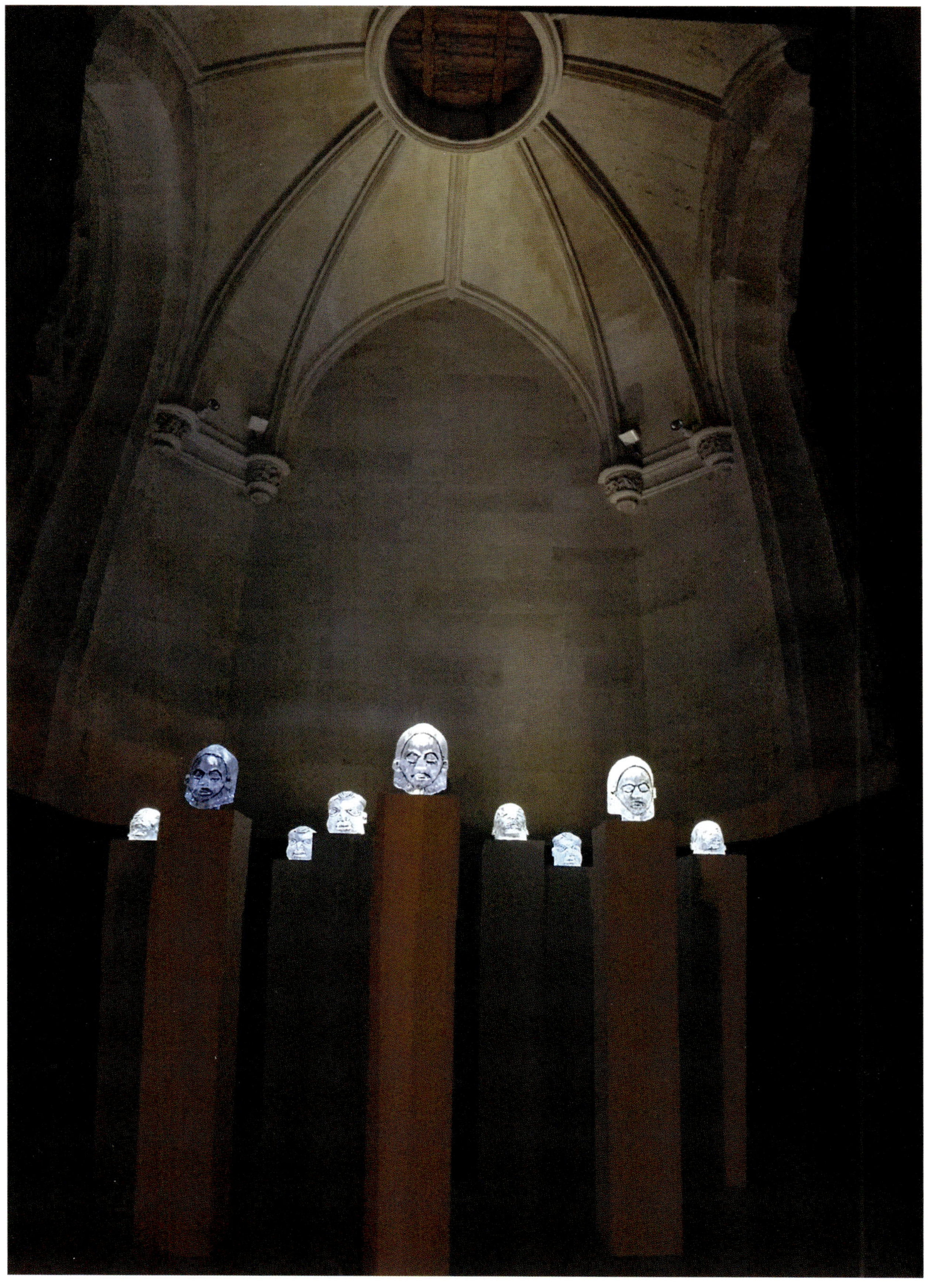

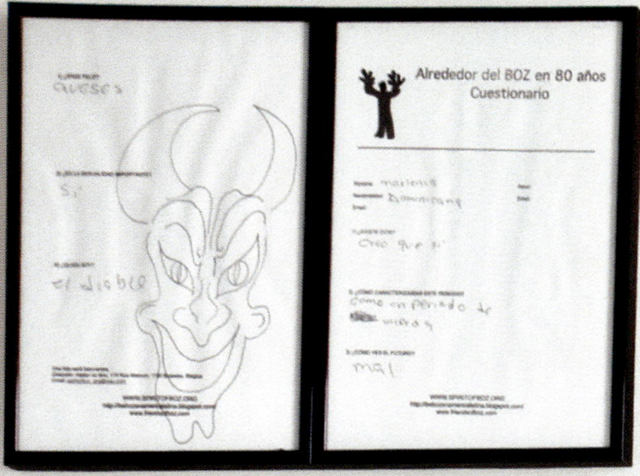
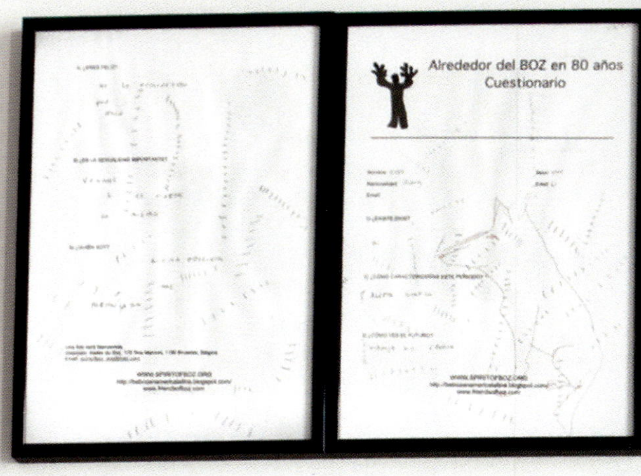
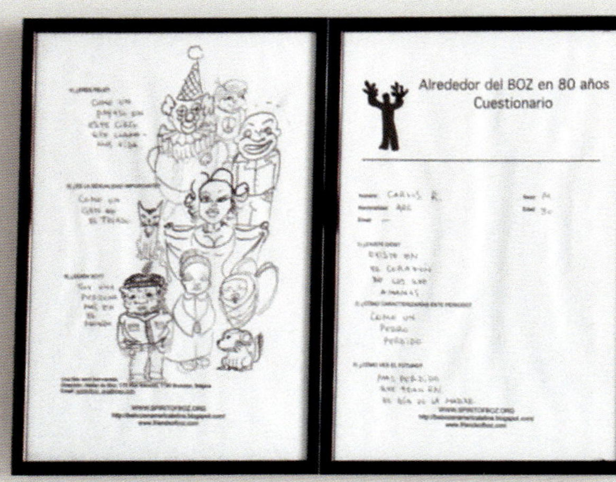
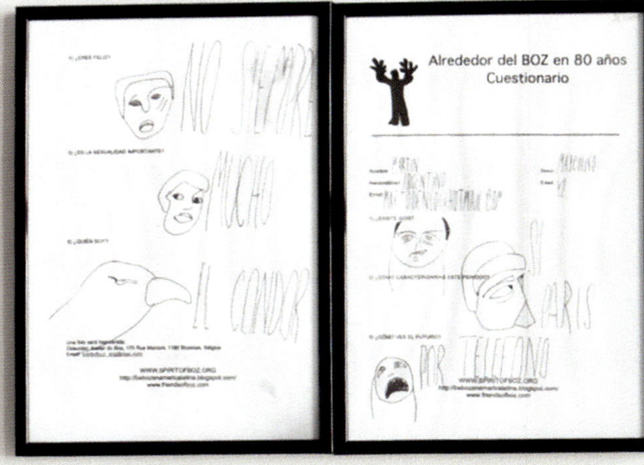
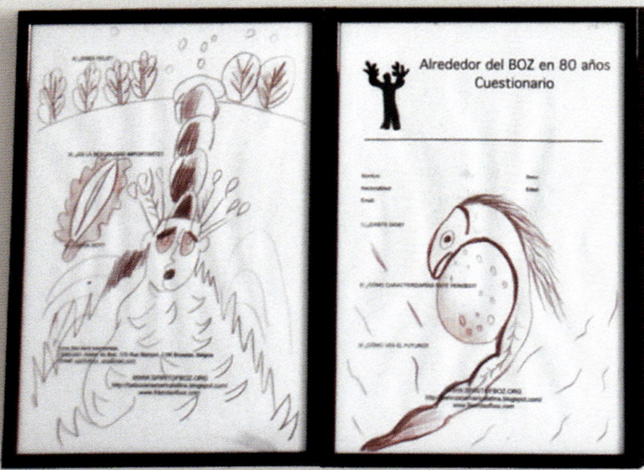
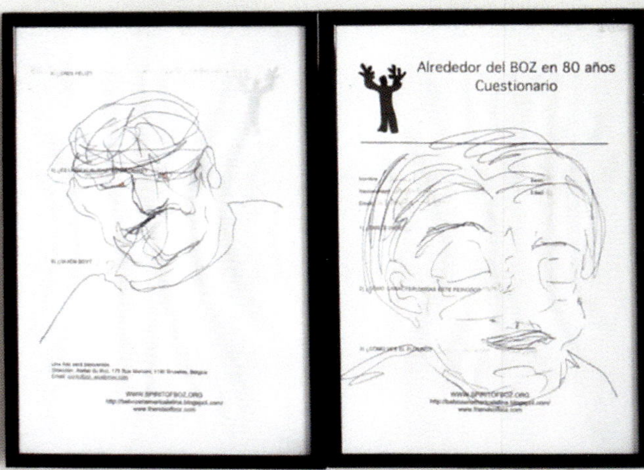

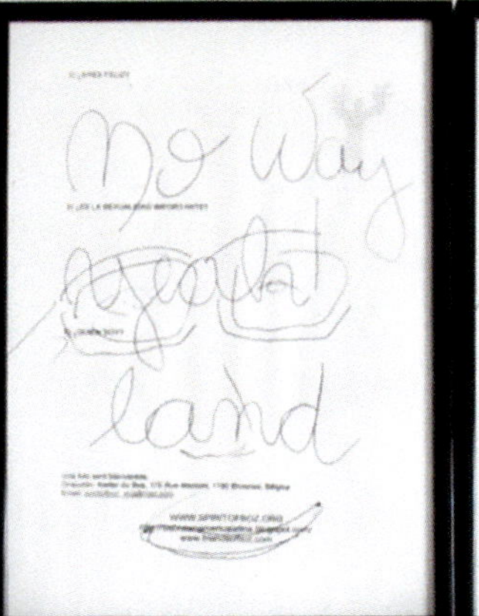
No Way
land

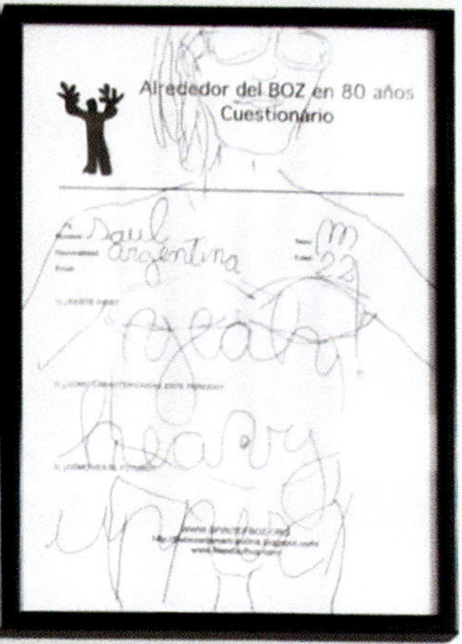
Alrededor del BOZ en 80 años
Cuestionario
argentina

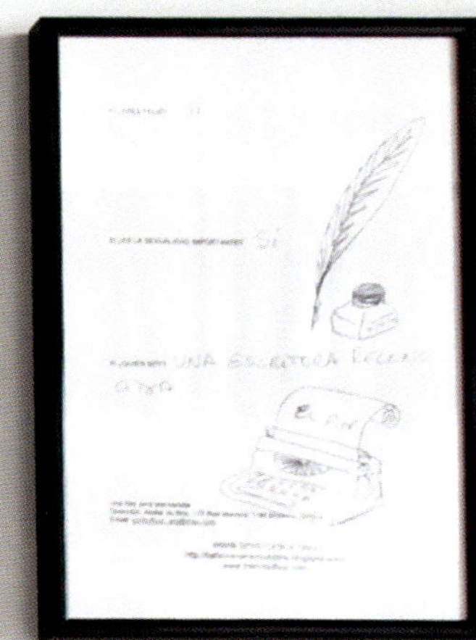

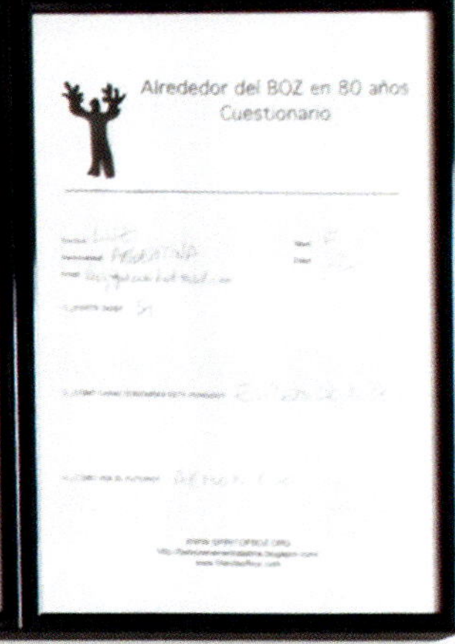
Alrededor del BOZ en 80 años
Cuestionario

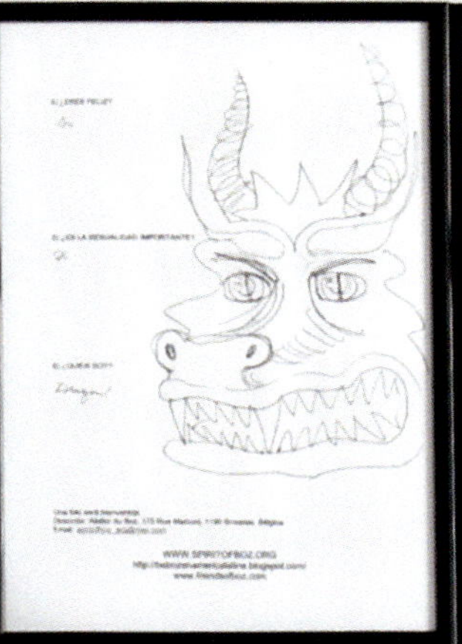

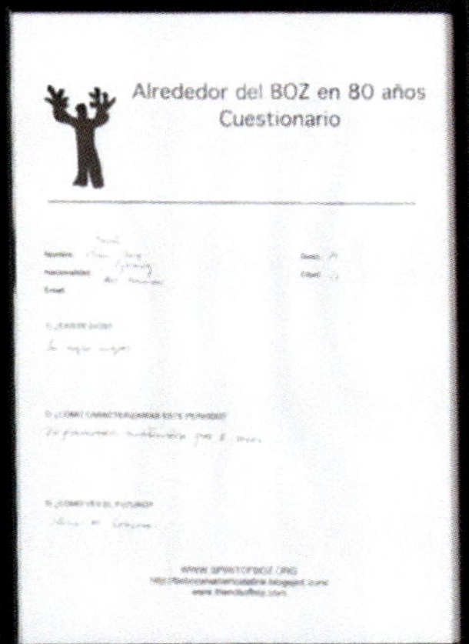
Alrededor del BOZ en 80 años
Cuestionario

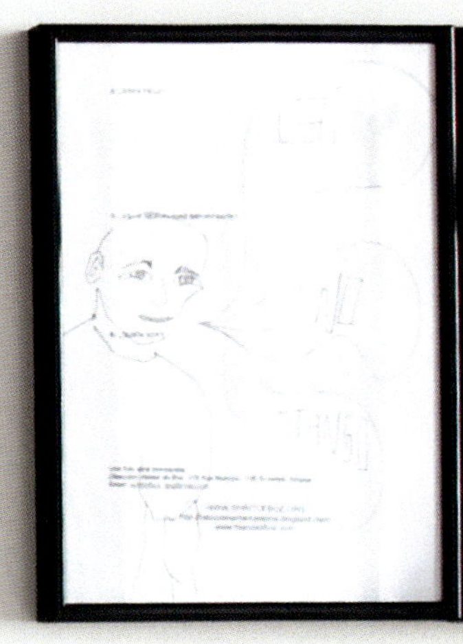

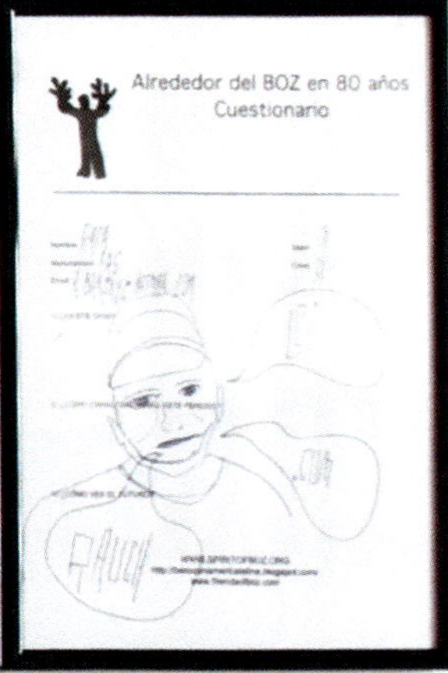
Alrededor del BOZ en 80 años
Cuestionario

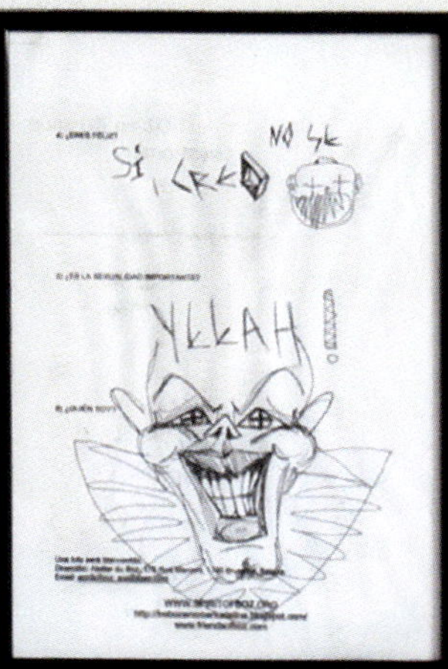
SI, CRRO   NO SE
YLLAH!

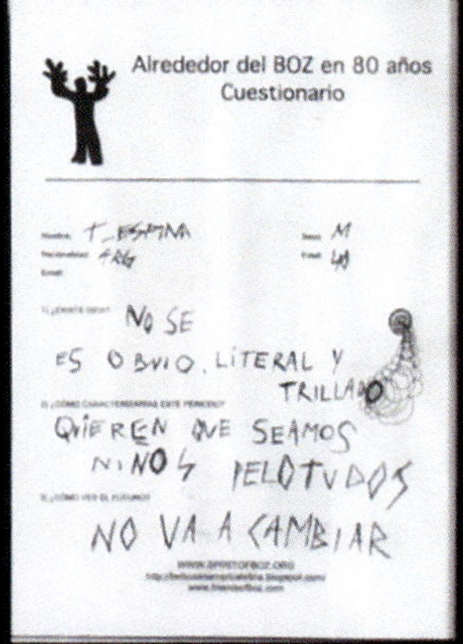
Alrededor del BOZ en 80 años
Cuestionario
T. ESPINA   M
ARG   LA
NO SE
ES OBVIO, LITERAL Y TRILLADO
QIEREN QUE SEAMOS
NIÑOS PELOTUDOS
NO VA A CAMBIAR

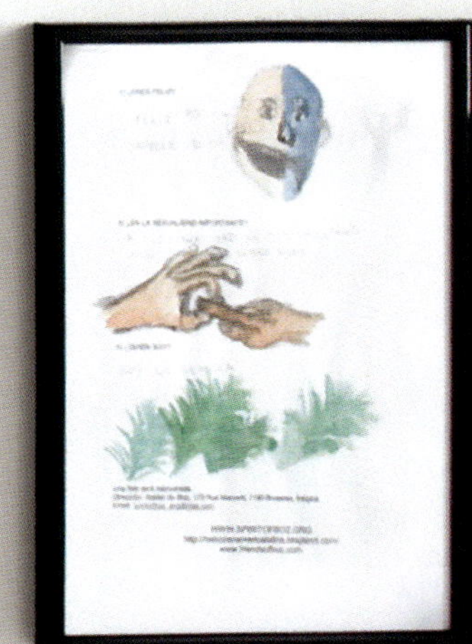

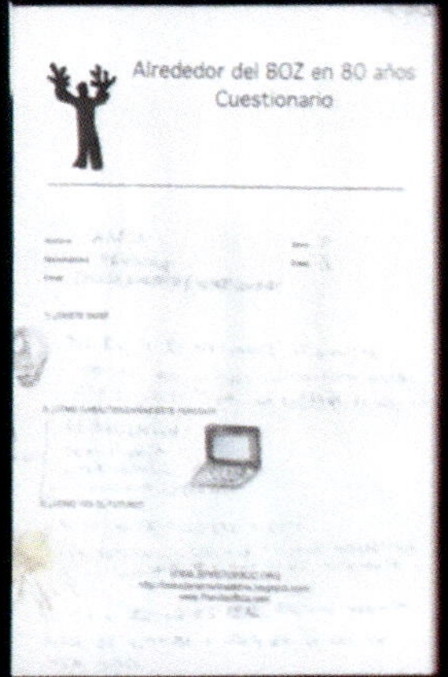
Alrededor del BOZ en 80 años
Cuestionario

Les Pierrots, 2019

12 black lacquered metal structures with painted masks
(variable height up to 1.6 m), variable occupied space
c. 3.5 x 5 m

Les Pierrots is a very recent installation, dating from late 2019. It is the culmination of reflection on the fate of contemporary man and the projection of the image of a disembodied, lost and nostalgic society. Friedler, for whom Pierrot is a necessary ally, stresses the archetypal value of this great figure of the *Commedia dell'arte*, the human comedy. Pierrot's mask symbolises the character's sincerity and naivety, which make him vulnerable. To us, the viewers, this vulnerability seems to be that of the artist (as well as of ourselves) who hides behind this representation so as to better convey the intensity of the drama that unfolds in the depths of our being. The development of this simulacrum is strictly linked to Friedler's mythology, who, through his character and avatar Jack Balance, had already invented a masked incarnation of himself that allows him to confront the existential problems he has to cope with.

The Pierrots are automata, a prefiguration of a mechanised and disembodied humanity, a reality that is almost actual today, in a world in which the drive to encode ever more of our existence, and thus endanger our own capacities, is growing. Friedler's suggestion is that it is an existential threat. The work is a parable of permitted alienation, of our submission to a connected and decerebrating world that compresses the individual into the formless and anonymous limits of a humanity ultra-dependent on the computer-based tools it has invented, thus locking itself into a mass culture that destroys thought, sterilises initiative and standardises all reflexes. The robotic schematisation of the figures' bodies emphasises the standardisation and mechanisation that dissolves individuality, a reality that the artist draws attention to through repetition. The reduction of the Pierrots' appearance to a metal skeleton illustrates the annihilation of life; humanity is lost, neutralised and reduced to a ghostly, emaciated substance, animated by a sad look. Only the souls of these figures, who still remember their luminous humanity, still roam in nostalgia, the intensity of which Friedler emphasises by tears. Highly expressionistic, the work is as moving as it is disturbing and questions the concepts of metamorphosis and mutation borne by a cyber-society that fantasises about dominating our ego and the proliferation of our capacities. Can we escape the tragic destiny that the artist sketches for us? The sad eyes of his Pierrots show us a more human despair… a regret.

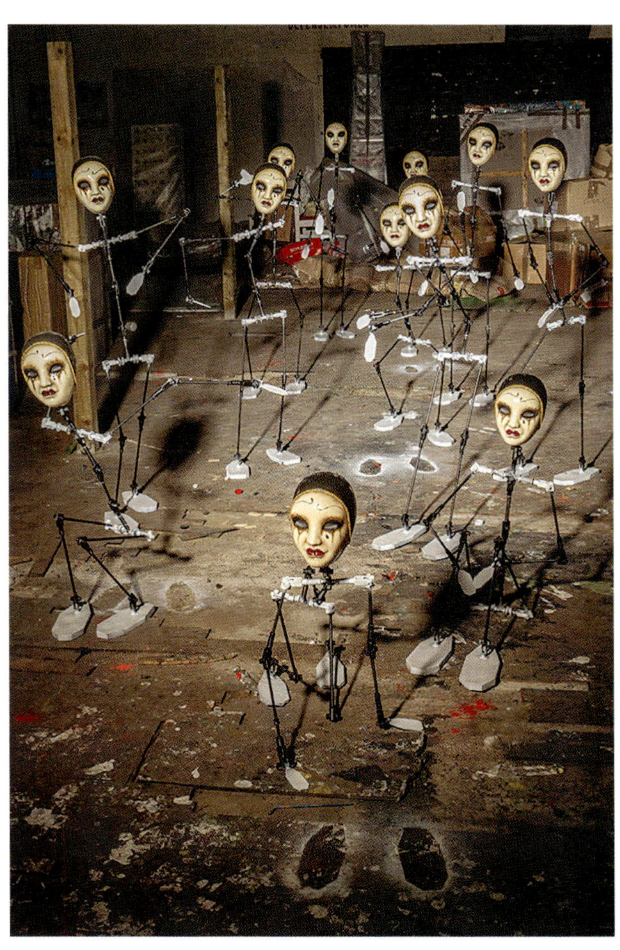 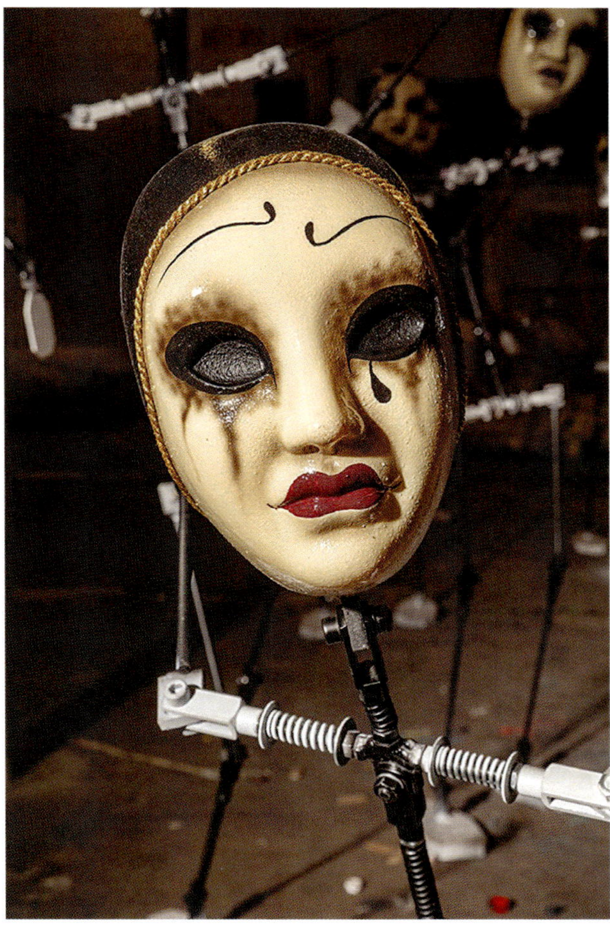

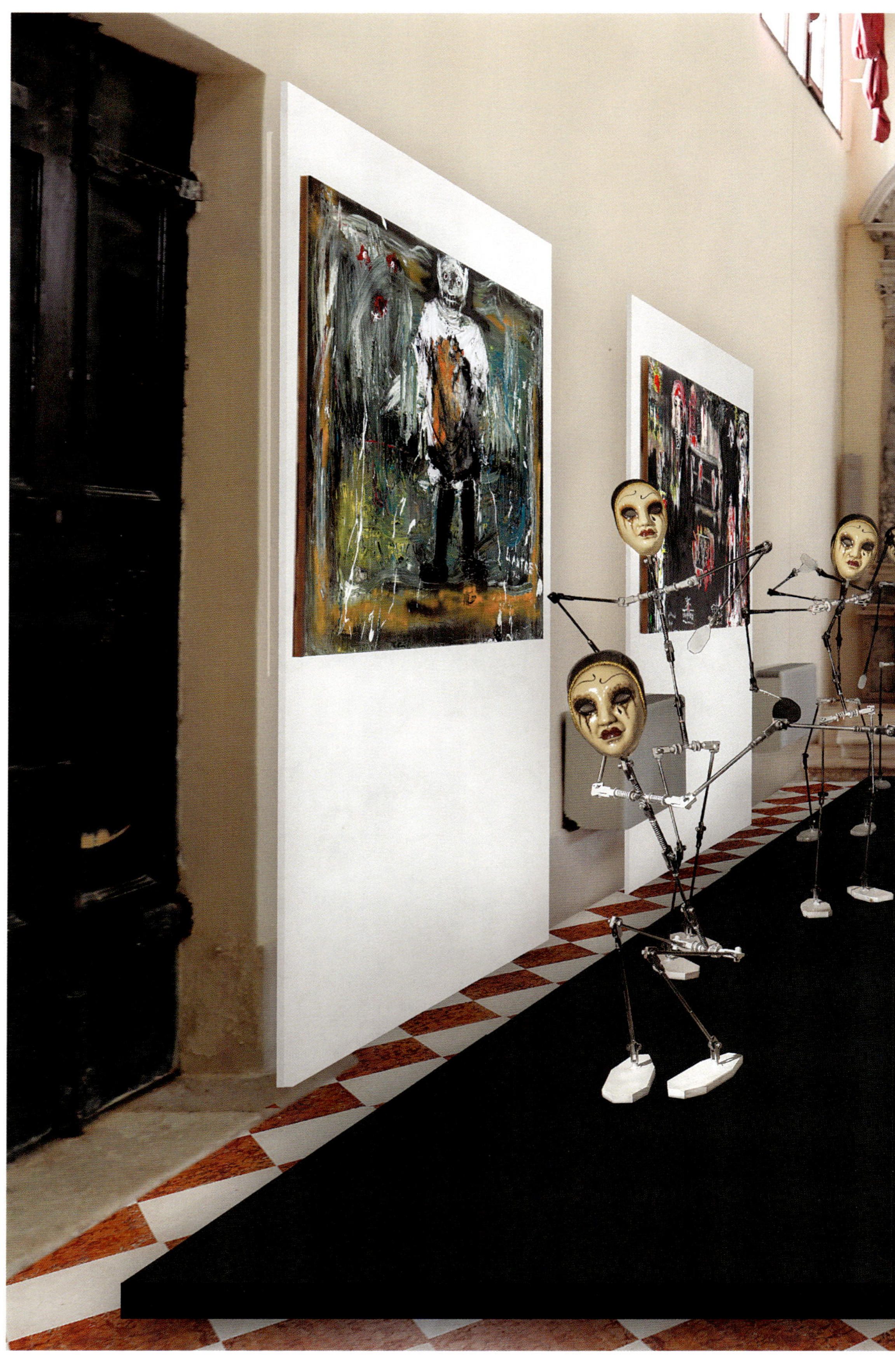

Les Pierrots, 2019
12 black lacquered metal
structures with painted masks
(variable height up to 1.6 m),
variable occupied space
c. 3.5 x 5 m

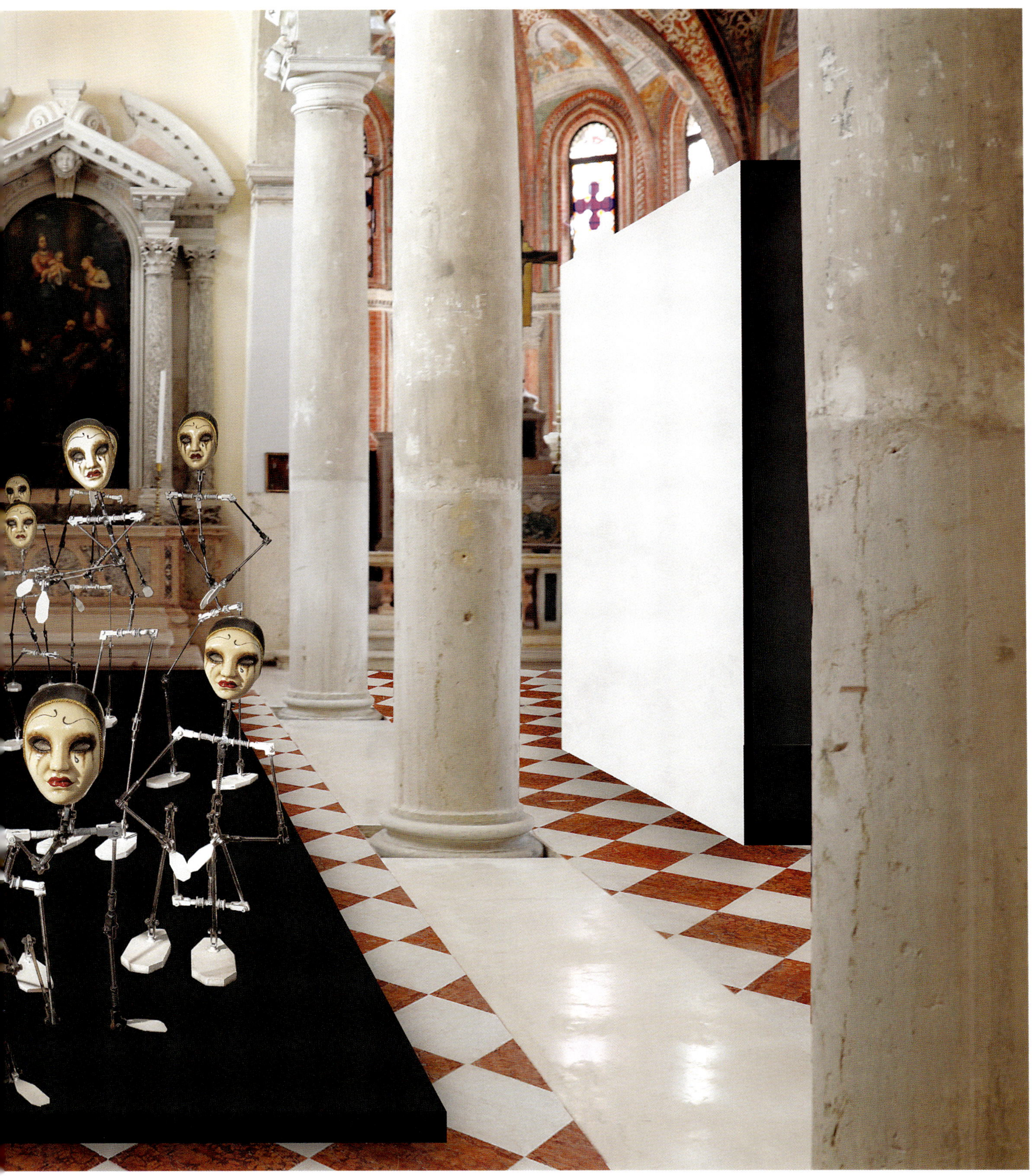

The paintings

The sequence of the *Pierrots* is accompanied by three paintings that suggest the existential darkness in which these beings dwell:

- *L'Autre*, 2018, acrylic and collage on canvas, 150 x 200 cm
- *Ode Satanique*, 2018, acrylic on canvas, 150 x 200 cm
- *Crucifixion*, 2016, acrylic on canvas, 200 x 300 cm
(displayed on the back of the wall of the *Forêt des âmes*)

These three works are emblematic of Julien Friedler's painting between 2016 and 2018. After an entire series of luminous works linked to nature and light that he painted from 2012 to 2016, his inspiration turned darker and more primitive. The matter is rough and the dark colours suggest darkness. A disquieting reality is established in these monumental works representative of Friedler's outlook. In them he explores the world that exists beyond what is perceptible and intelligible, giving rise to secret connections with invisible dreams buried deep in the unconscious. This is here that Friedler arrives, at this slow and visceral introspection that accompanies his gesture — or which is instead accompanied by his gesture — and erases all Cartesian belief in human reason, giving way to mystery. It is an immersion in the irrational that explores the depths of the infinite and of becoming. Julien Friedler's painting might be described as follows: it arises out of the psychoanalytical practice of exploring the unconscious, but once all dogmatism has been abandoned, he gives himself over to a meditation that challenges the world of forms, habits and behaviours, and thus embraces the splendour of the abyss. It is here that one discovers the depth of the soul which, reflecting itself, projects itself onto the canvas to become a painting. Friedler writes: 'What purpose do our paintings, sculptures and installations have? If not for this: a combination of opposites, a paradoxical description, an insertion of the flows that pass through the *Spirit of Boz*. Here, the universe will expand until it reaches a point of interruption: pure synchrony, hidden under the mass of creations, in which all means merge. In the end, every disjointed, separate work, visible to everyone, will only be a detail, an image, the isolated manifestation of a global phenomenon: a single painting seen from different angles. A painting capable of recomposing itself in the minds of all those who devote themselves to it. There is no difference between the subjective microcosm and the universal macrocosm'.
Friedler is motivated by a higher aspiration that illustrates the infinite dimension of art and demonstrates its capacity to reinvent the world.

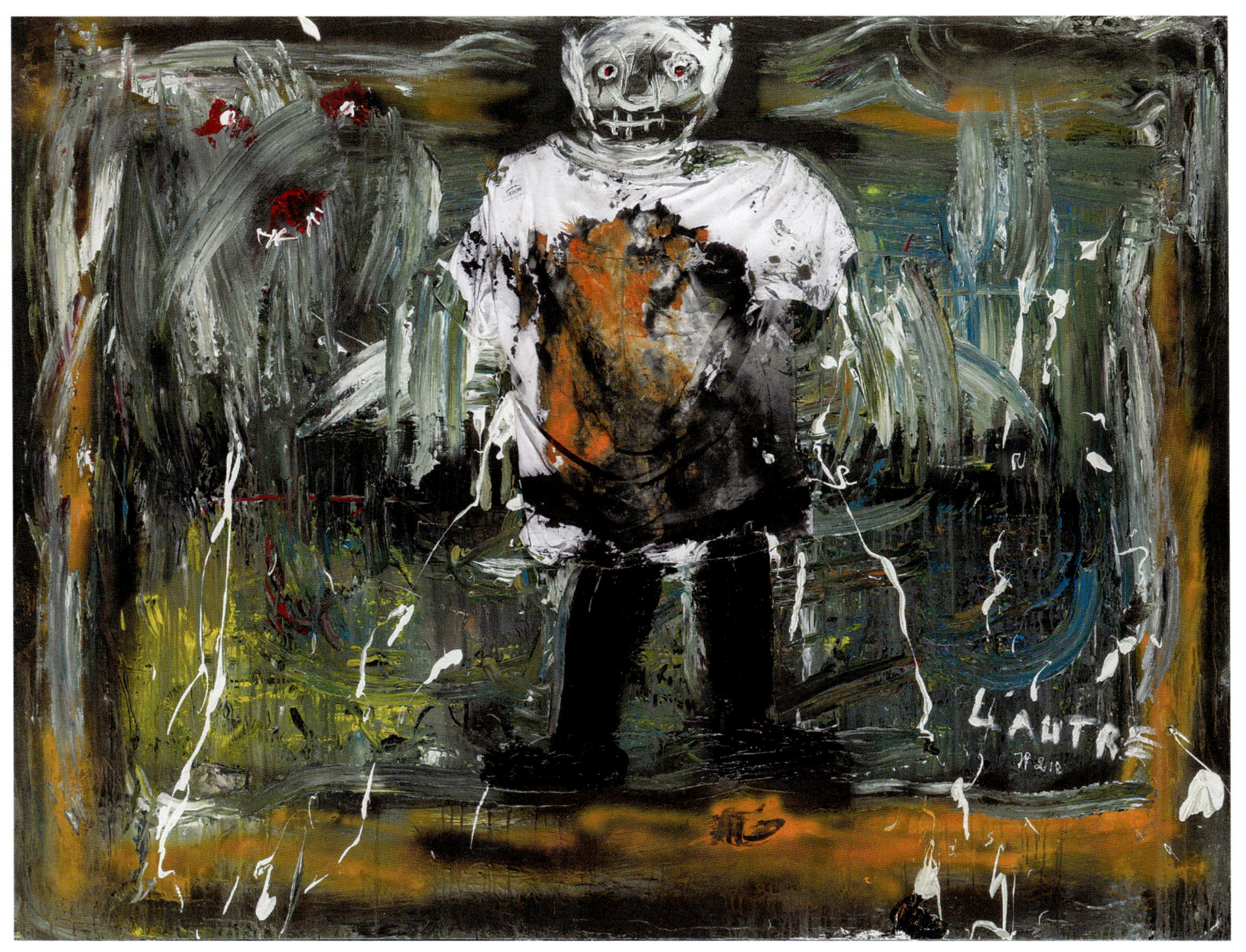

L'Autre, 2018
Acrylic and collage on canvas,
150 x 200 cm

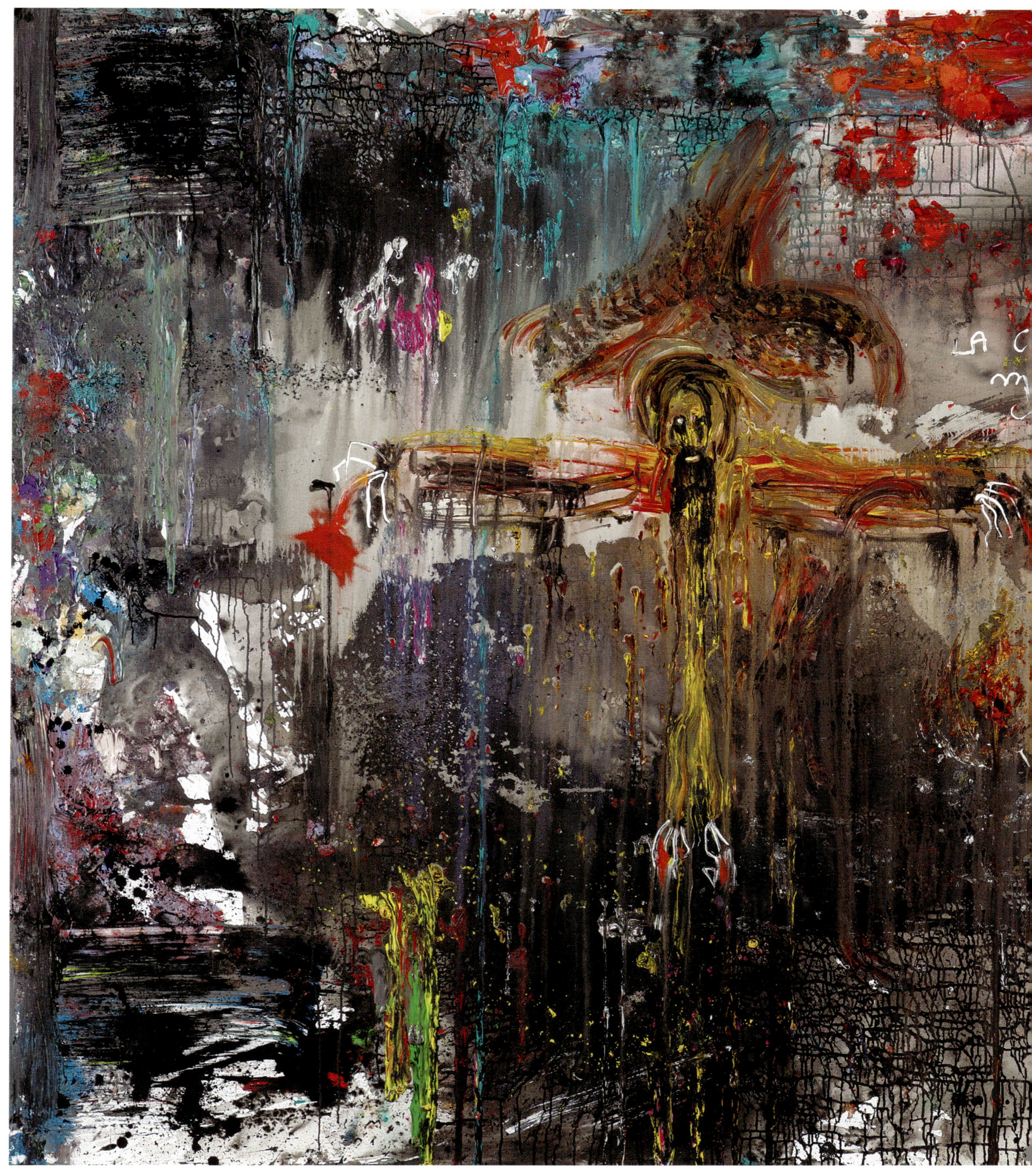

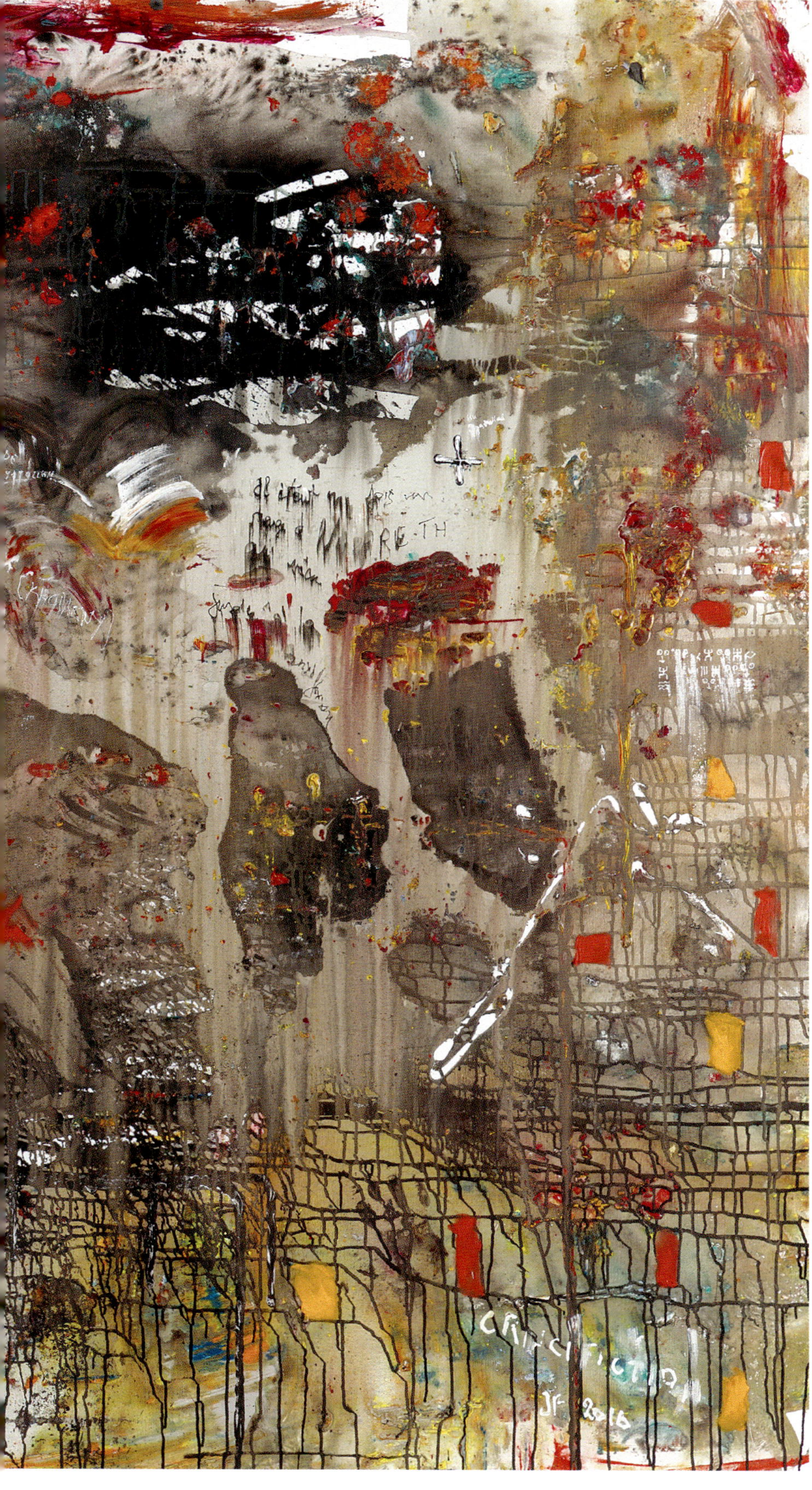

Crucifixion, 2016
Acrylic on canvas, 200 x 300 cm

Ode Satanique, 2018
Acrylic on canvas, 150 x 200 cm

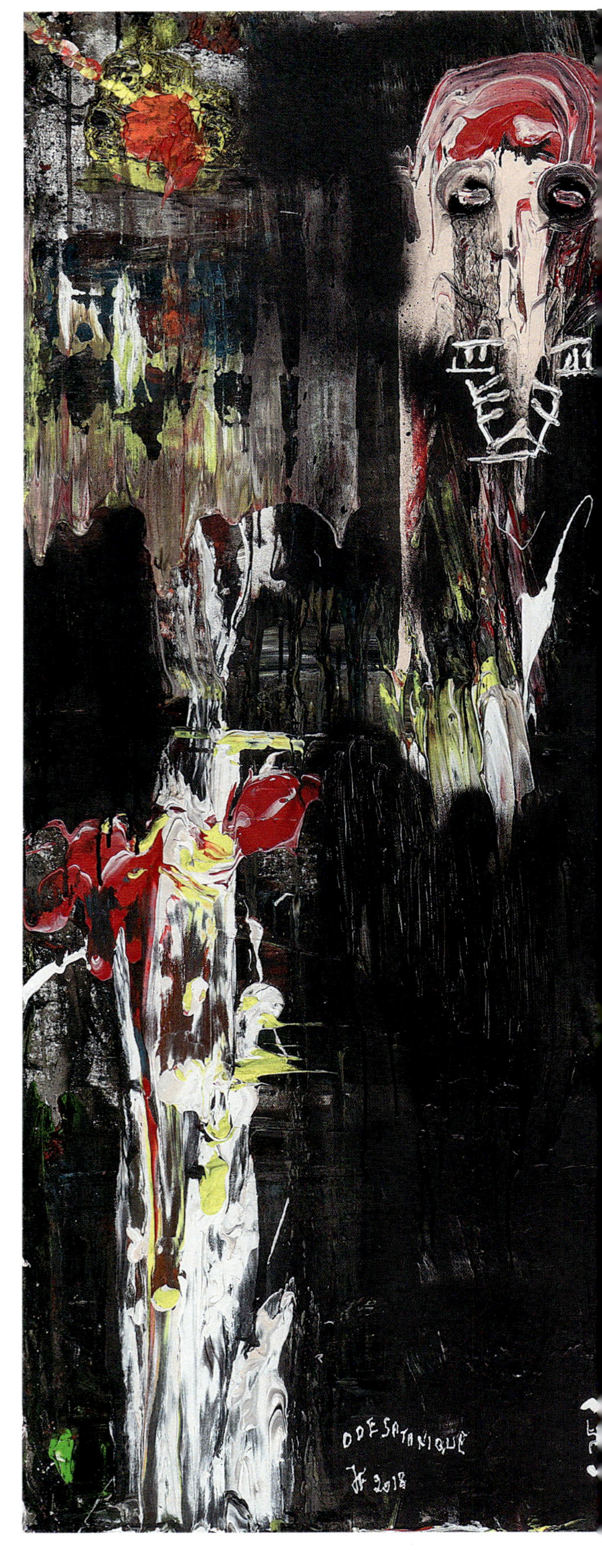

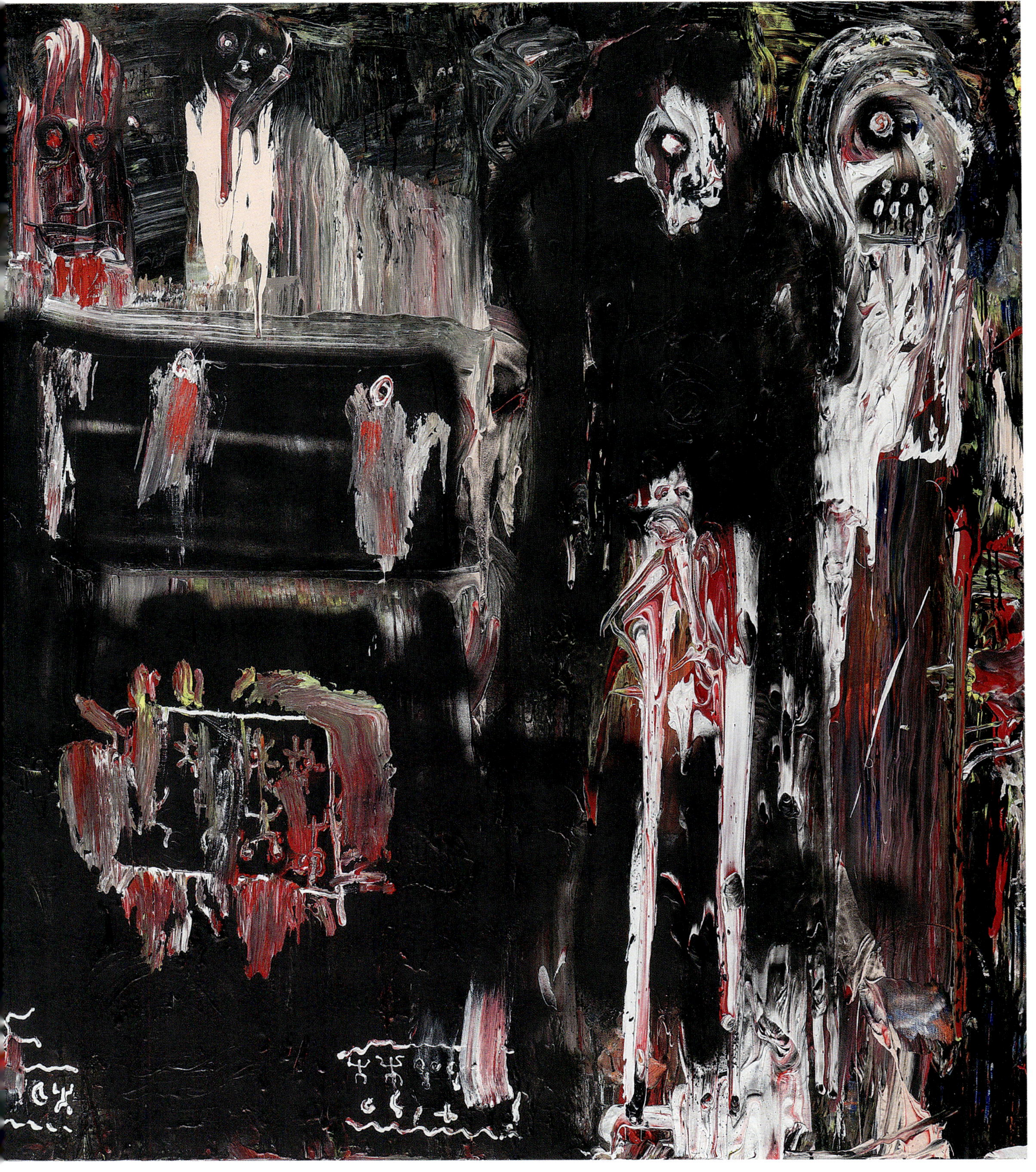

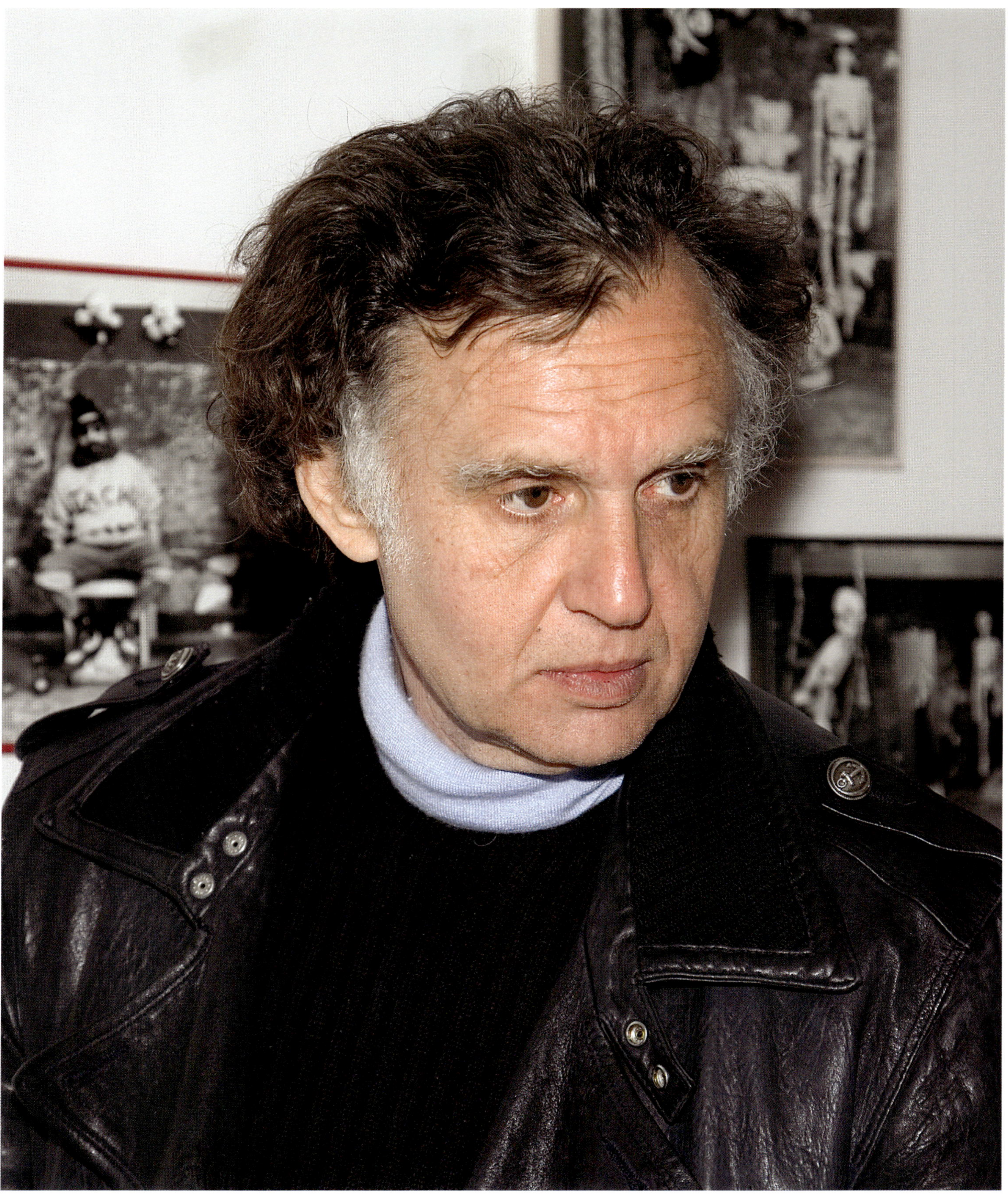

Biography

Dominique Stella

'My work is the inscription of the Divine in a microcosm (*Spirit of Boz*) with universal springs.' J. F.

The son of Jewish parents, both of Transylvanian origin, Julien Friedler was born in Brussels in 1950 and currently lives in Monte Carlo. He received a careful religious education, respecting the precepts of Judaism. After studying philosophy and ethnology, he followed a course in psychoanalysis in Paris; at that time he adhered to the post-structuralist theories laid down by Jacques Lacan, while beginning a personal psychoanalysis with the latter.
Julien Friedler is a complex character and the construction of his art is founded on certain traumas that are still painful and that have long haunted his family. The Second World War, still so close, left indelible scars on his family, who suffered the tragedies of those who were deported or vanished in the Nazi camps. Living in pain and remembrance, his mother never recovered, and thus instilled in her son a deep anxiety by which he would forever be tormented.

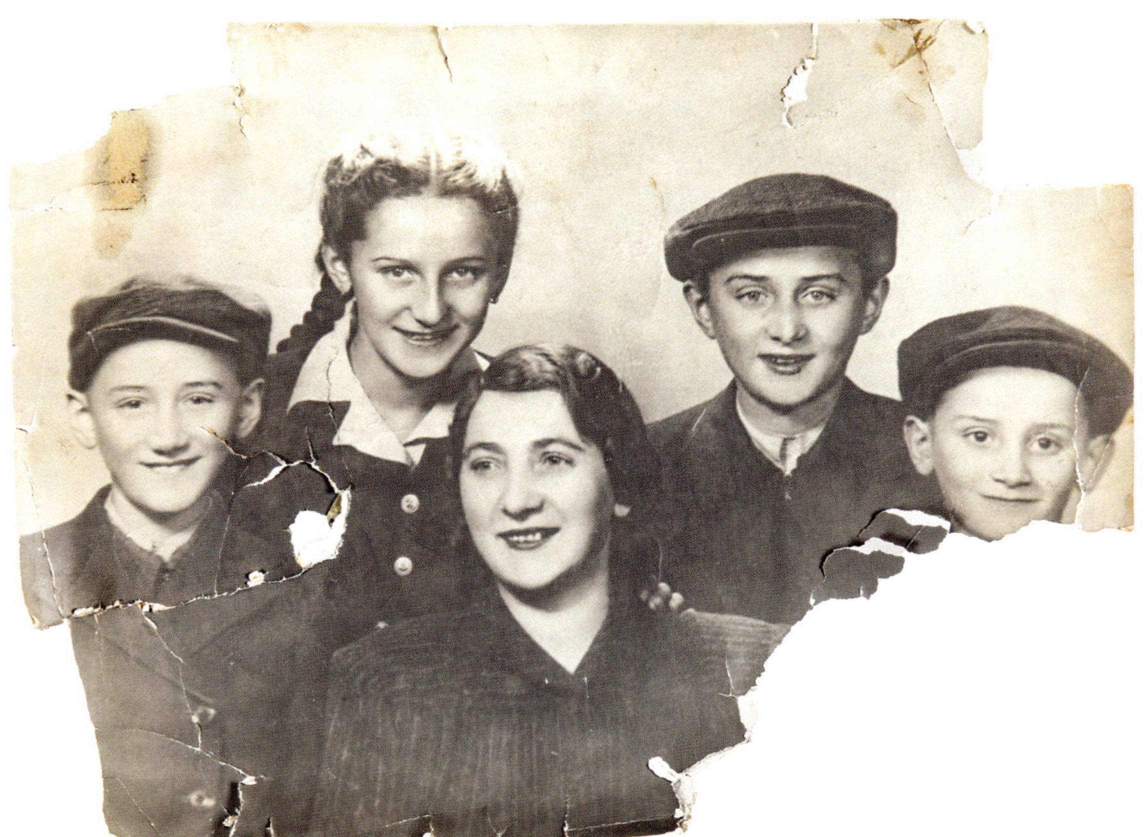

Portrait of Julien Friedler, Munich, 2008

Julien Friedler's grandmother (centre) with her three sons and her daughter (Julien Friedler's mother). The three boys were deported and disappeared in the camps. The mother and her daughter escaped deportation

On Lacan's death in 1981, Friedler was denied his daily session with the famous psychoanalyst, and thus the possibility of assuaging his malaise.

During the 1980s, he searched for a personal path to follow; he travelled and, through his jeweller father, discovered the business world in which his partner Lutty de Geest was also involved, whom he married in 1984. Throughout this period, he nonetheless devoted much of his time to writing. In 1982, he published his first book, *Mosaïque*, a poetic tale that features a variety of fictions whose purpose is to lead the reader astray in the labyrinth of thought. His next book, *L'Ombre du rabbin* was published in 1985 (Lieu Commun, Paris), which tackles the Shoah through characters whose questioning of the tragic fate suffered by the martyred Jewish people is analogous to that of the artist. The mythical and epic word 'Quest' illustrates the journey undertaken by the book's heroes, figures representative of Friedler's questioning.
1988: birth of his daughter Tatiana.

During the 1990s, Friedler's studies focused on an exploration of the psychoanalytical field. But the fundamental torment by which he is inhabited found no respite and opened the way to an exhausting quest for Meaning manifested in the elemental questions that the artist poses and attempts to elucidate in his writings and plastic works. The artistic work he undertook about 1996 acted as an extension of his questioning of the Unconscious and of the artistic saga he was engaged in, which he generically named *Spirit of Boz*, thus encompassing all aspects of his personal narrative, which, together with his art works, represented a search whose essence, as he reminds us, 'will forever remain my inner life and its relationship to an enigmatic, elusive Creator'.
In spite of the advent of painting in his work, Friedler continued to write. He published three books during the 1990s. In 1995, *Psychanalyse et neurosciences: la légende du boiteux* (PUF, Paris). In this, the author takes up the question posed by Sigmund Freud's *Project for a Scientific Psychology*, by engaging in a comparative analysis in the light of current knowledge developed by neuroscience. Appreciated by an informed public, the book earned him praise. In 1998, in succession there appeared *Tirésias*, a poetic drama (Caractères, Paris) and *L'ivrogne* (Éditions de Janus, Paris), the cover of which bears an illustration of one of Friedler's first paintings, *Le Petit homme jaune*.

In the second half of the 1990s, painting became a permanent feature of Friedler's production. For him, art became the source of 'a bearable truth' which, by its expressive force, allows 'the myths of humanity to be told in images'. His first and sometimes clumsy works attest a spontaneous approach already dominated by bright colours, and which rapidly found personal expression in a series of paintings, for example *Le Petit homme jaune*, the *Miroir de la Princesse*, and *Le Cheval fou*. The artist's pictorial will asserts itself with a sometimes naive and expressive forcefulness, resembling graffiti art in which the written sign very quickly imposes its insistent presence.

During the 2000s, painting was still present in Friedler's practice. *Le Shaman* (2000) became the symbol of Friedler's process of transformation, but he never forgot his point of departure. He viewed art as a synthesis of ideas and actions, and the poetic writings included in his early canvases illustrate the passage from the pictorial to the sign, with the latter very quickly developing into a cryptic language in the series of works titled *La Parole des Anges*. This cycle of paintings, produced between 2000 and 2002, has a conceptual dimension in its content and an aesthetic dimension in its form. These works are the medium for Friedler to deploy a coded, esoteric and primordial language based on symbolism attributed to the sign. In Friedler's words, '*La Parole des Anges* is a mystical doctrine, a

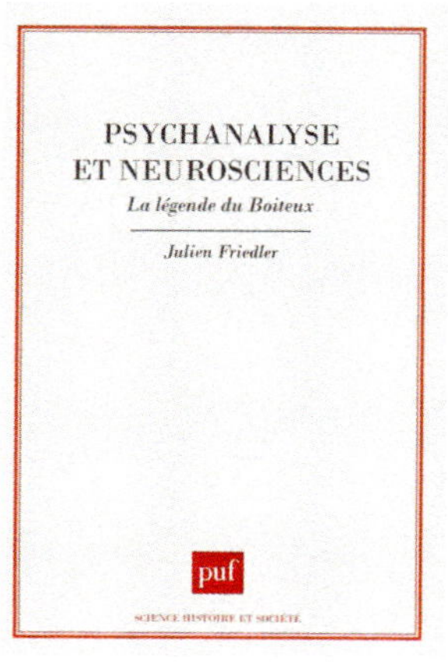

Cover of *Psychanalyse et neurosciences* (Paris: Puf, 1995)

Le Petit homme jaune, 1997
Acrylic on canvas, 118 x 73 cm

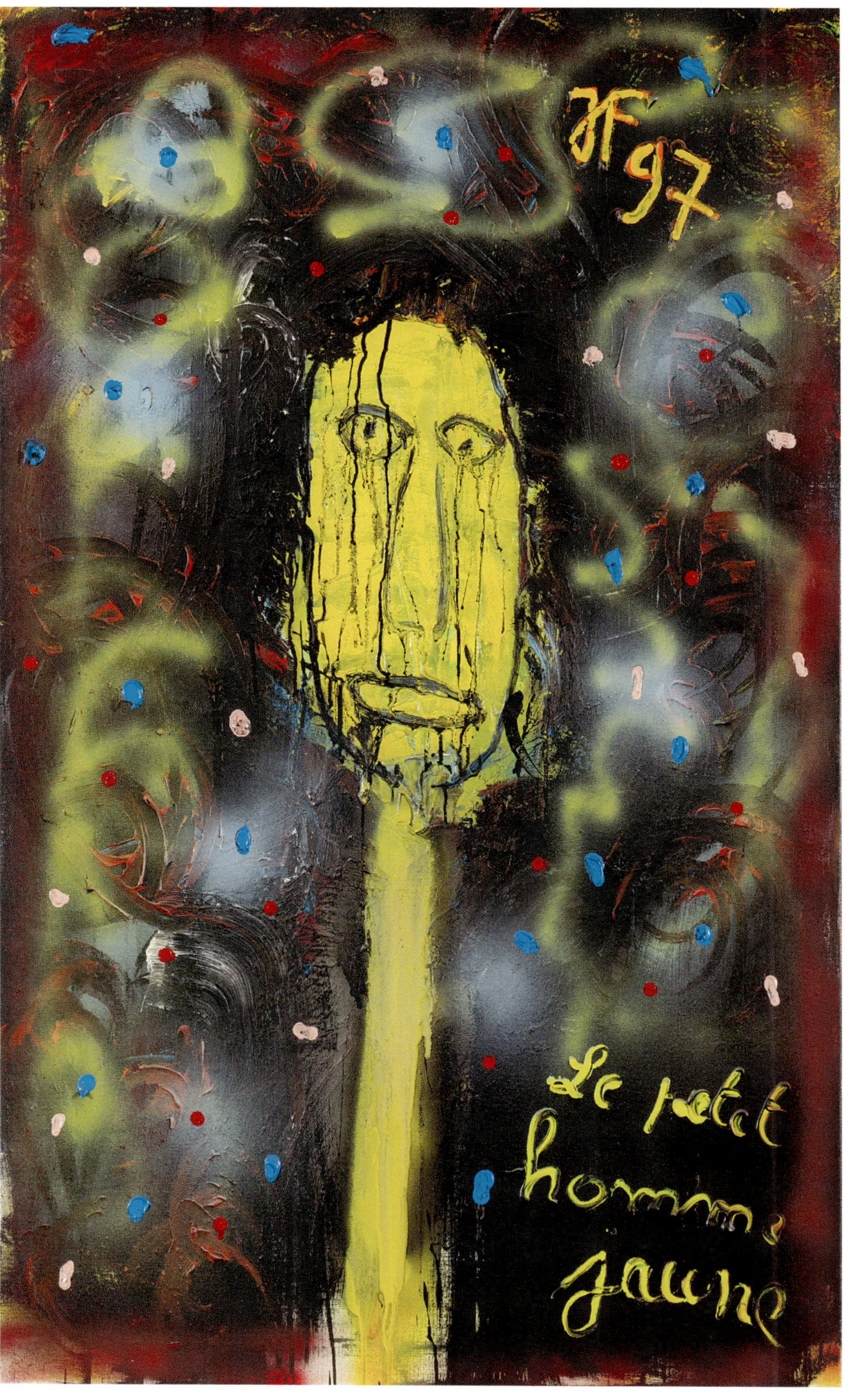

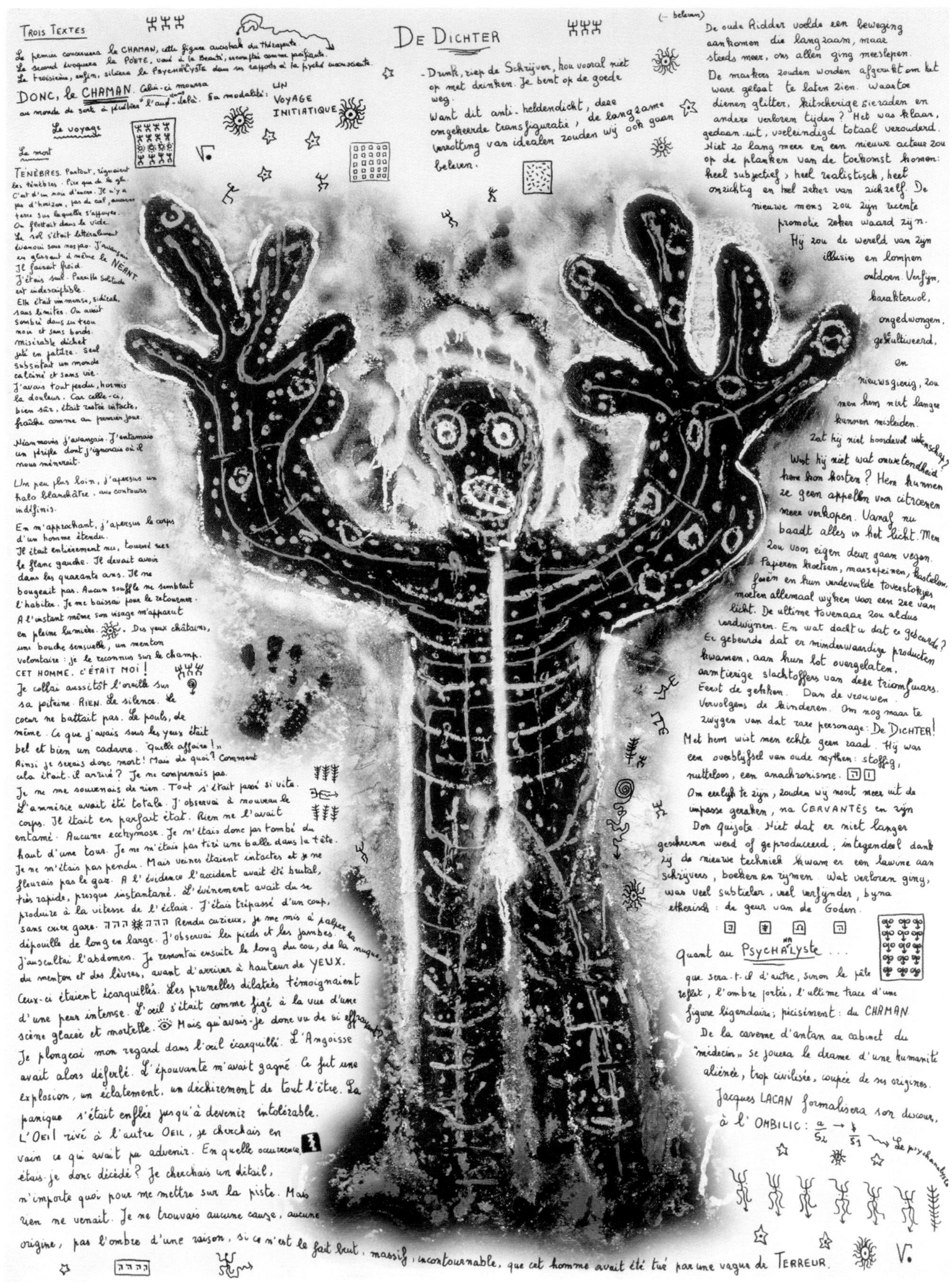

Le Shaman, 2000
Ink and acrylic on canvas,
118 x 73 cm

All Over II – La Parole des Anges, 2002
Acrylic on canvas, 200 x 300 cm

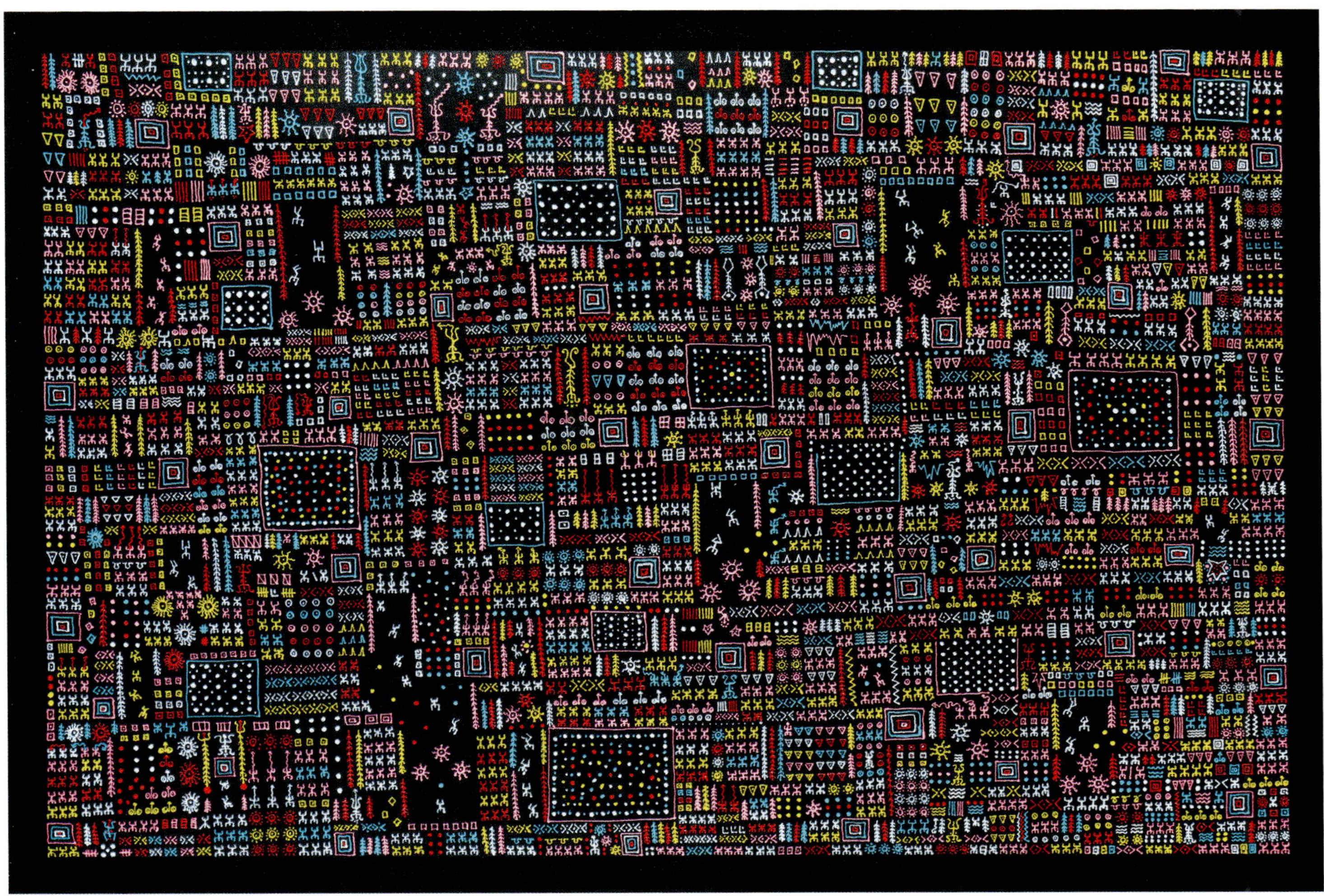

fundamental language that underlies the proliferation of discourses, each sign, or even the entire painting, can therefore be the subject of meditation'. Through the adoption of this language, Julien Friedler establishes a cartography of concepts that question humanity on the idea of the Sacred, whose mysteries he attempts to interpret by means of quasi-religious writing. A retrospective of this cycle of paintings would take place in 2018 at La Cité Miroir in Liège, accompanied by a catalogue that included the major works of *La Parole des Anges*.

In 2000, his studio was occupied by *Les Innocents*. A barbed-wire enclosure measuring 11 by 9 metres surrounded stuffed animals and school benches, in a mise-en-scène that was certainly tragic but also playful. The installation was monumental. Friedler explains: 'I used a language of extremes: childhood and death, it's the Shoah, of course, but also a metaphor of imprisoned childhood… of all the children in the world killed and wounded in their innocence'. The installation quickly became a point of reference in the artist's work, conveying the idea of an art of sharing, and inviting inquiry. Viewers passing through the installation are confronted by the fundamental questions of the world. Successive versions of *Les Innocents* have since travelled to numerous exhibitions dedicated to the artist.

It was during this period (2000) that Jack Balance came into being (http://rebelle.blogspirit.com/archive/2021/04/29/julien-friedler-dealer-d-utopies-3251717.html). Jack Balance is another key figure in Friedler's mythology: he expresses the notion of setting new targets for oneself, he is the artist's social double, an alcoholic and depraved, aware of what surrounds and oppresses him. He occupies the cage at the centre of *Les Innocents*. 'Jack Balance is necessary for me', says Julien Friedler, 'probably because I like to remain in the background. I'm shy and solitary, so I have produced a dummy that allows me to say and do what I myself would never be able to express or do'. Jack Balance symbolises man's struggle to exist in terrible dependence on his Creator. He attempts to proclaim himself a 'subject', but to do so he has to overcome the limits that have been imposed on him, such as mutism. He therefore has several modes of communication: writing and painting, but also breaking the law of silence when his creator is inattentive. Jack Balance is also shut in a cage, from which he escapes to travel the world. In order to exist, he needs constantly to cheat, protest and rebel. Jack Balance is a frustrated clown who asks himself existential questions, travelling the planet on a mystical quest. He embodies the Conscience.

2003: Friedler turned himself into a facetious clown and his studio began to fill with ghostly characters, the walls became covered with writing, and this immense place, in the heart of Brussels, became the den where Julien Friedler's expanding universe — which he named *Le Boz* in 2003 — had its origin. And it was there that *Spirit of Boz* was developed in 2006: a metaphysical quest, an invitation to extend art into life, a unique work that obliges us to come out of ourselves and to dissolve into it. For, outside of his prolific, radiant and sometimes disturbing work, Friedler invites us to modify our awareness of being. Art is a source of self-revelation, a place for sharing and exchange, an invitation to dream, a quest for meaning, an escape from the mediocre realities of everyday life, a path towards the inaccessible truth of life, a metaphysical adventure: 'The expression of the unspeakable', says Sonia Bressler.[1] 'Julien Friedler's force', she clarifies, 'consists in having his creative gestures in his space and *Spirit of Boz* as their extension in the space of the world'.[2]

All this Friedler explored through his actions, his performances, his installations and his paintings. His questioning was becoming increasingly deep and required an opening onto the world. The artist, and more often his double, left the studio and entered onto the stage. We became the spectators and were invited to become the actors. The world of Boz began to organise itself. Jeanne Zeler joined the adventure to coordinate its development.

[1] In Sonia Bressler, *Julien Friedler. De la Métaphysique de l'errance* (Mariac: Jacques Flament Éditions, 2013), p. 75.
[2] *Ibid.*, p. 76.

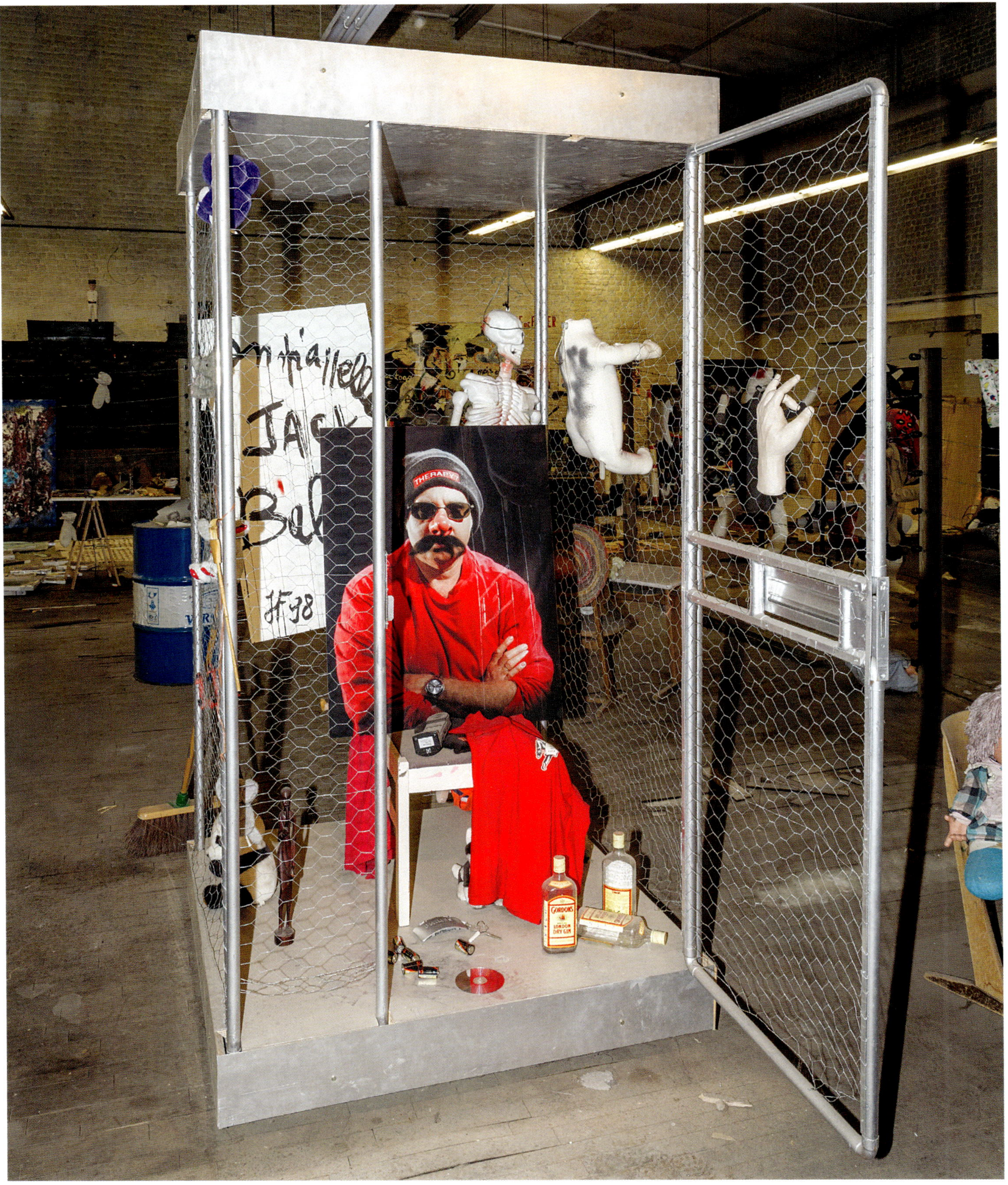
JACK
Bel
JF98
THERAPY
GORDONS
LONDON
DRY GIN

The studio and *La Poupée juive*,
c. 2003

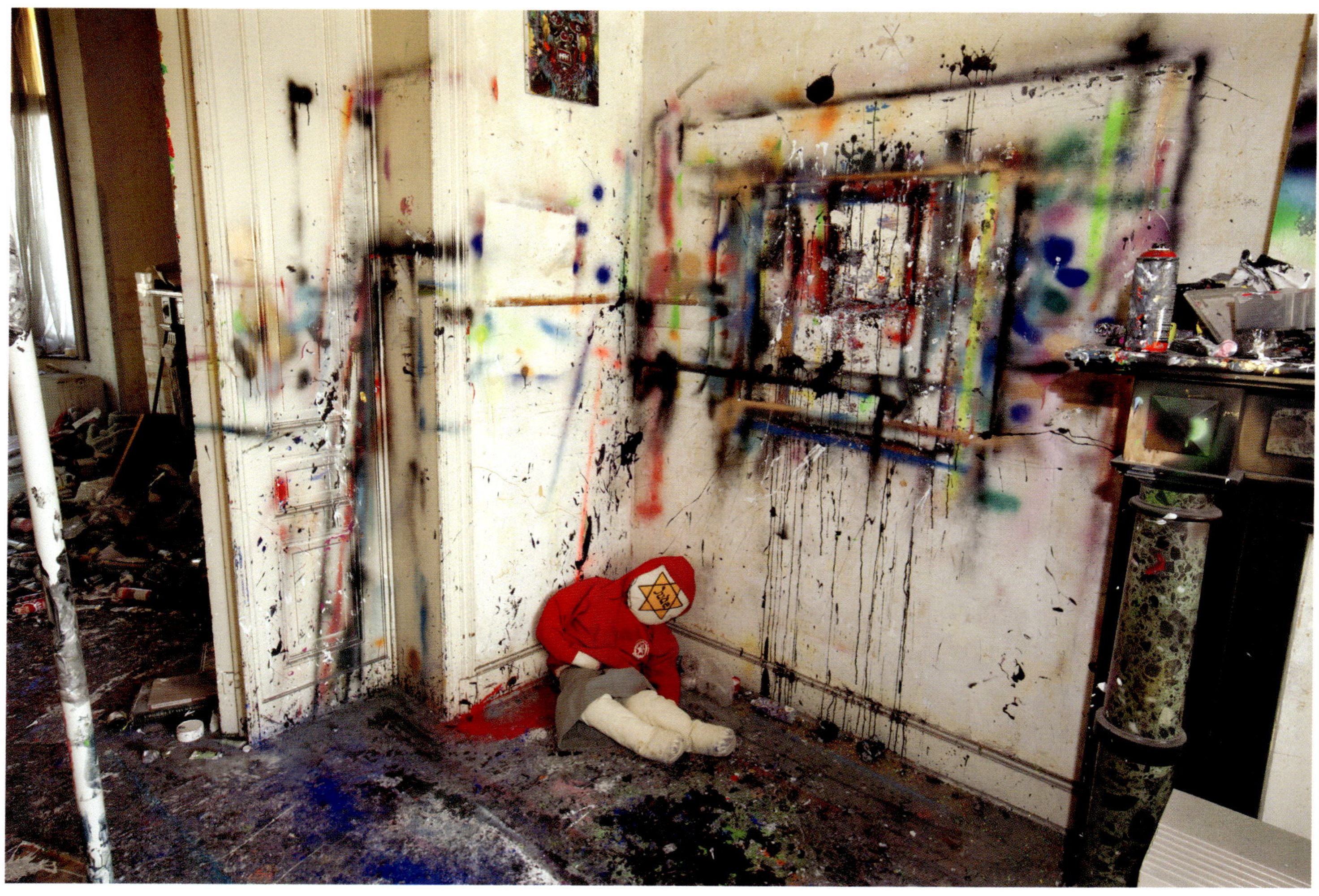

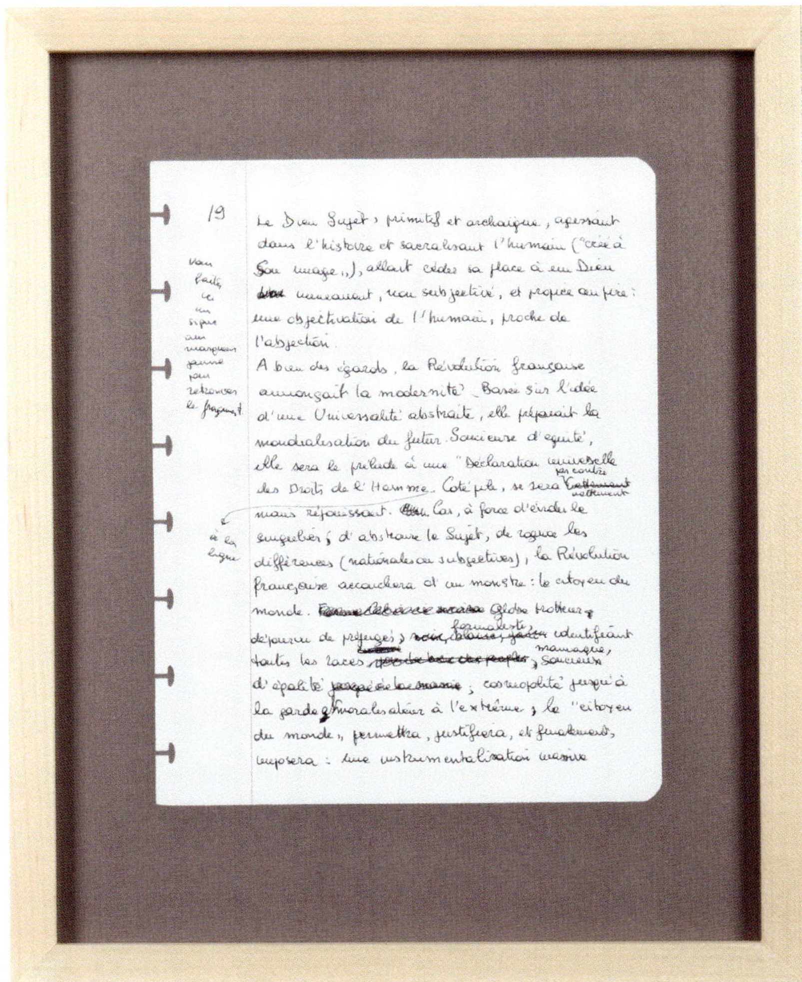

Then came the start of the writing of the *Livre du Boz*, which went in parallel with the maturation of the *Boz* philosophy. The book is a hunt, a quest, an epic, a meditative and ambitious work, whose writing filled the next few years. Friedler defined the book in the *Fundamentals*: 'Three clowns – Jack Balance, the Scribe and the Mirror Man – are caught in their own trap: a vision that unwinds and slips through their fingers. Watching them evolve, we have the impression of a waking dream. The story is non-linear, open-ended and cleverly broken up. It unfolds simultaneously on several levels, fitting the stories into each other like a set of Russian dolls. The expression of time fluctuates and is largely unpredictable. Space is hazy. The plot is not always evident…'.

2003: First exhibitions. *L'infanzia dell'arte*, solo exhibition at the Fondazione Mudima, Milan. Paintings from the series *Parole des Anges* and the installation *Les Innocents*; speaking on Rai 3, Philippe Daverio was enthusiastic about the work. Arturo Schwarz spoke at the opening, praising the power of Friedler's work, particularly *Les Innocents*. The catalogue included numerous photos of the Brussels studio.

Friedler's work was included in two art fairs: Art Brussels with the Damasquine Gallery, and the Basel Fair with the Pailhas Gallery in Marseille.

Creation of the first installations, featuring the theatrical and burlesque character Jack Balance, who began to win his independence in Friedler's universe: *BB Jack Balance, Jack Balance dans son transat*. The world of *Boz* was coming together and the studio gradually became a place that Friedler wanted to expand to embrace the world.

2004: continuing to write, he published *L'Œil d'Œdipe* (PUF, Paris). Friedler's goal was to deconstruct the myth of Oedipus so as to turn it into a fantasy, so in this book he denounces the overdevelopment of the unconscious and cites the need to go in the opposite direction — from the fantasy to the myth — which presupposes the elaboration of new 'mythemes'. We recognise here the concerns of the artist, the builder of a legendary mythology that he develops through a mythical universe anchored in both reality and the unconscious.

2004 also saw two more solo exhibitions: *Paroles et Paraboles ou le Mythe en question*, at the Passage de Retz, Paris, and *Memories* at the David Di Maggio Gallery, Berlin. Friedler also took part in two group shows: *De leur Temps – Collections privées françaises* at the Musée des Beaux-Arts, Tourcoing, and *Vanitas, Eitelkeit der Eitelkeiten* at the IKOB, Eupen.

2000–2009: after *La Parole des Anges*, painting dominates this period. The emergence of *Spirit of Boz* stimulated a creative force that transcended Friedler's pictorial work in a spontaneous and irresistible surge that imposed painting as a source of energy that was both introspective and effusive. *La Parole des Anges* already contained all the aspects of the thought that would give rise to Friedler's ensuing work. In premonitory fashion, it outlined the complexity of his production to come, triggering all the different aspects of Julien Friedler's character — Friedler as psychoanalyst, as writer, as poet, and as artist. They all tend towards the same goal, that of reactivating myths in an unstable society so as to find meaning in them. It was in this spirit of recourse to the great founding mythologies that Friedler painted a series of emblematic and legendary figures, fabulous and entrancing giants, imaginary personifications of our unconscious fears. *Le Foudroyer* (2004), *Ecce Homo* (2009), *Le Cavalier de l'Apocalypse* (2009), *Le Clown androgyne*, *Le Guerrier* (2010), but first of all *Le Shaman* (2000), a powerful figure in the Friedlerian universe and especially significant in his work. This image could be a self-portrait. The shaman is traditionally a poet, scholar and sorcerer who passes a message to the living from the beyond. During these years, Friedler produced three important works: *Les Demoiselles revisitées* (2005), an installation featuring three resin sculptures freely inspired by Picasso's *Demoiselles d'Avignon*. These were exhibited in 2007 at the Francis Naumann Gallery in New York. He also created two hyper-realist sculptures: one, *Le Juif errant* (2004), is an archetypal image of a figure that is both terrifying and forlorn; the other, a representation of *Arafat* (2004), which was sold at Phillips de Pury & Company auction house in London in 2005. These works demonstrate a critical realist outlook on society, reminding us that Friedler seeks to retranscribe striking images.

2005: *Les Innocents* was shown in an original presentation called 'La Fin des temps', produced during the 2005 Flanders Festival and accompanied by Olivier Messiaen's *Quartet for the End of Time* and words by Primo Levi. This moving installation asked viewers to reconsider the Second World War and to rethink the present. Also in 2005, the pictorial cycle *La Parole des Anges* was shown at the Galerie Philippe Cazeau - La Béraudière, Paris.

Nor should it be forgotten that the end of 2005 marked the naissance of the template of Julien Friedler's entire thought process, *Spirit of Boz*, a concept that is essential to the expansion of the discourse on art to all those in search of themselves and others. *Spirit of Boz* is the crucible where our environment is analysed and where awareness of the turmoil that troubles our world is developed; it is also the place of action and proliferating thought that feeds on the rumours of our societies so that we may all fight them together, in defence of a founding utopia of a society in which art would be our saviour.

2006: in parallel to painting, Julien Friedler continued his work on the legendary *Boz* epic and created the *Spirit of Boz* association. In an attempt to project the field of art into the social domain (and not the other

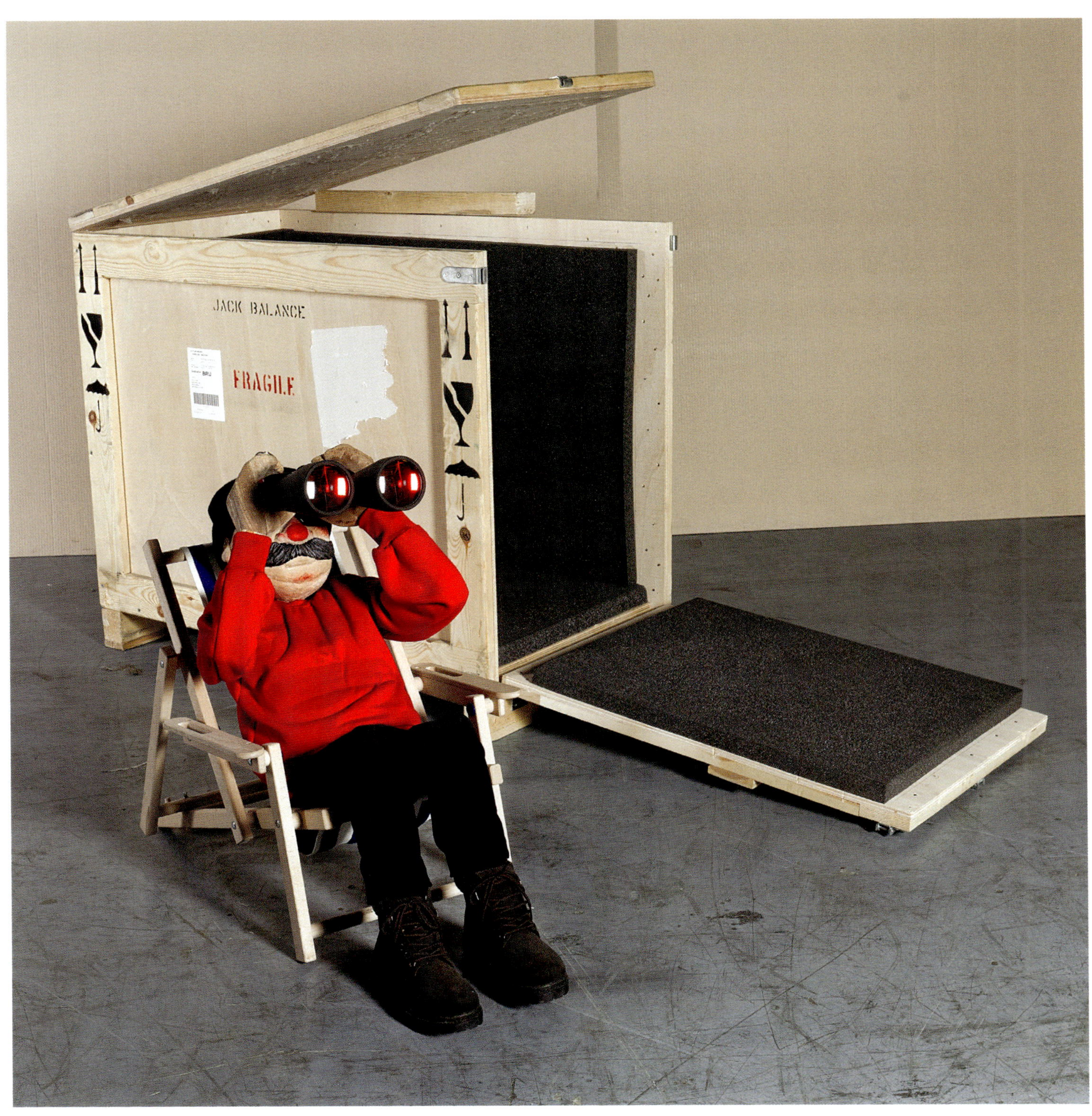

JACK BALANCE
FRAGILE

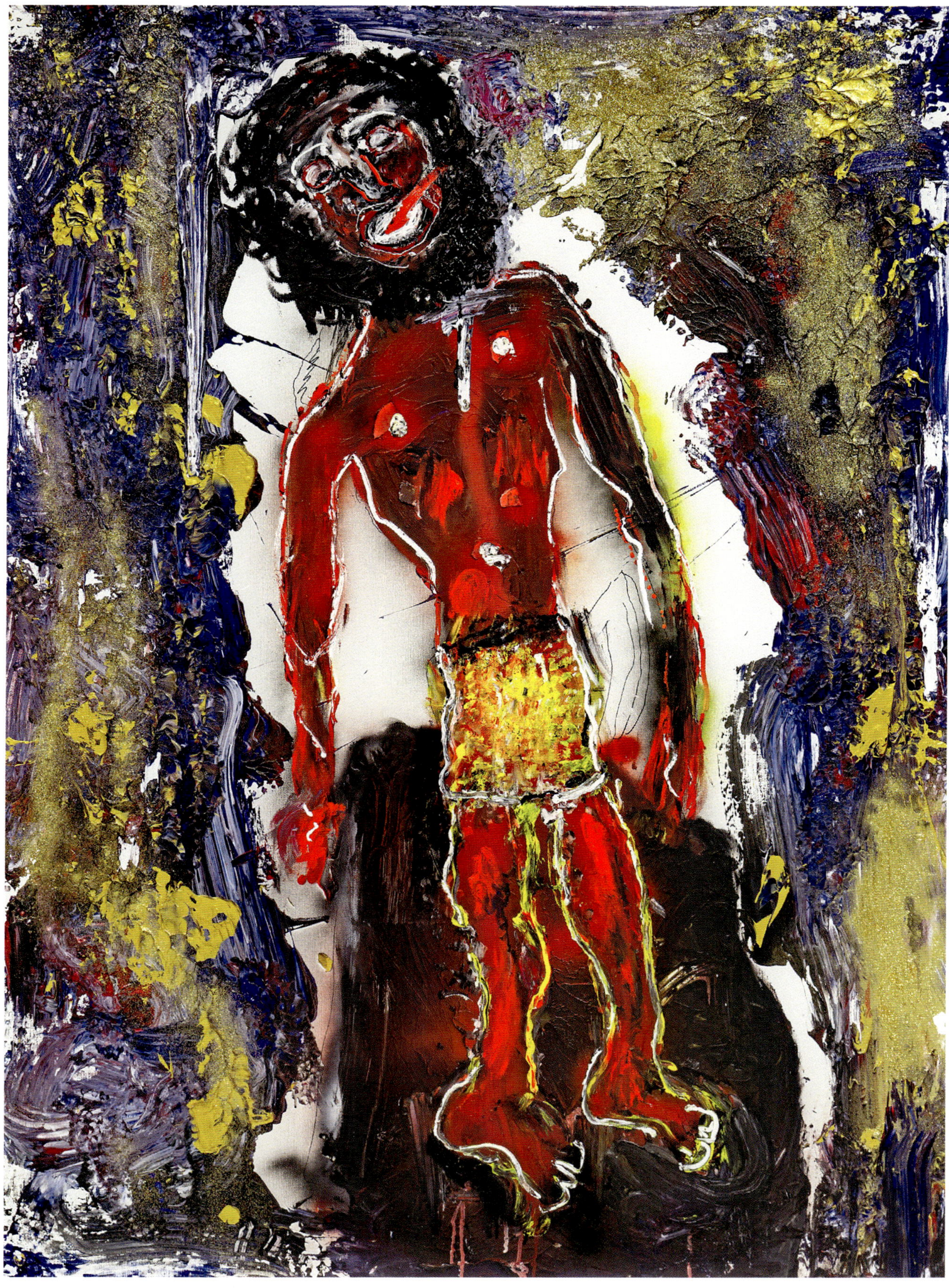

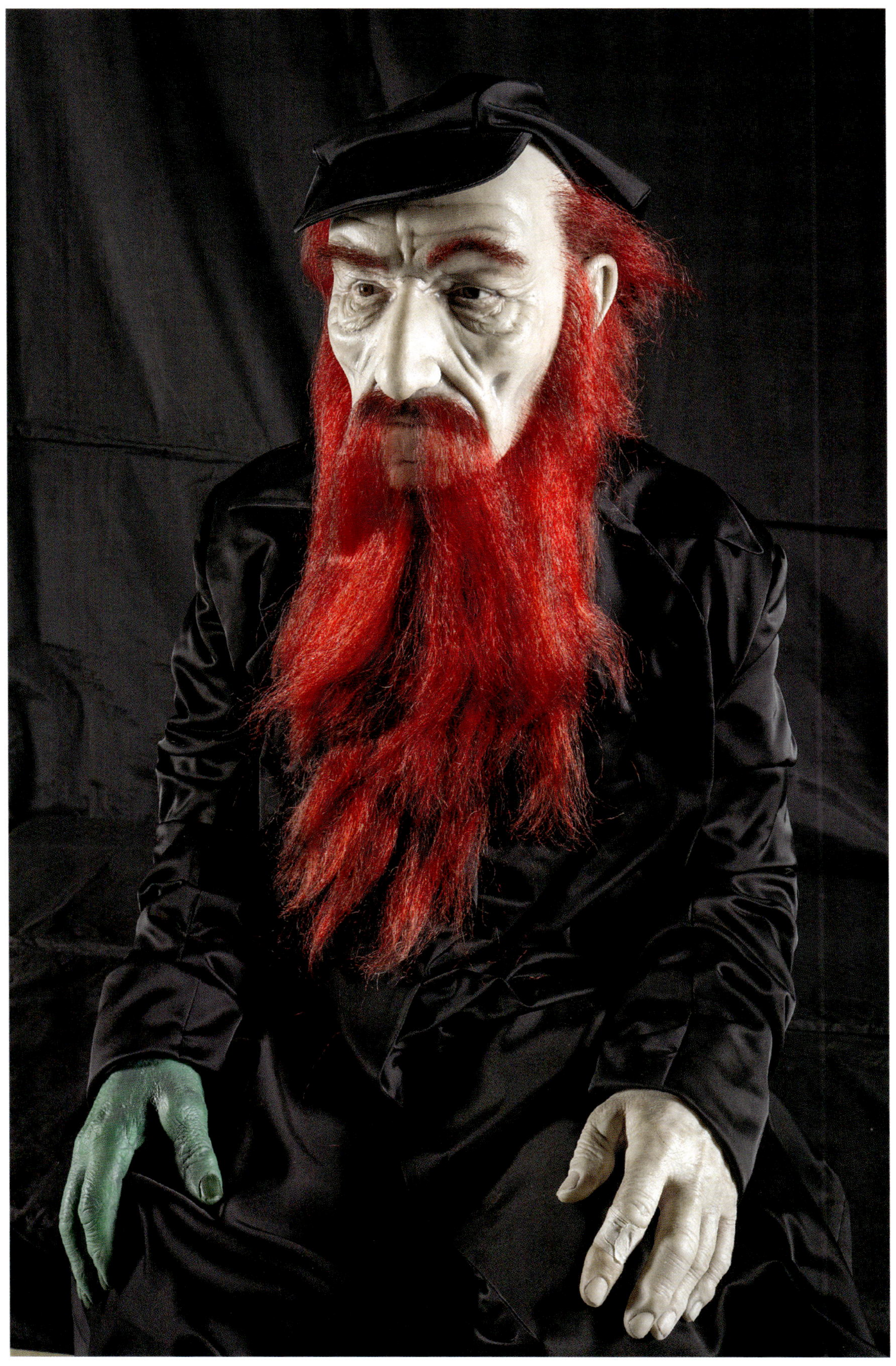

Ecce Homo, 2009
Acrylic on canvas, 200 x 150 cm

Le Juif errant, 2004
Sculpture in resin and mixed
media, h. c. 120 cm

Les Demoiselles revisitées, 2005
Three sculptures in resin,
100 x 100 x 50 cm each

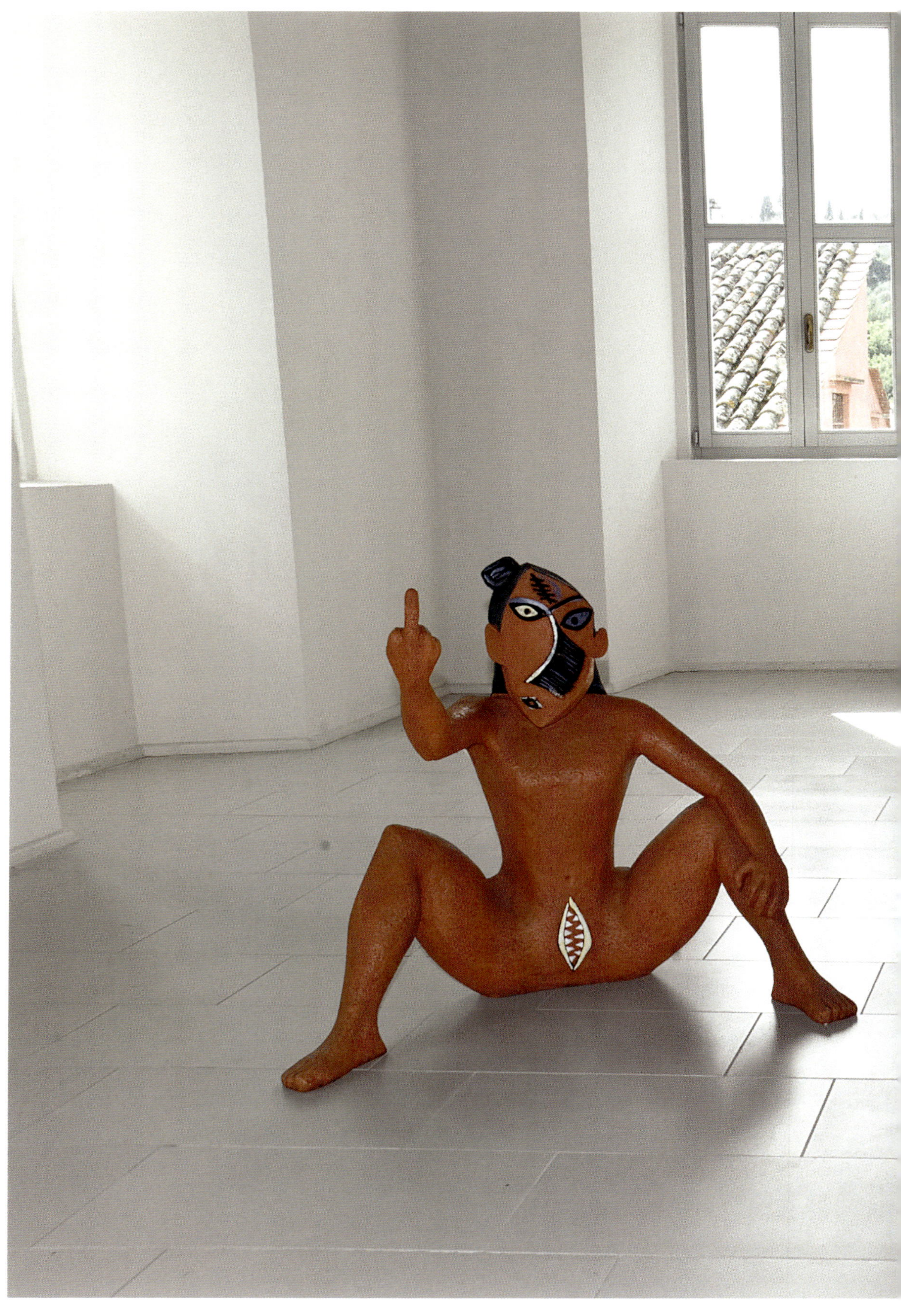

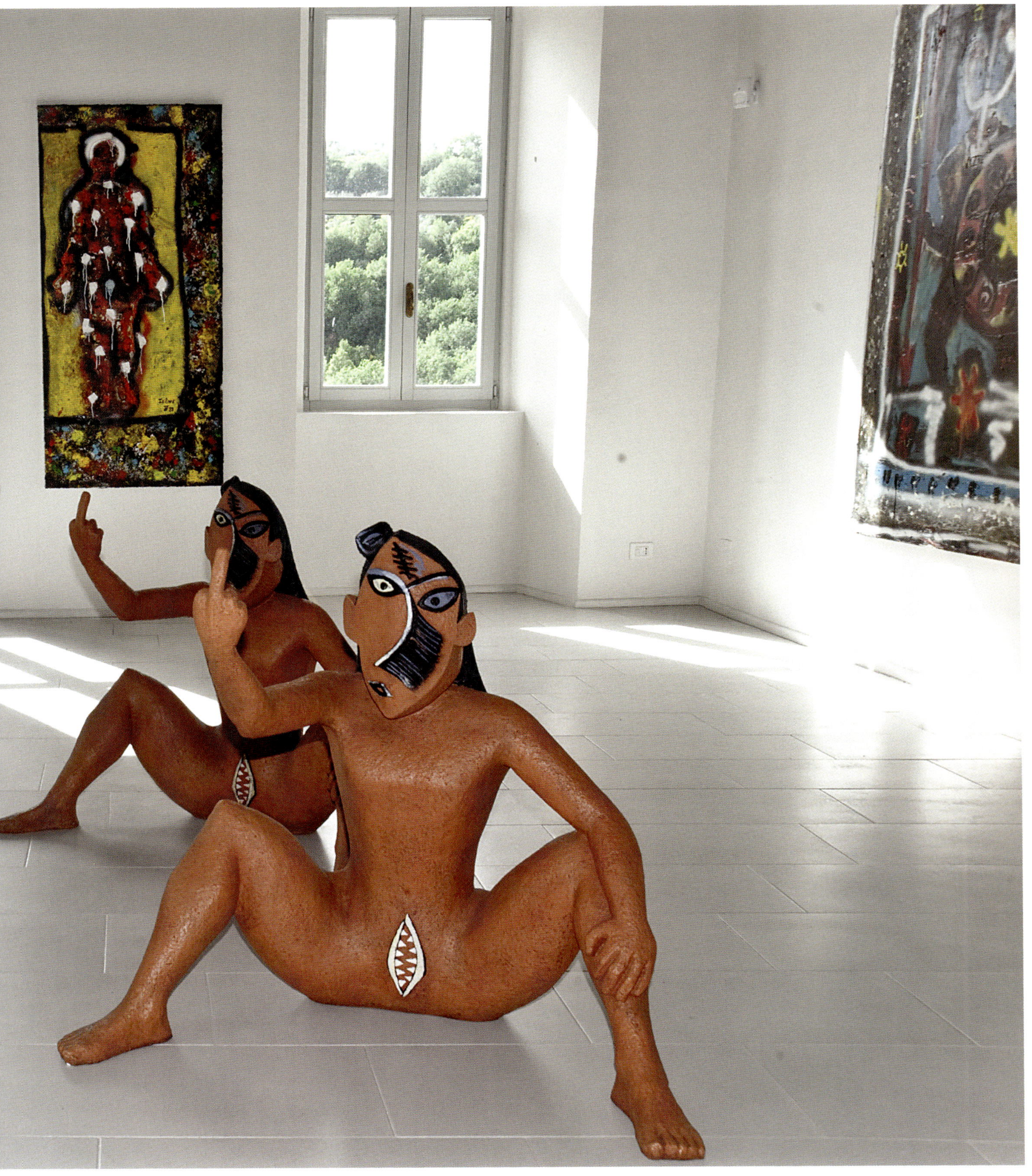

way round), Friedler created *Be Boz Be Art*. The main objective of its complete programme — artistic, humanistic and philosophical — is to create or generate creative flows. In this universe, both imaginary and real, he constructed a labyrinthine, hypertextual and multimedia work that connects a set of energies whose purpose is to reveal instances of secret complicity between the most disparate and geographically distant beings through his actions performed through *Spirit of Boz*. Sonia Bressler has this to say about it: 'Julien Friedler's most complex work is not the one that can be seen… His work is a global gesture, there is a beginning, an impulse, then there is its momentum, its mechanism, then there is its spatiality and finally its extension. He likes to speak of work in rhizome. Julien Friedler's work is *Spirit of Boz*.'[3]

2 December 2006: (http://rebelle.blogspirit.com/archive/2021/04/29/julien-friedler-dealer-d-utopies-3251717.html) *La Nuit du Boz* took place at Le Canal in Brussels. Advertised in the streets of Brussels as a happening, the evening promised to be lively. Sonia Bressler recounts: 'Everyone is having fun, there's music playing and champagne, a sweet poetic intoxication takes hold of the dancers for one night against a background of electronic music. Is this a projection of our life today or a contemporary allegory of the cave? It is here that *La Forêt des âmes* begins'. The event, an interruption to the banality of ordinary life, introduced to the attendees all the projects designed to help us reconsider the world in accordance with the logic of art, of a moment dedicated to meditation, on the other side of our beings, far from the contingencies and the materialistic injunctions of our society. Friedler invited everyone to *Be Boz Be Art*. This is the title of an apolitical, philosophical programme. It is a movement dedicated to art-seekers. Its associated actions encourage artistic expression to be created where it seems to be lacking. The programme is based on the lines of three works: *La Forêt des âmes*, *Le Clochard Céleste* and *Give up*. This part of Friedler's multidisciplinary and collegial work is an attempt to merge different forms of expression. Here, art is the medium of exchange and communication, embodying the end of certainties and the beginning of a creative era, and inviting everyone to be a part of it.

2006–2009, establishment of *Spirit of Boz*'s founding concepts (https://docplayer.fr/200236625-La-foret-des-ames-de-julien-friedler.html).
La Forêt des âmes - Le Tour du Boz en 80 ans is the first action that leads to the construction of *Spirit of Boz*. It is a questionnaire distributed during *Boz* happenings, to which everyone is asked to give answers. There are six questions that introduce the path of deep thought, collective action and self-questioning: 1. Does God exist? 2. How would you describe this epoch? 3. How do you see the future? 4. Are you happy? 5. Is sexuality important? 6. Who am I?
The questionnaire was presented to the public for the first time on 2 December 2006. Friedler's intention is for the experiment to continue for 80 years, ending in 2086, 'beyond our lives' he says like a sort of vanitas, the aim being to collect the answers to these six questions. Since 2007, those involved in this project have travelled to countless places in the most unusual regions of the planet to collect the deeply considered or fleeting thoughts of the thousands of participants in answer to these six questions, which remain unchanged regardless of the society in which they are asked. From Togo to Santiago de Chile, via New York, Milan, Rome, Paris, London, Moscow, Kathmandu, Lhasa and Beijing, *La Forêt des âmes* invites everyone to stop by.

2007: the questionnaires arrive from Rwanda, Morocco, Bulgaria and Brazil. Prisoners, the sick, schoolchildren and students offer to share this moment of eternity either through writing or drawing. Because that is what it is all about. The questionnaires received will be sealed in columns that together

Arafat, 2004 (sculpture in resin
and mixed media, h. 160 cm), and
studio of *Boz* view

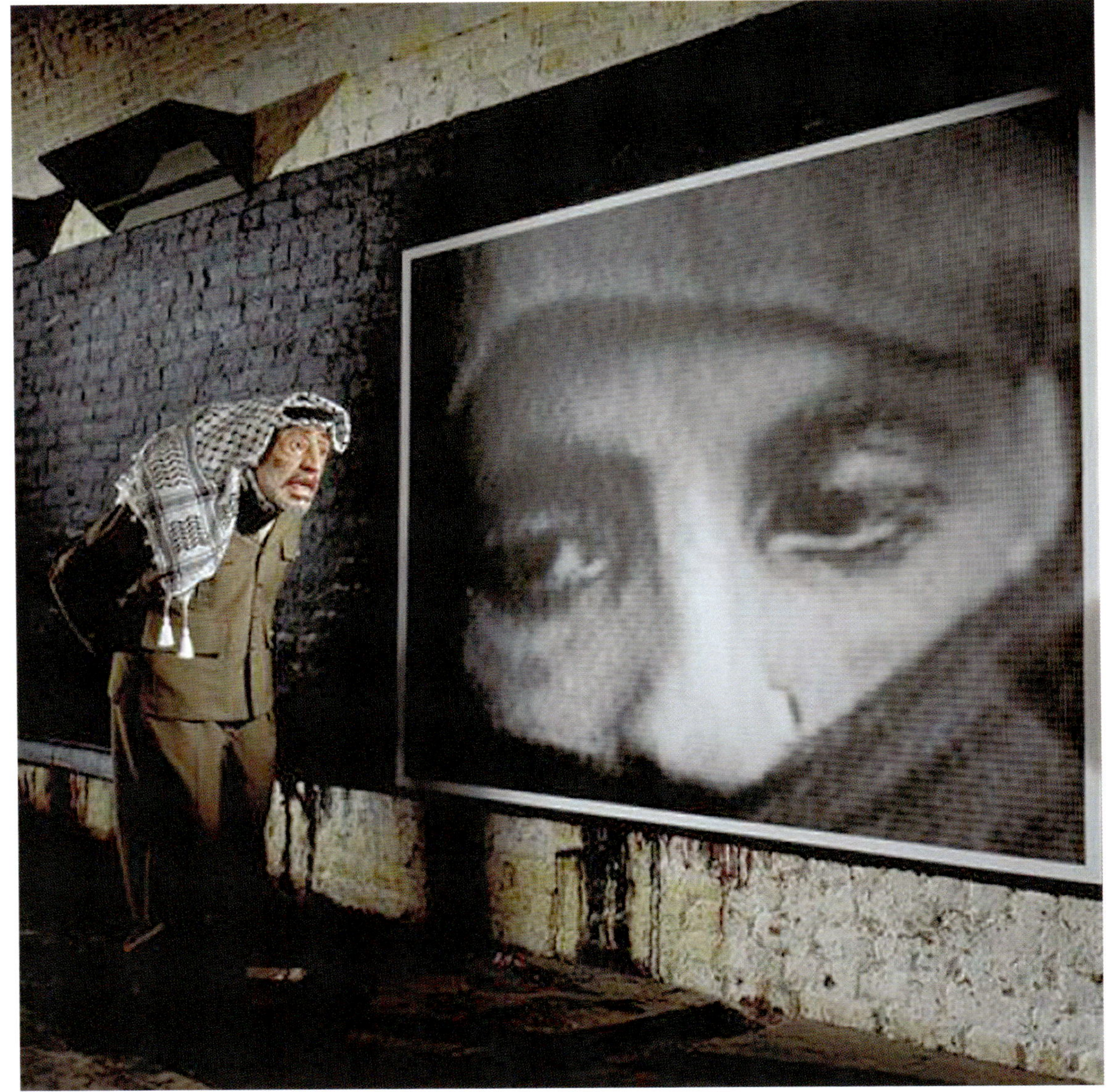

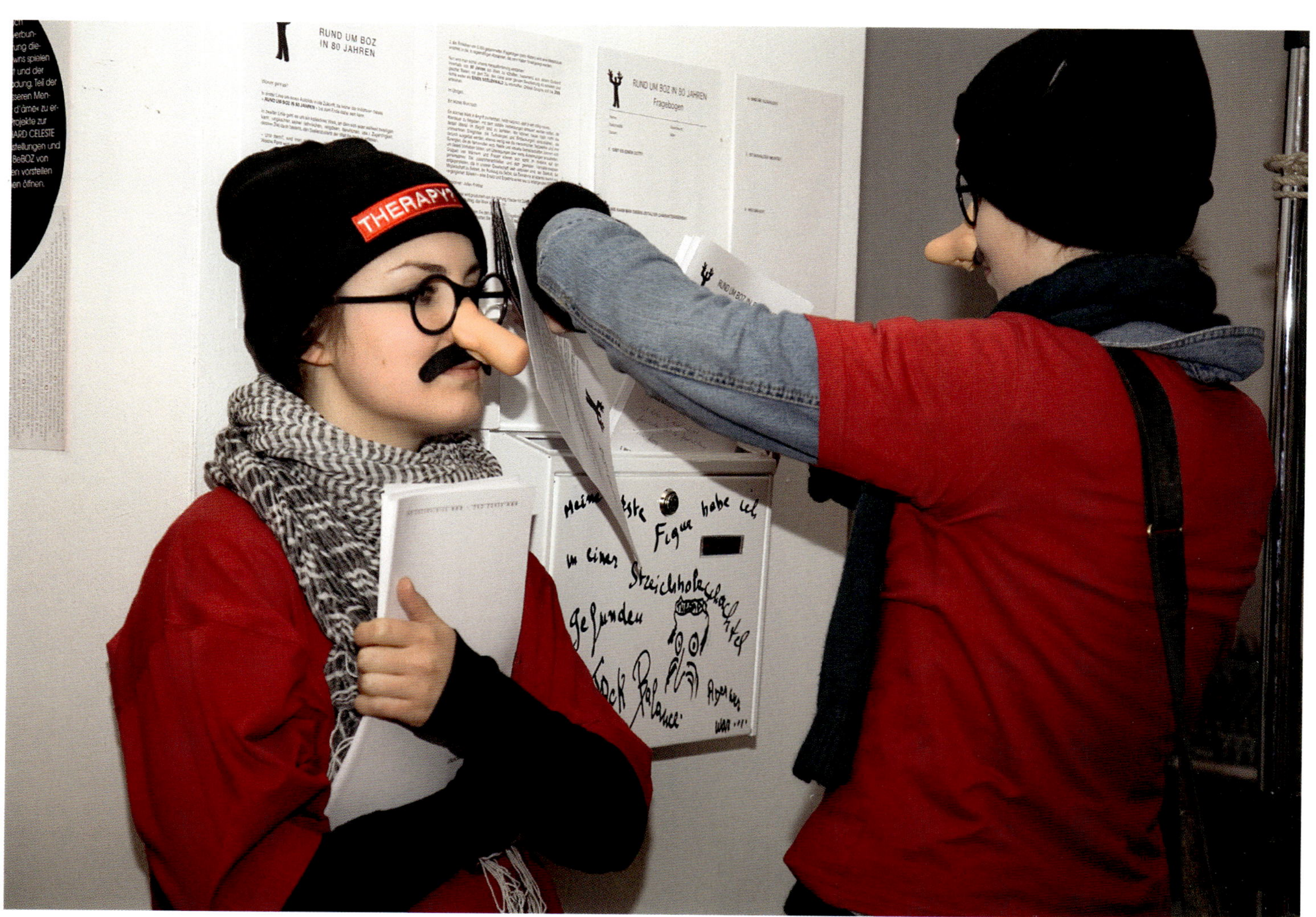

Performance questionnaires:
*La Forêt des âmes - Le Tour du
Boz en 80 ans*, 2008

Poster of *The Night of Boz*,
2 December 2006

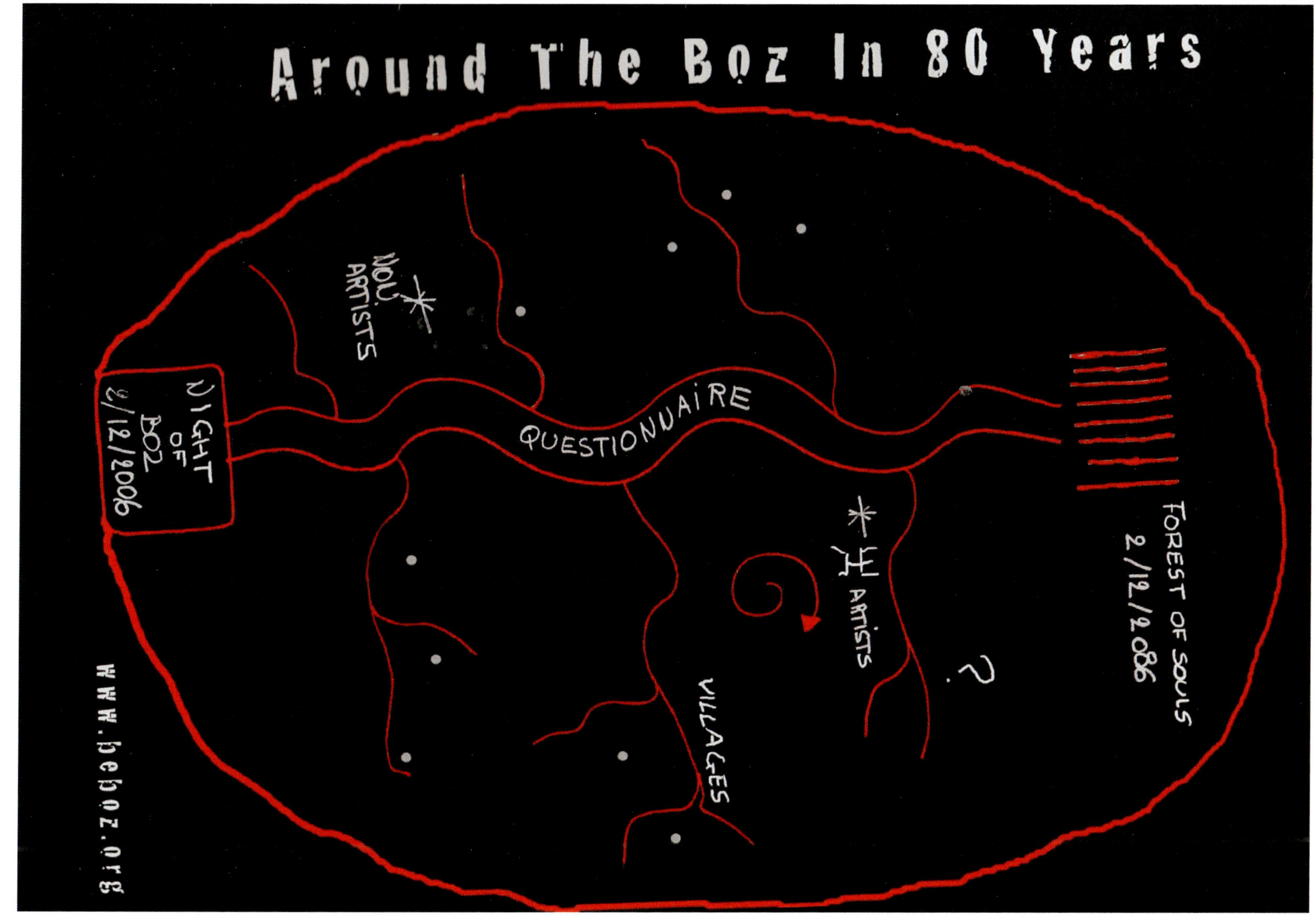

Around The Boz In 80 Years
NOU. ARTISTS
NIGHT OF BOZ
2/12/2006
QUESTIONUAIRE
FOREST OF SOULS
2/12/2086
ARTISTS
?
VILLAGES
www.beboz.org

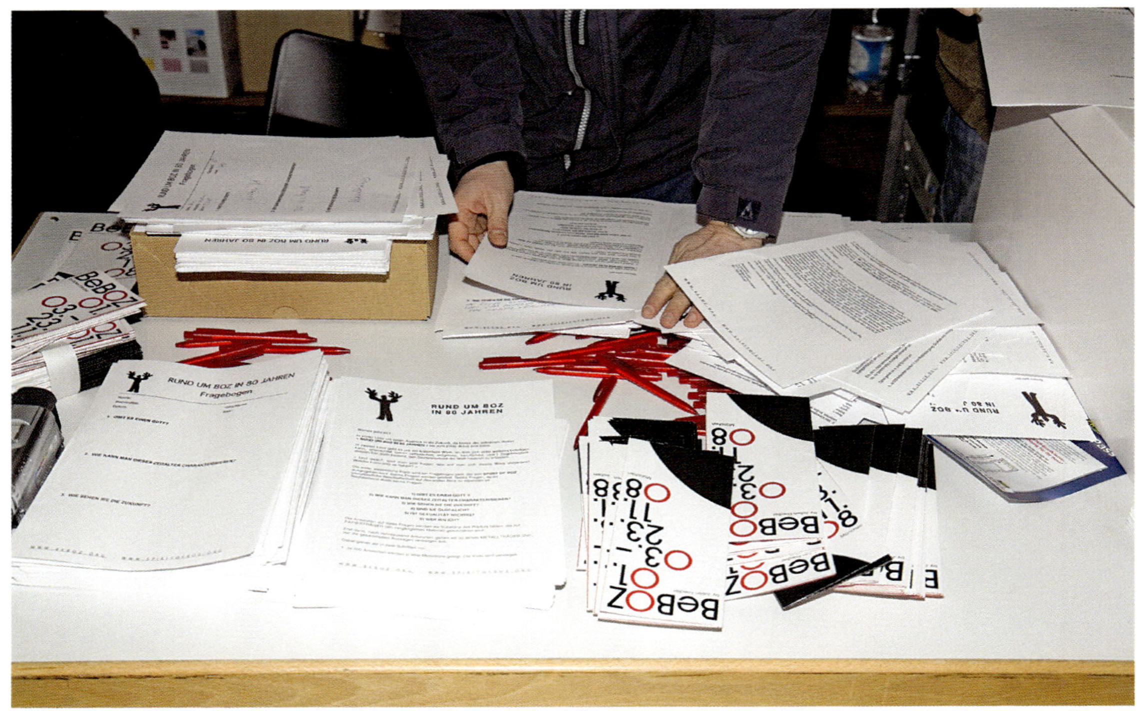

will create *La Forêt des âmes*. In September 2007, Carmen Ferreyra travelled through South America. With her teams, she brought back answers from Buenos Aires, Córdoba, Rosario, Loncopué (province of Neuquén), Gualeguaychú, Santiago de Chile, Montevideo, and the favelas of Belém in Brazil.

2007 also saw the inception of *Give up* and the first objects that were given and received as part of an exchange programme that has grown over 10 years. It is a project based on giving, letting go. The donation can be of anything, an everyday object or even a work of art. The programme was first developed in Togo and Argentina, then in Indonesia and Europe. One of the most significant actions of the *Give up* 'journey' occurred in Loncopué, Argentina, where the population of this small town of 6000 people, completely unaware of artistic concerns, was invited to share a facet of their daily lives by making drawings, paintings or donating some object. They also filled in the questionnaire for *La Forêt des âmes*. A competition led to the selection of twenty-five of the hundred or so works collected, which were then integrated into the *Boz* collection, constituting the most eloquent evidence of the impact of the reflection on art among people who have no experience of it. The drawings by Ida Leandro are remarkable.

Also in 2007, in the programme called *Le Clochard Céleste*, the *Spirit of Boz* proposed exchange and dialogue with the most ignored individuals in our society: 'Whether in the streets of Brussels, the outskirts of Jakarta or with street children in Rwanda, the *Clochard Céleste* programme consists of giving the means of artistic expression to people living in distress or precariousness — artistic expression as it can arise anywhere.'

The exhibition *In Quest* was held at the Galerie Philippe Seghers in Ostend (curated by Michael Dewilde). The exhibition was accompanied by a performance by Jack Balance on Ostend dike (https://www.paperblog.fr/209641/la-cabine-du-boz-performance-a-ostende/ – https://www.youtube.com/watch?v=xshbcF0DZLl). 'Around 2pm, an armada of Jack Balance look-alikes spread out around the booth. Dressed in a black cap, glasses, false nose, moustache and a red T-shirt, and with the *Tour du Boz* questionnaire in hand, they went to meet the onlookers, whom they asked to fill in the questionnaire'. Let's go back to Julien Friedler, who set up this *Boz* programme at a time when he was questioning the fundamentals of his artistic action. Although he had already been painting for several

[4] Julien Friedler, *Les Fondamentaux* (Paris: La Route de la Soie - Éditions, 2020), p. 7.

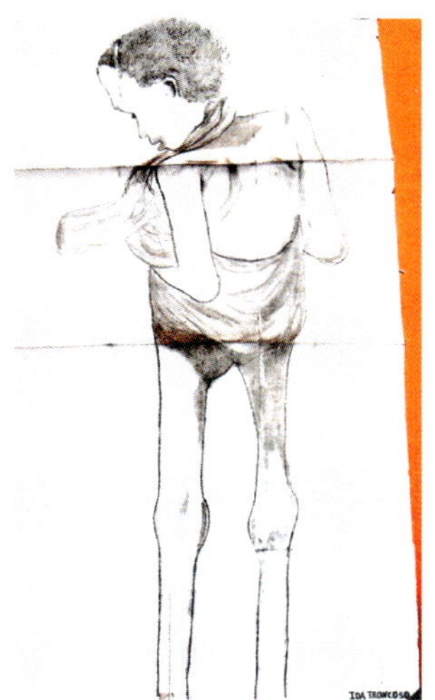

Drawing executed by Ida Leandro for *Give up, Spirit of Boz*, 2007, Loncopué City (Argentina)

Performance *Jack Balance*, Ostend, 2007

years, he went to the farthest origins of our civilisation, to sources that have been least altered by preconceived ideas, to find the answers to his questions: 'What is it all about?' asks Friedler. 'Instead of giving an abstract definition, which is always reductive, I will try to illustrate here a place of propagation: an amalgamation of affects, thoughts and sensations, arising out of a chain of acts that question the status of the artist'.[4] It is this status that interests him, that legitimises his work and that of so many others.

In spite of all the vivacity produced by the world of *Boz*, Julien Friedler continues his personal work. His studio continues to be filled with his paintings, sculptures and installations. His painting, which arises from letters and signs (*La Forêt des âmes*, 2007), continues to develop its ritual themes, akin to experiences of trance and hypnosis. Friedler scrutinises and delves into the matter to extract its vital sap. The pictorial form is close to graffiti. These are primitive works created with rugged, magmatic matter.

2008: The *Spirit of Boz* programme continued. Information given by analysis of the first elements collected around the world reinforced Friedler's conviction that art is the mover of our lives and generates a force composed of light and truth. On 18 June 2008, the works created in Loncopué, a small village in the remoteness of Patagonia, were presented at Sotheby's in Munich in an exhibition of the drawings, paintings, sculptures and questionnaires to collectors used to highly rated works by established artists. The event provoked questions. Friedler replied that it was the result of 'going to look for art where it is not expected'. In parallel to the exhibition at Sotheby's, a *Be Boz* performance was given at the Heilig-Kreuz-Kirche in Munich. During the church service, the priest invites everyone to think about the questions in the *Forêt des âmes* questionnaire. In his sermon he emphasised: 'The questions of being and becoming, of appearance and truth are not foreign to the *Be Boz* project. It is a questionnaire in which the answers are perhaps of less importance than the questions'. The six questions were inscribed above the church choir, while the installation *L'Envol* (2008), where questionnaires are rolled up in a spiral movement, was set at the highest point of the nave. A *Give up* event with the title 'Out There in the Middle of Nowhere' was held at the Galerie der Künstler in Munich, when visitors were encouraged to offer an object that symbolised their personal desire, placing it in a ring of ashes. The Munich trilogy marks an important moment in the emerging history of *Spirit of Boz* and a video is available of it at https://www.dailymotion.com/video/x4pj56

2008: Friedler created the installation, *La Forêt des âmes*, composed of nine wooden columns topped with African-inspired masks made from transparent resin, which are illuminated from the inside by

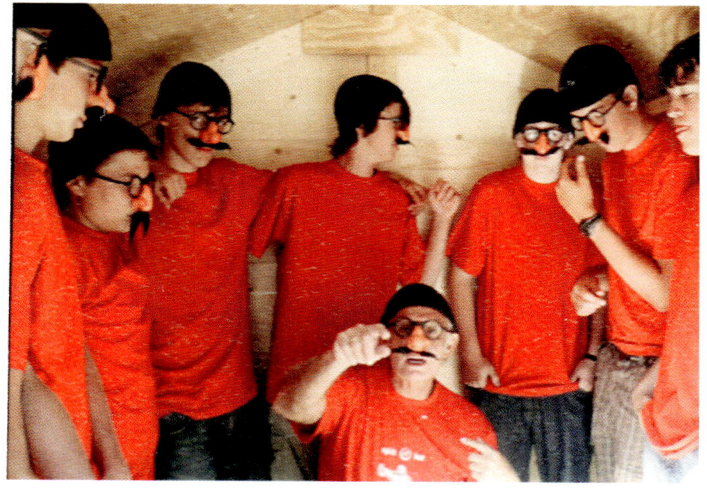

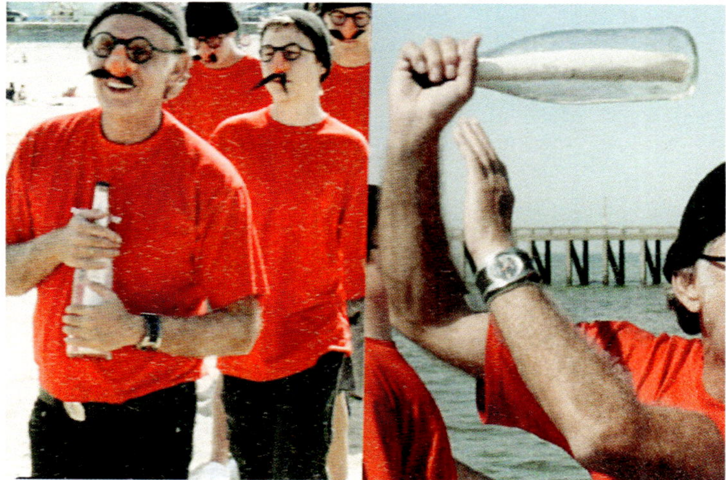

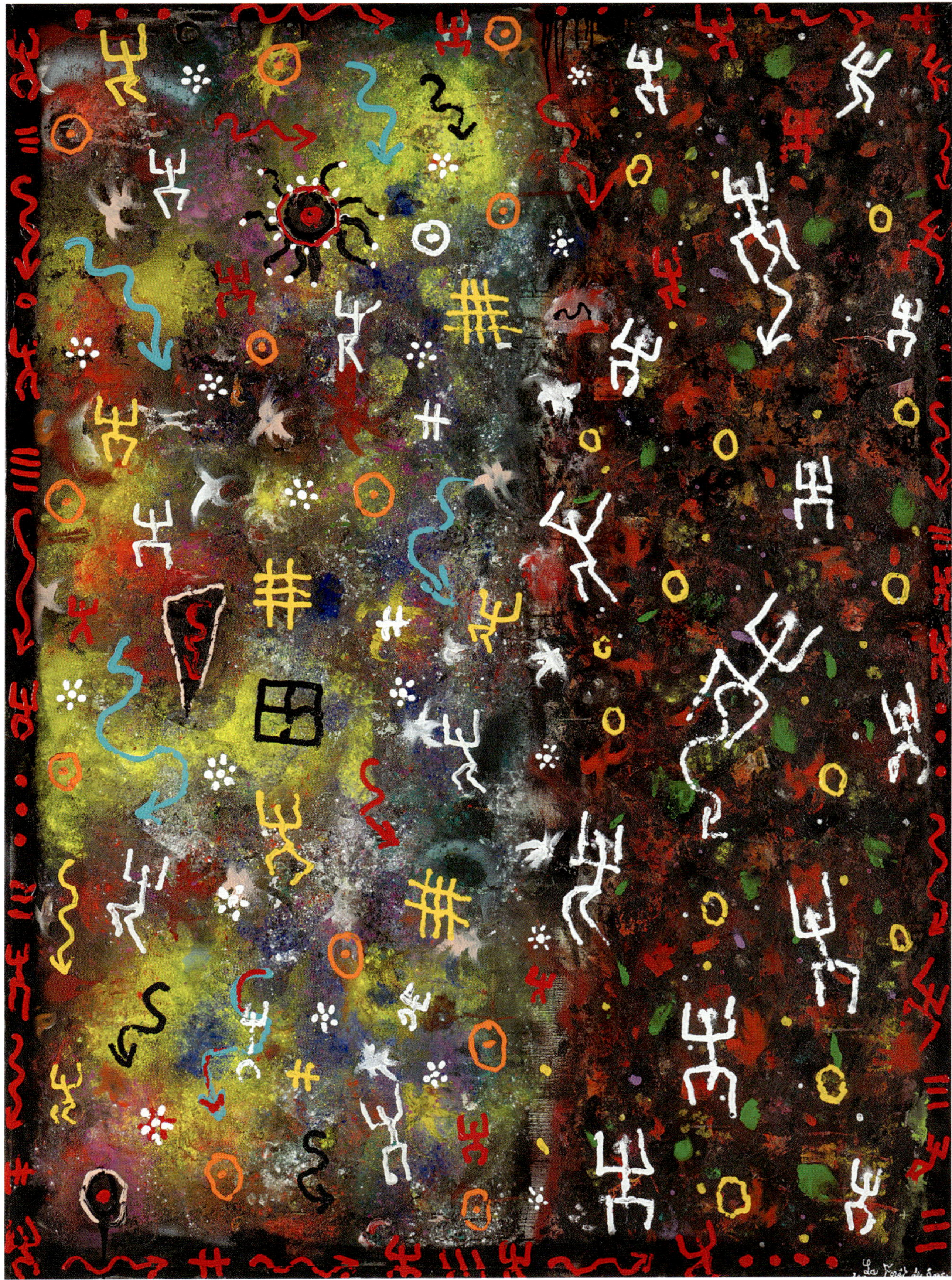

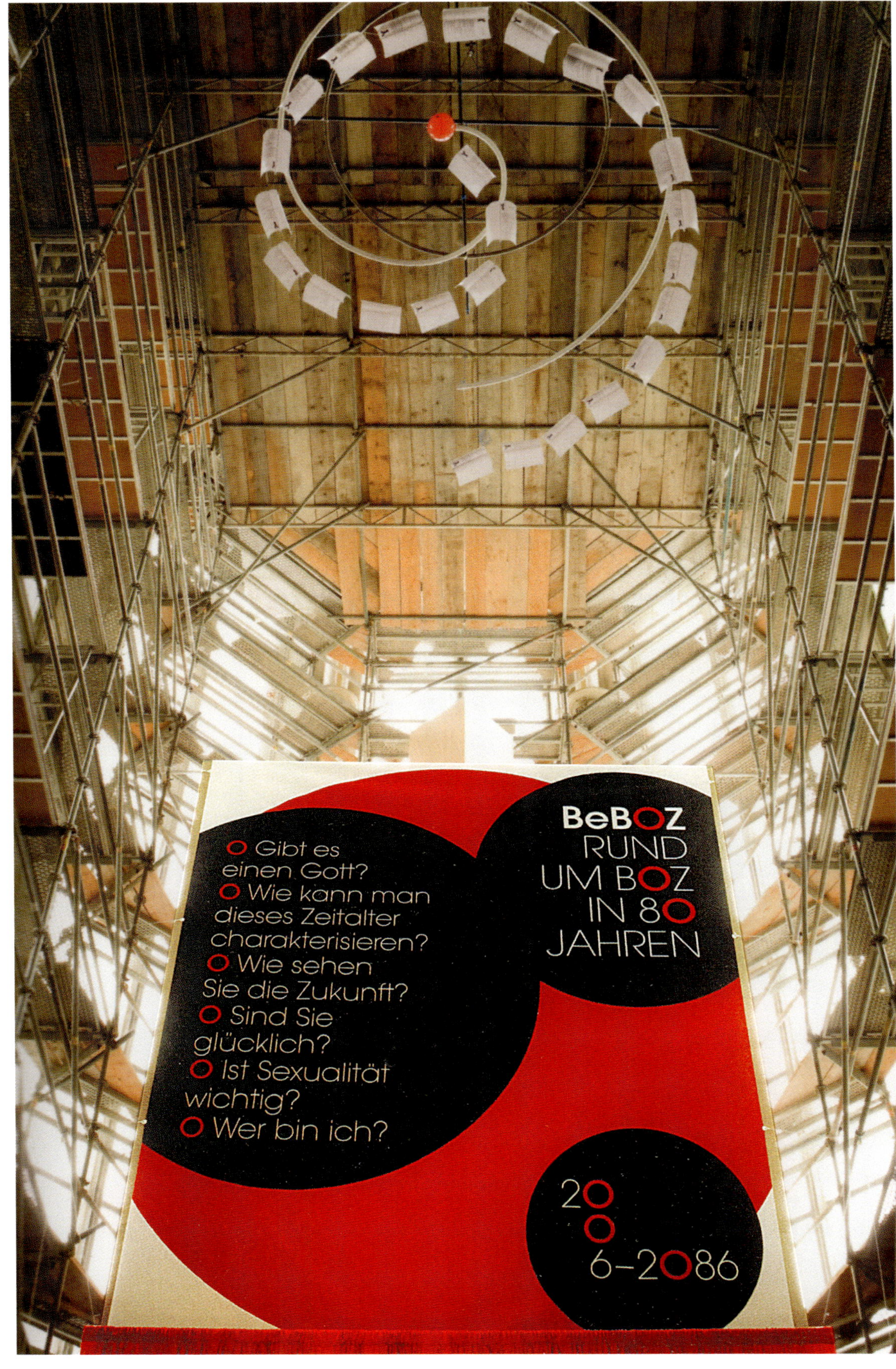

La Forêt des âmes, 2007
Acrylic on canvas, 200 x 150 cm

The installation *L'Envol* and the sign presenting the six questions about *La Forêt des âmes* in the church choir (Heilig-Kreuz-Kirche, Munich), 2008

a LED light. The effect is striking and the accompanying music invites the public to meditate. This installation heralded a set of monumental columns in which the questionnaires collected from around the world will be sealed.

In 2008, the *Give up Togo* action was held. Agnès Mukarubayiza, who was in charge of the *Boz* programme in the country, collected a great many symbolic objects, including the *Statuette des jumeaux*, which became the starting point for a performance by Belgian artists at the *Boz* workshop in Brussels in 2010.

2009 was an important year for Jack Balance. The Christopher Henry Gallery in New York presented Julien Friedler's first solo show in his gallery, *Who is Jack Balance?*, which was curated by Gabrielle Bryer. The press release stated: 'Spread over two floors of the gallery, the exhibition takes us on a discovery of Jack Balance and the World of Boz. Through his writings, paintings, sculptures and happenings, Friedler's conceptual project takes us on an adventure in a parallel world where the artist confronts us with haunting questions for which we have no answers… There is spirituality in Friedler's imperfect world: he helps us see, understand and accept the unacceptable imperfection of our human condition. To do so, he has invented an allegorical figure of himself — Jack Balance — whose adventures allow the artist to distil his message.'

Two other exhibitions were held that same year, one of which was at the MUBE (Museu Brasileiro da Escultura), São Paulo in Brazil in October (https://www.julienfriedler.com/exposition/mube/). This huge retrospective showcased Friedler's work. Permeated by philosophical concepts and

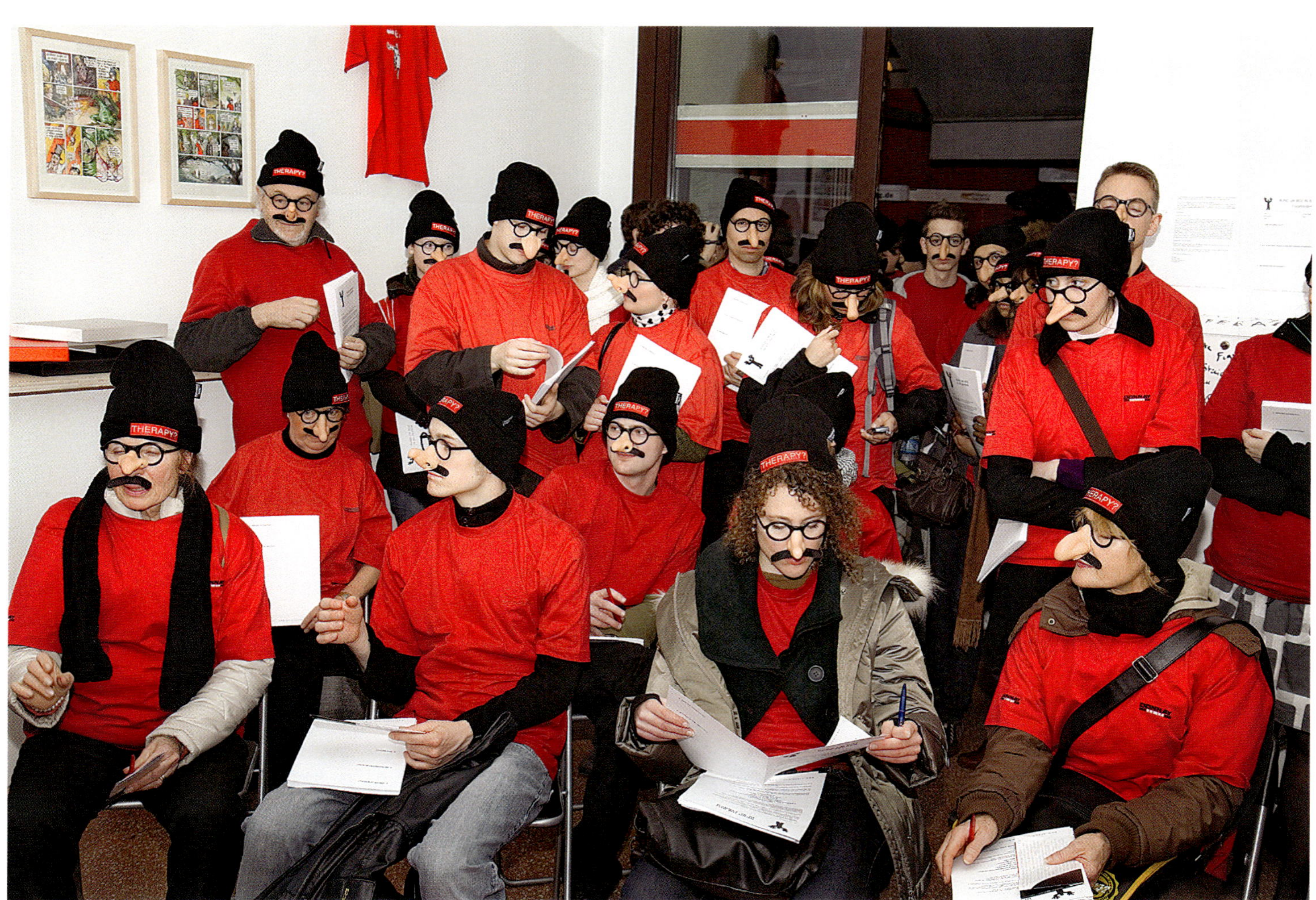

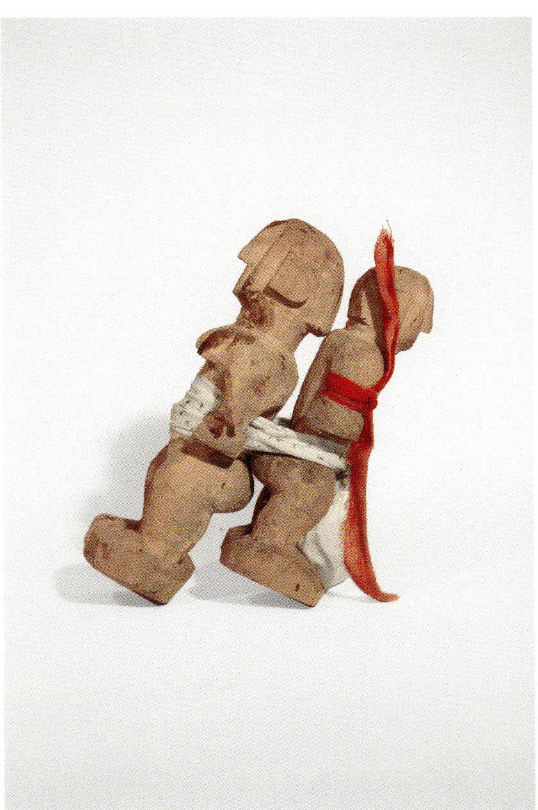

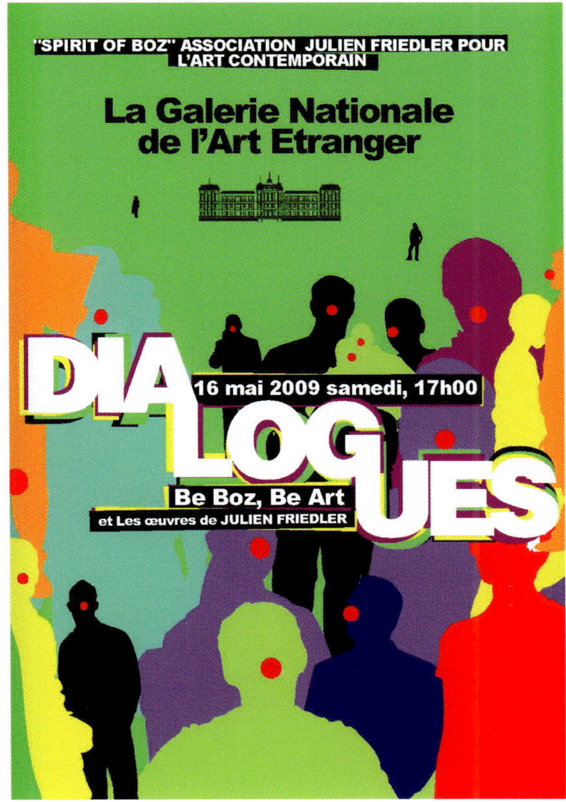

references to art history and Pop Art, it drew attention to the coexistence of several mythologies.
In the manner of the term *Boz*, a construction with no real meaning, the project was permeated by
playfulness and humour, but it also had a psychological dimension. The shows featured some thirty
works that covered the fields of painting, sculpture, literature, video, photography, installations and
performance.

Julien Friedler's presence in Brazil was also the occasion for street performances during which
everyone was invited to fill in the questionnaire, give an object or propose a drawing. The *Boz* collection
was growing.

The other exhibition in 2009 was held at the National Gallery for Foreign Art in Sofia, Bulgaria, from
May to June. The exhibition was called *Dialogues* (https://www.spiritofboz.com/julien-friedler/julien-
friedler-artwork/sofia/) and contrasted Friedler's works with the *Be Boz Be Art* project. Conceived as
a conceptual and atypical exhibition, Julien Friedler made it a dialogue between the singular and the
universal, the dream and the ideal with reality, modernity with tradition, the written with the visual, all
with the goal of making visitors react and participate. They were of course also invited to answer the six
questions in the *Tour du Boz en 80 ans*.

2009 was also the year in which the installation *La Forêt des âmes* was exhibited for the first time.
Isolde Brielmaier presented it in a group show at the Jack Shainman Gallery in New York. The
exhibition illustrated the important role of African or African-influenced artists on the world scene, and
was presented as part of the *Spirit of Boz* project.

In spite of the need for constant travel, Friedler continued his painting, producing *Ecce Homo*
(2009), *Le Cavalier de l'Apocalypse* (2009) and many other works illustrative of his introspective
power in his Brussels studio. By this time, Friedler had developed his own pictorial manner,
distinguished by an openly subjective style that passes from Appel, through De Kooning and arrives

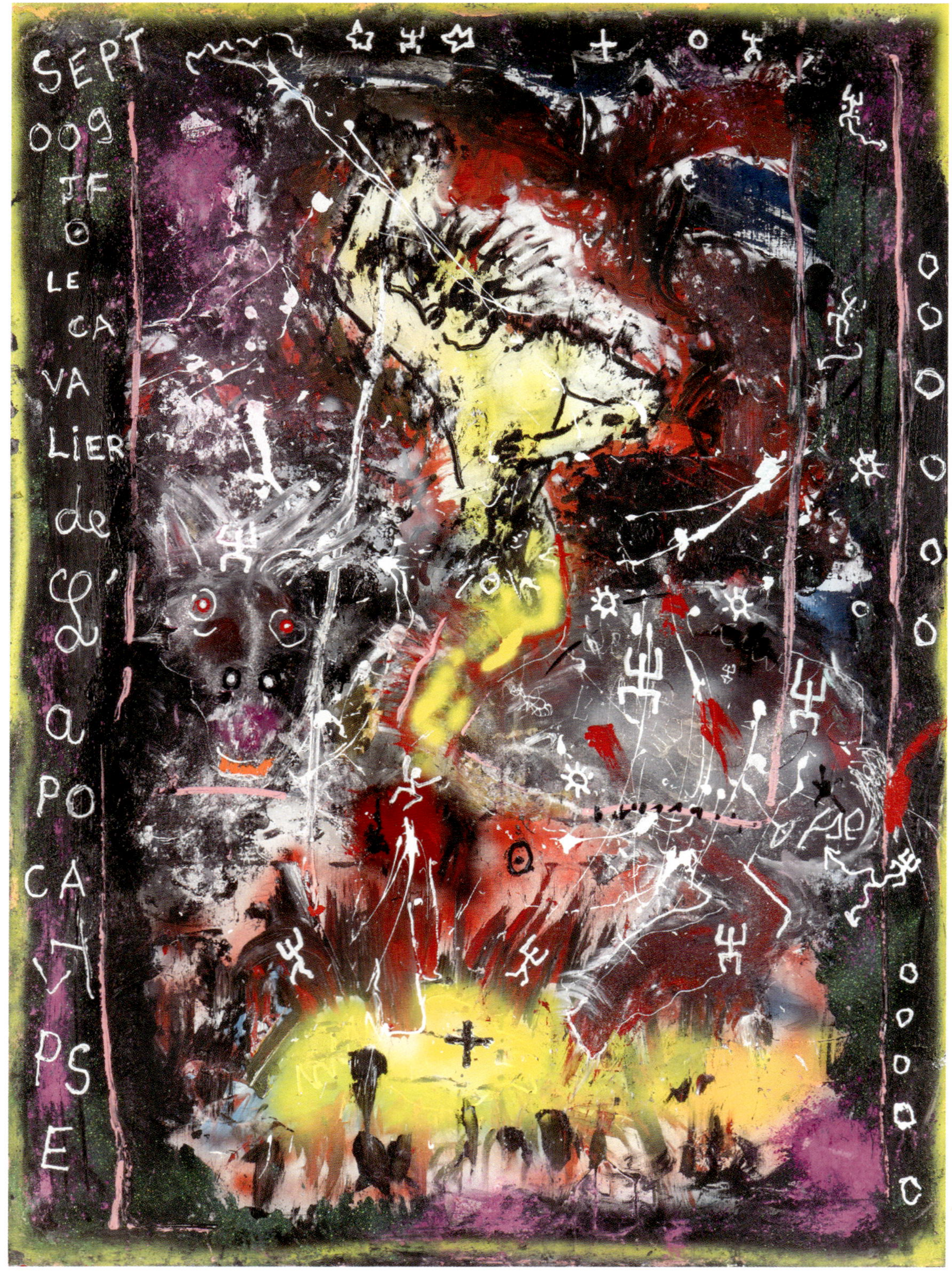

Le Cavalier de l'Apocalypse, 2009
Acrylic on canvas, 200 x 150 cm

La Chute du Joker, 2010
Acrylic on canvas, 300 x 200 cm

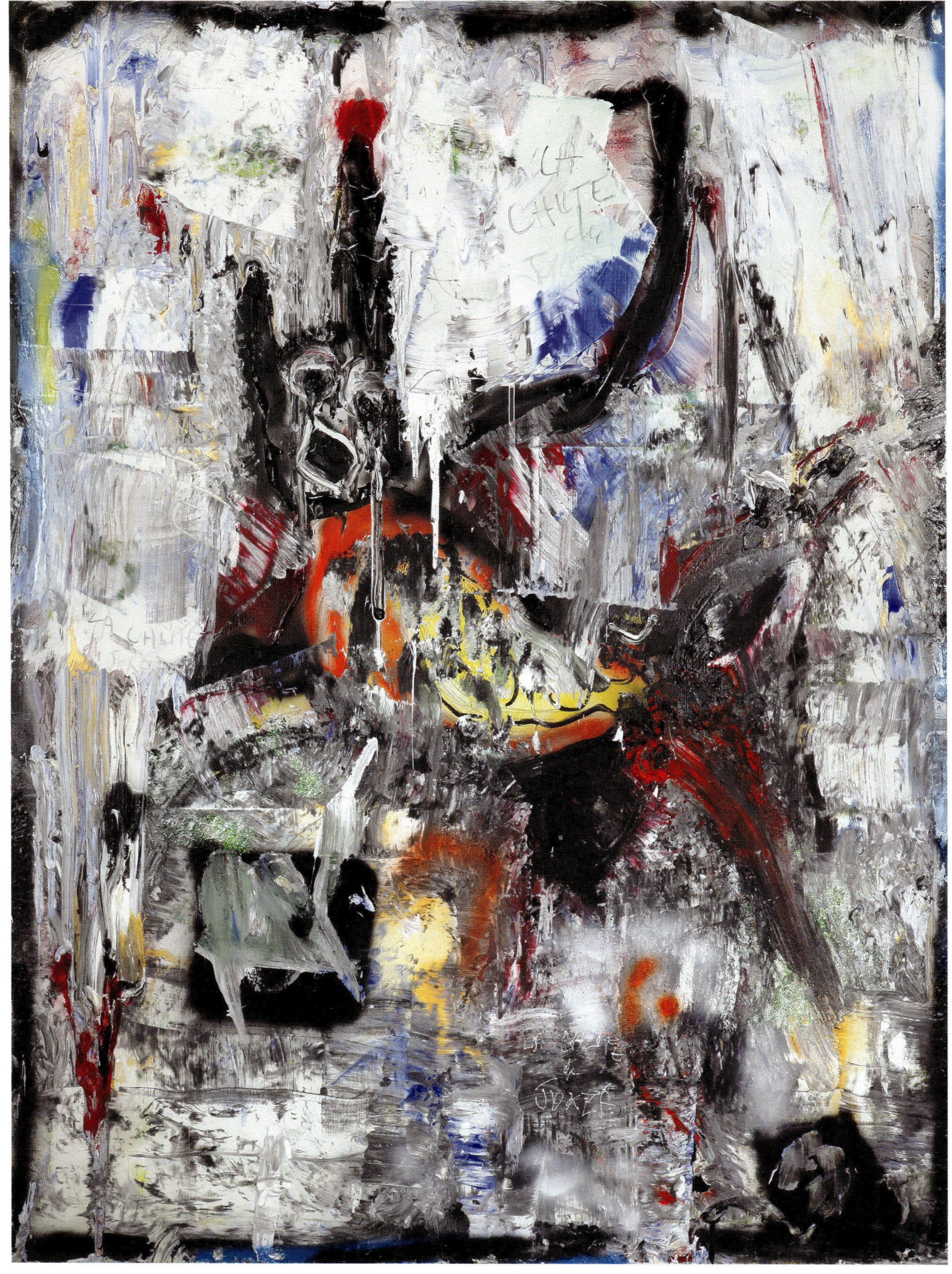
LA
CHUTE
du
LA CHUTE

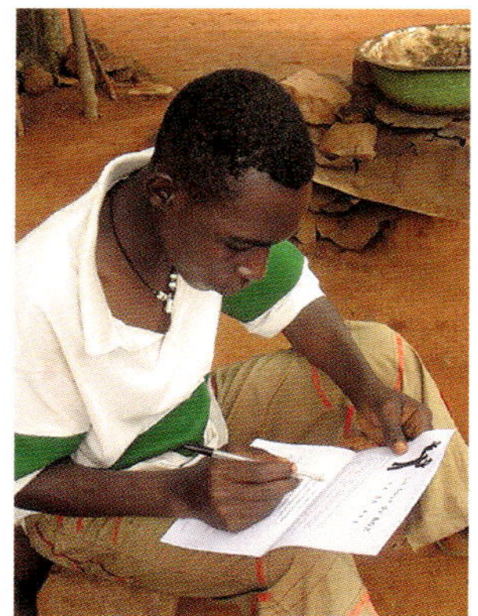

Young Togolese completing the questionnaire of *La Forêt des âmes*, 2010

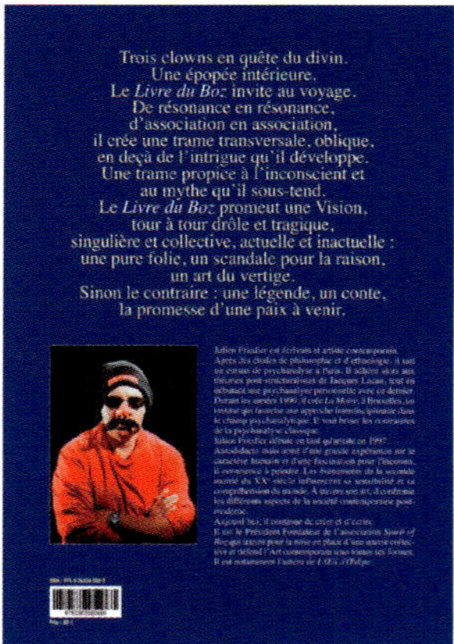

Cover of *Le Livre du Boz* (Mariac: Jacques Flament Éditions, 2013)

at Basquiat, however whose subject is no longer the torment of the self and the ecstasy of the artist ('tragedy, ecstasy and doom', proclaimed the Abstract Expressionism generation) but includes fluid, erratic forms, idols and totems, constellations and animals, abysses and battles.

2010: *Spirit of Boz, the Truth of the Labyrinth* exhibition, CW Gallery, New York, on the legend of Boz and its projection in the literary reality of the *Livre du Boz.* This multi-faceted book suggested an interpretation in the form of a comic strip featuring three clowns on a quest for the divine. It included a bit of burlesque and some tragedy in their adventures which, via a series of parallels and associations, created a transversal and oblique framework within the plot it developed, a framework favourable to the unconscious and myth it underlay.

Friedler developed his text *La Vérité du Labyrinthe*, which would later give rise to debates and be published in 2017.

2010 was also the year for the conference/debate on the *Spirit of Boz* held in Monaco in July. *Give up Togo* also continued its adventure. After her journeys to Rwanda, Agnès Mukarubayiza returned to Africa as part of the *Tour du Boz en 80 ans* (https://www.spiritofboz.com/be-boz-be-art/the-program-around-the-world/togo/). The inhabitants of Tovegan suggested they rename their village *Boz.* A great number of questionnaires and objects were gathered.

10 October 2010, an important performance occurred in the *Boz* studio in Brussels: *Give up Togo/ Brussels – La performance des Jumeaux.* A group of local artists inspired by the objects brought back from Togo entered into an artistic dialogue in particular with the statuette of the twins, a small and symbolic sculpture from Togo. They painted three works in an action that combined delirium and trance (https://www.spiritofboz.com/be-boz-be-art/the-program-around-the-world/togo/).

Julien Friedler returned to the studio in 2010 and intensified his pictorial output. He painted *La Chute du Joker*, a major work whose technique was close to dramatic abstraction, and continued writing the *Livre du Boz.*

His work was included in a group exhibition at the Galerie Gourvennec Ogor in Marseille. For its inauguration, the gallery brought together artists from different generations. Poetic, magical and sometimes disturbing, the show had the goal of rediscovering a panorama of different aesthetic choices and of reconsidering themes as varied as human relations, politics, reality and its metamorphoses, the history of art, space and illusion.

From 2011 to 2015: further *Give up* and *Forêt des âmes* actions were held in Togo, as well as in Brussels and New York (2012). The philosopher and writer Sonia Bressler set out on a journey through Asia from which she brought back painted works, symbolic objects, and questionnaires. She went first to Jakarta in Indonesia in 2011, then to Lhasa in Tibet in 2012. Two years later, she was in Bombay in India, and Kathmandu in Nepal, from where she sent back papers, drawings, collages and unusual objects to join the *Boz* harvest. In 2015 she travelled to Gansu in China and more recently among the Uyghurs (2017). These journeys feed her own work as an ethno-philosopher: 'I observe the metamorphoses of humanity', she commented, 'so as to better understand and transmit it'. As a result of her involvement, the project's exchanges and dialogues have diversified, with art serving as a medium for communication in accordance with the *Boz* theory. Interviews and reports are included as part of a programme of listening to and discovering others, and also of exchanges that she calls *The Wall of Humanity.* It is a specific study within the world of *Boz* that the philosopher has now carried out in France, Indonesia, Tibet and China, and which she has been pursuing since 2012.

During these years, two books were published on the world of Julien Friedler. In 2012, Norbert Hillaire's *Double vue, 50 fragments pour Julien Friedler* was published by Somogy (Paris). 'Faced with Julien

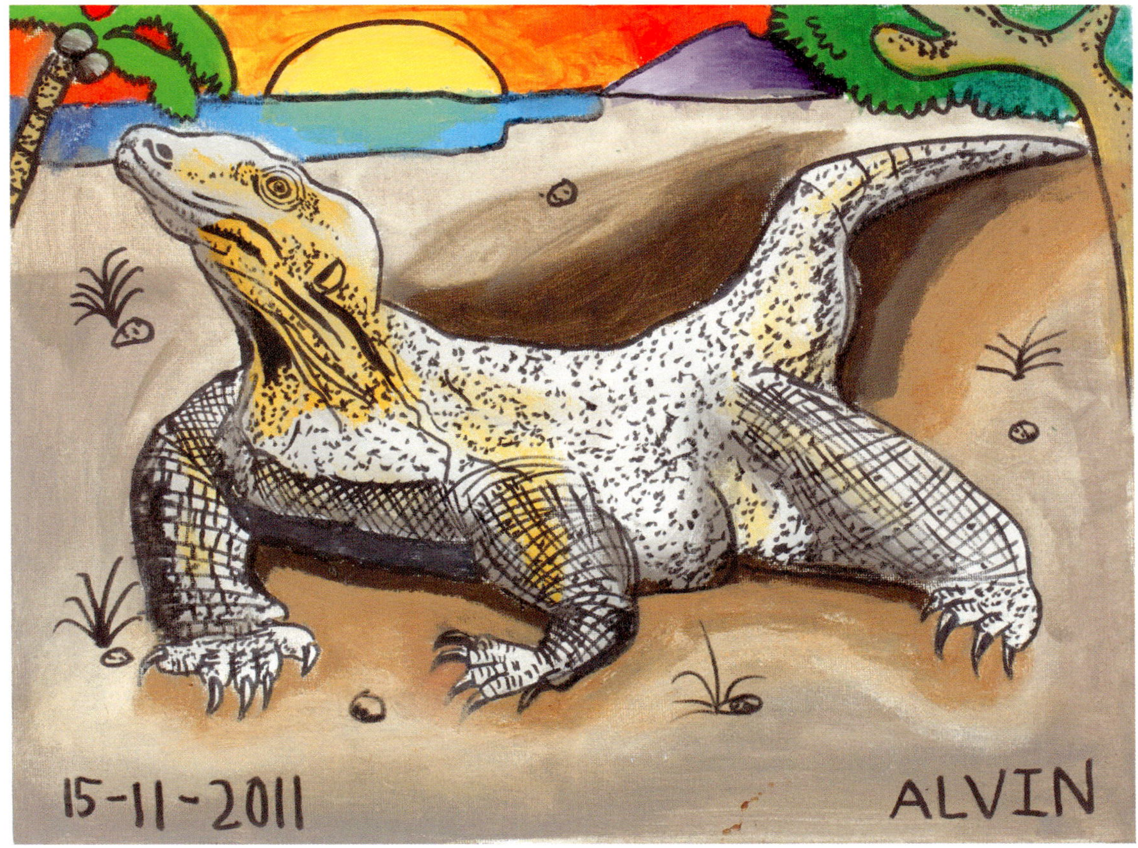

Be Boz Be Art at Jakarta, Indonesia. Student at Jakarta Hadiprana Art Centre, Alvin Kennet Cheng, realised the painting *Komodo* for *Give up* action, 2011

Friedler's universe,' Hillaire writes, 'at the frontier of the social, the aesthetic and the sciences of dreaming, we wanted to share the challenge.' On 1 September 2012, the solo exhibition *Les Disparus* was held at the Gourvennec Ogor Gallery in Marseille (https://www.julienfriedler.com/exposition/les-disparus/). Exhibiting a series of photographs taken in his Brussels studio in spring 2012, Friedler takes viewers into the intimate confines of his work, into the private world of his memory as a man and an artist. By revealing the traces of his heated creative process, and irradiating the space with materials and pigments, bodies and signs, Friedler reveals his inner battlefield. The photographs do not reveal real paintings, just traces of their existence are visible, like the remnants of a work of art that are not enough to tell us whether it is really completed or not. In the middle of the exhibition viewers were confronted with the doll bearing the Jewish star, a witness to the atrocities and individuals who have disappeared forever, and whose existence only continues thanks to memory. Nor does the artist appear, he is present only by his own absence.

On the evening of the show's opening, Julien Friedler, or rather Jack Balance realised the *Performance des allumettes*, featuring matches, alcohol, a pair of scissors, cloth and a bowl. The cloth was cut into small pieces. A match was struck, then another and the cloth set alight. It was allowed to be reduced to ash. The performance was an allegory of a programmed disappearance, an inquiry into the vanity of things. The artist continued on his journey as a propagator of ideas.

2013: publication of *Le Livre du Boz* by Jacques Flament Éditions. Julien Friedler comments: '*Le Livre du Boz* is neither a book, nor a poem, nor a tale, even less a drama or an essay. It is nothing, apart from the style by which it is inspired and haunted. There are no points of reference here.

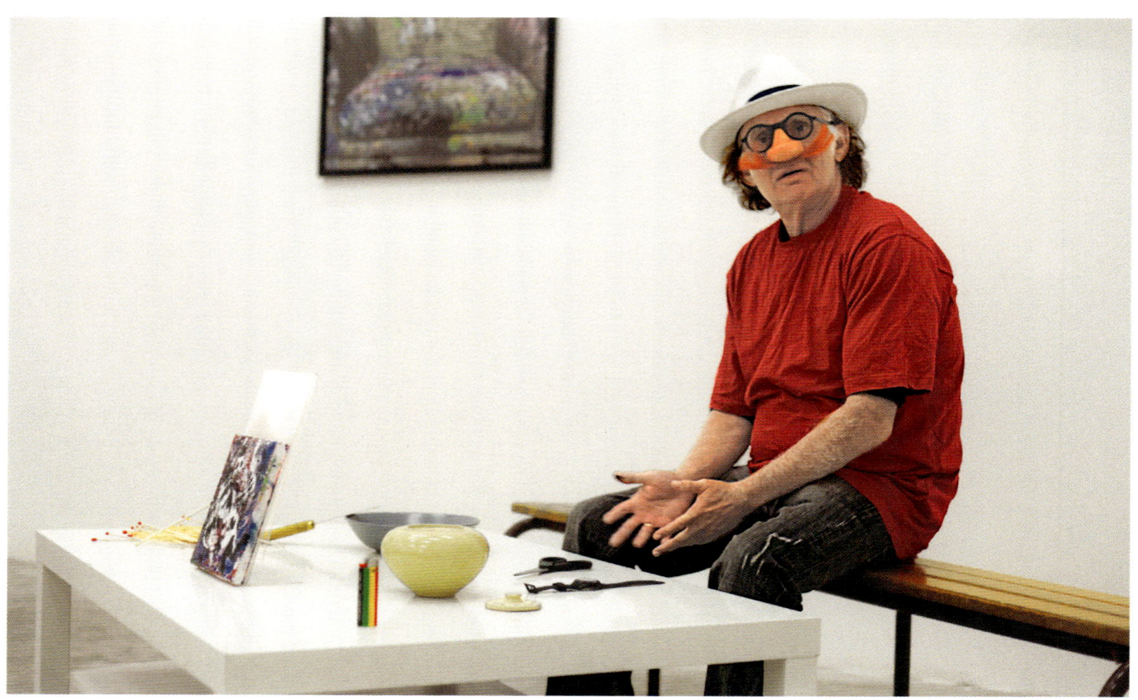

No beacons. We sail with the wind. The stories are woven, finished, reborn with the flow, before
a storm comes up to carry us away to the threshold of a new vision. For such is the book of Boz,
an unusual, unclassifiable work, created by a wanderer for other wanderers.'
2013: Sonia Bressler published a book on the work of Julien Friedler: *Julien Friedler. De la Métaphysique de
l'errance*, Jacques Flament Éditions: 'Neither time nor space as we know them', she writes, 'are sufficient to
grasp the form and the material of Julien Friedler's thought and creation… We must accept that art (in the
sense of creativity) should be placed at the heart of life, of the social and economic construction. His work
is to listen to the extent of the world's movement, it is about defining an alternative'. Sonia Bressler travelled
to Nepal, where she organised a *Forêt des âmes* choreographic workshop, run by Marylin Alasset. She also
went to Bombay (conference + questionnaires – video and meetings with artists).

2012–2015, painting: Friedler painted important works in this eventful period. A retreat was
necessary, to work, paint, and invent in the studio. Sheets of canvas, metal plates, cardboard and
everyday objects became settings for microcosms that sprang up sporadically and disquietingly,
able to encapsulate the lurches, syncopated rhythms, feverish states and opacities of a mixed
universe in which life is given to aggregations of small spirits and coils (*Saturnins*, 2012), lemurs
and enchanted landscapes (*Le Parapet*, 2012), sandblasted colours and muffled screams (*La Chute
du Joker*, 2010), fireworks and cosmogonies (*Planète Alpha*, 2012), creeping bestiality and refined
decorum (*Maou*, 2011). The omnipresent space of Friedler's painting hosts a torrid world whose
tiny cells, subject to undulating movement, are engaged in a dance of sinuous forms and signs that
suggest the palpitations of nature. It is a proliferating world — intense and dramatic but also joyful.
Landscapes, light, glitter, Friedler's work releases a creative energy that explodes in coloured bursts
on the canvas.
2012 also marked the start of a period of nomadism for Julien Friedler. Between 2012 and 2018
he abandoned sedentarism and began an itinerant lifestyle that led him to stay frequently in
hotels. On these occasions, continuing his pictorial meditation, in six years he produced over 300
works on paper in small formats easy to produce and transport. They arose from his meditative

Planète Alpha, 2012
Acrylic on canvas, 150 x 200 cm

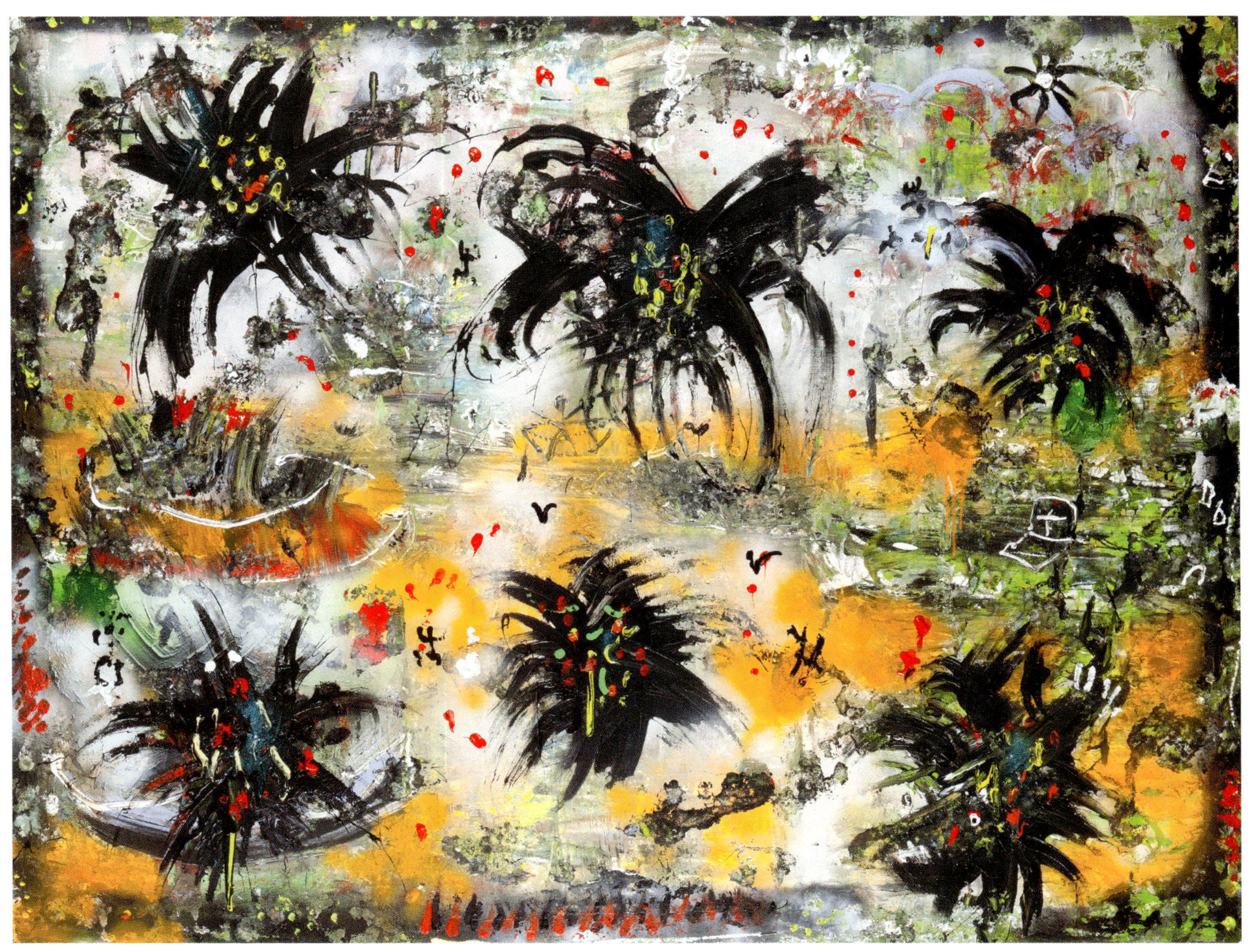

and colourful inspiration that alternates between figuration and abstraction, in which roaming ghosts inhabit uncertain universes. These small works are related to the large studio paintings he produced during the same period and convey the same strength, energy and mystery.

2014: *Voyage* exhibition, held at the Museo Civico Archeologico Girolamo Rossi, Forte dell'Annunziata, Ventimiglia, in Italy. Jacques Flament Éditions published the catalogue for this exhibition. The show presented large archetypal, primitive works from the series of emblematic figures produced in 2008–2011, works from Friedler's series of landscapes, planets and enchanted universes (2010–14), and a series of the works on paper that he executed during his travels. *Voyage* was an illustration of a personal meditation, an inward journey that Friedler had rendered in an evocative and poetic body of works. The paintings interacted with the permanent installations in the archaeological museum, in a timeless dialogue dating back to the origins of art.

Friedler's travels continued, but alternating with periods spent in the studio. Meetings relating to the text *La Vérité du Labyrinthe* were held in Brussels.

2014: performances were given by Carmen Ferreyra on the theme *La Vérité du Labyrinthe*, one at the Armory Show in New York, and the other at the Untitled Art fair in Miami.

Also in 2014, new works were produced using a new technique that might be described as 'liquid painting', an expression used by the Italian critic Gianluigi Colin in an article in the newspaper *Corriere della Sera* in 2016. *Totems* (2014), *Le Patriarche* (2014), *Ecstasy* (2014), *Le Totem et les deux Chevaliers* (2014), *La Grotte aux résurrections* (2015) and many others were indications of Friedler's activity. During the period 2012–15, the artist's Brussels' studio was populated by *Schnarks*, ghostly and pathetic clown figures, the deformed or fantastic personification of the most disturbing dreams, but also fabulous heroes and legendary beings who inhabit unknown worlds. Such figures as *L'Homme poubelle* (2014), *Démon* (2014), *Le Noir Chevalier* (2014) are created out of rags and found materials. Born from objects, they identify themselves with an ordinary but also exceptional story recounted to us by Julien Friedler; they are also characters in legends constructed by Friedler and exhibited at the same time as the paintings.

2015: this year saw three solo and three group exhibitions. *Amok & Kalinka* at the Riflemaker Gallery in London displayed the 'liquid paintings', installations of *Schnarks* and paintings from the years 2012–14. A solo show called *Mania Boz* was held at the Fondazione Mudima in Milan, with a catalogue with texts by Dominique Stella and Gianluca Ranzi, covering works from *La Forêt des âmes* to the most recent paintings and the *Schnarks*. And the third solo show in the former Anglican Church in Bordighera, Italy, exhibited three works from the series of landscapes (2012–14) and *La Chute du Joker*. In a discussion on these works, Philippe Daverio and Julien Friedler exchanged on the theme of the *artist-shaman* (https://www.bordighera.tv/2016/06/spoleto-julien-friedler-%E2%80%9C-retro-boz%E2%80%9D/).

Also in 2015, in Bologna, Friedler's text *La Vérité du Labyrinthe* was taken as the basis for an exhibition-dialogue between Friedler and Rebecca Ballestra at the Spazio Testoni gallery. Since 2010 Julien Friedler had been writing *La Vérité du Labyrinthe*. 'The objectives of *La Vérité du Labyrinthe* are those of every honest man in search of a modern spirituality', wrote Friedler. 'Through my experiences and research, I have sought to weave a path that leads to peace and serenity. To get out of the chaos, one step at a time, we have to understand what we are all made of. As the texts go on, the noise and the fury become more distant'.

In Venice this time, *La Parole des Anges* was exhibited in Palazzo Molin to coincide with the 2015 Biennale. The show once again brought together Julien Friedler and Rebecca Ballestra, the organiser of the event, who unveiled her cycle *Journey into Fragility*.

Julien Friedler's work was also included in the Bienal de las Fronteras Tamaulipas on the Mexico-US

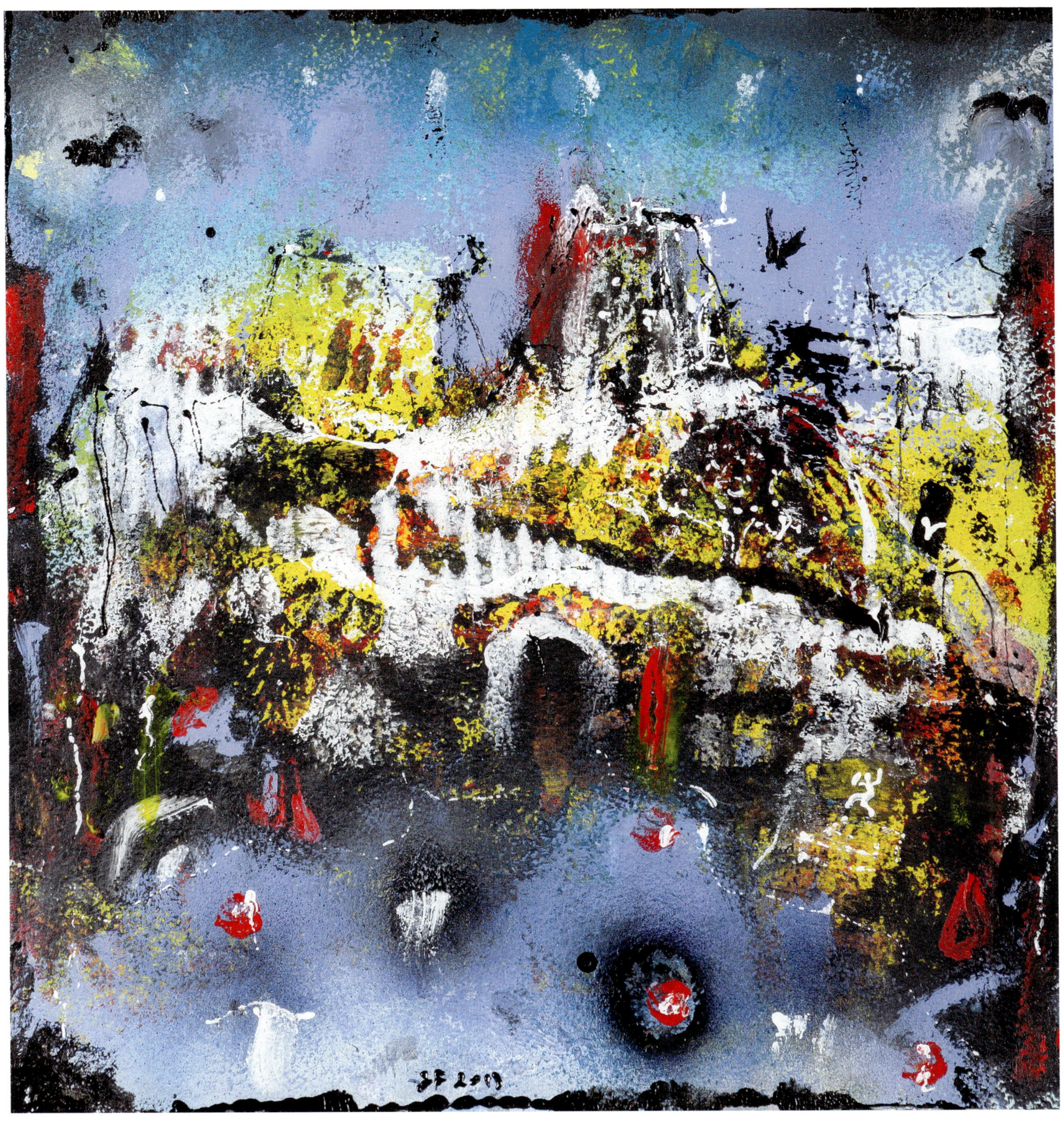

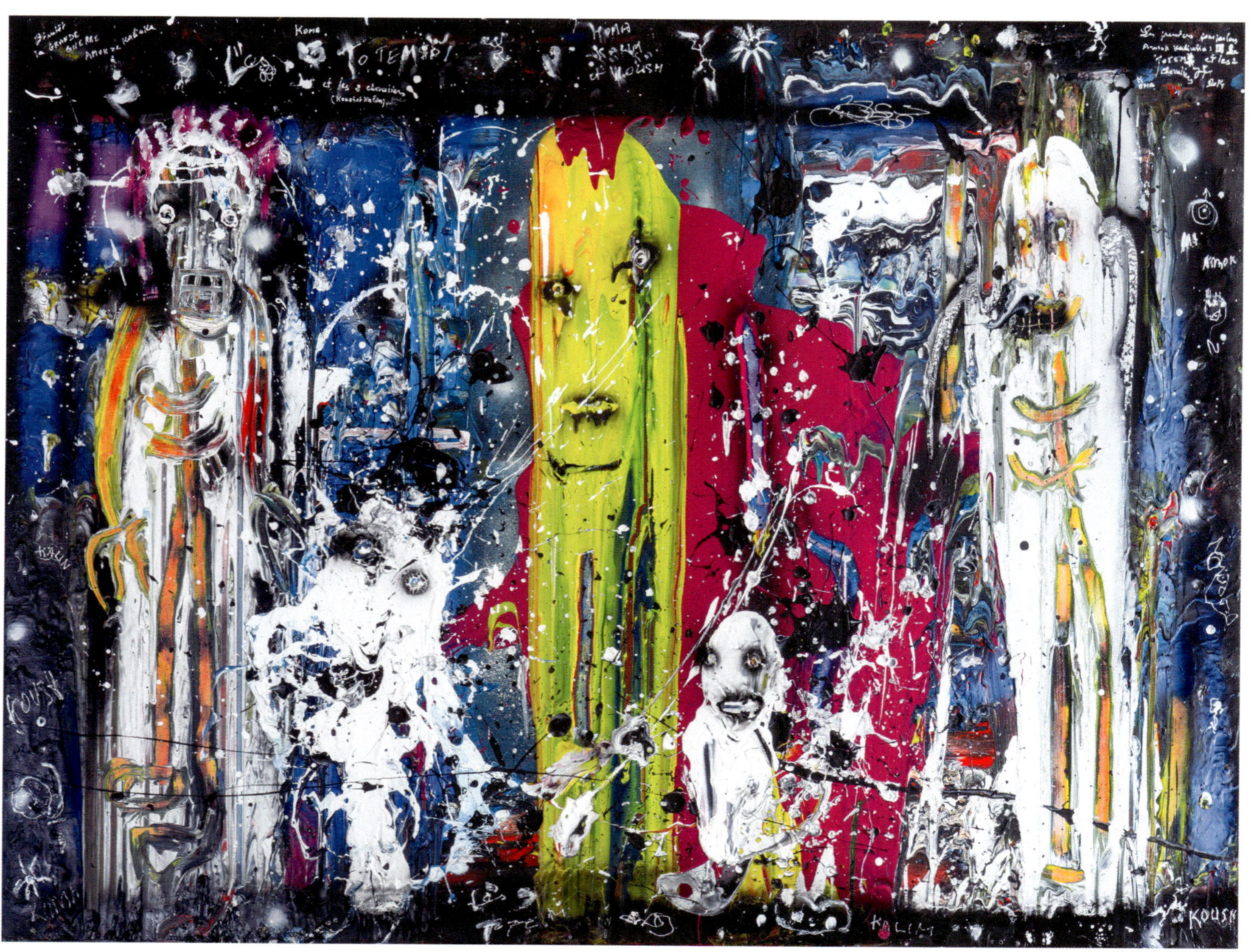

Le Totem et les deux Chevaliers, 2014
Acrylic on canvas, 150 x 200 cm

L'Homme poubelle, 2014
Mixed media, 138 x 96 x 30 cm

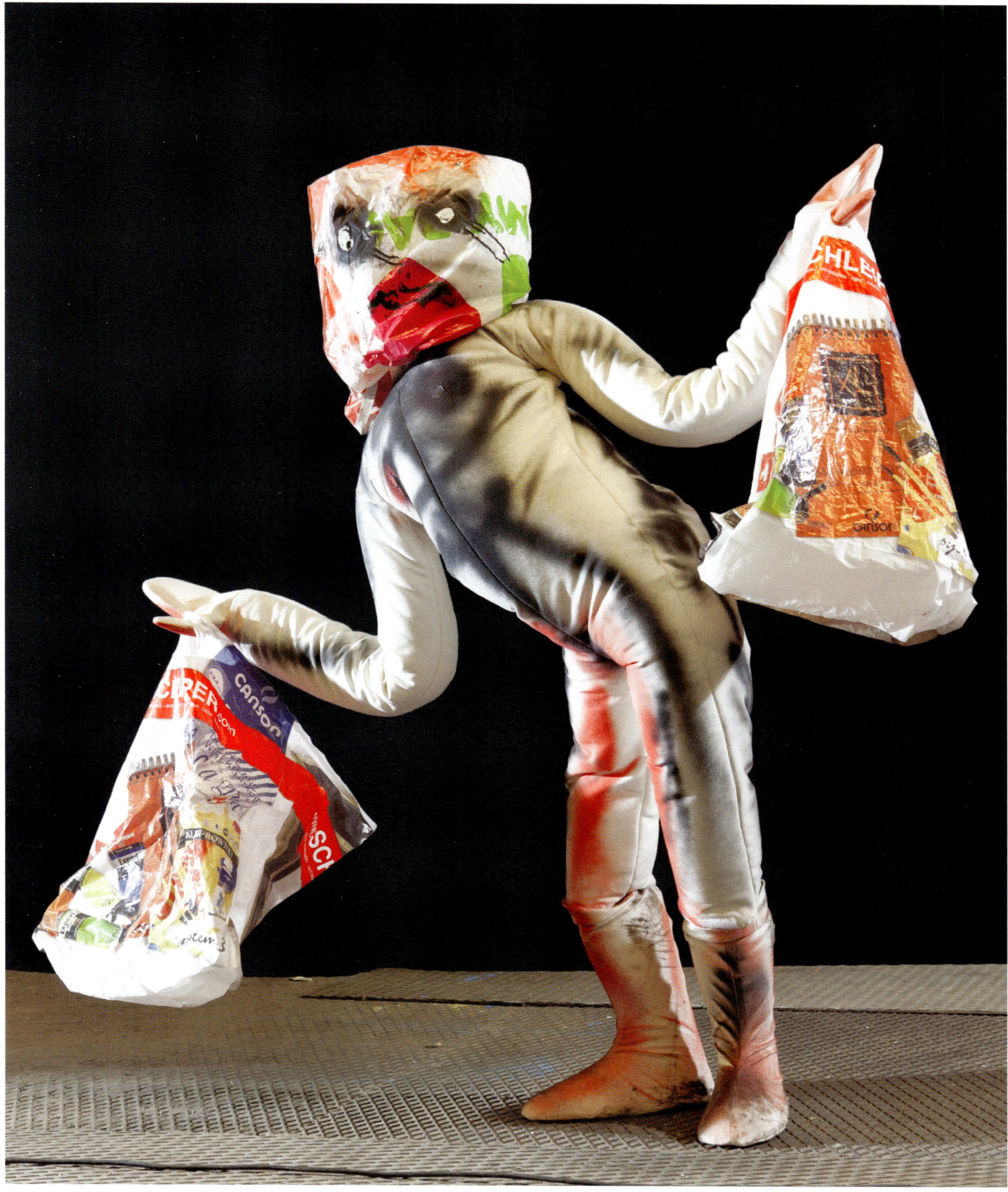

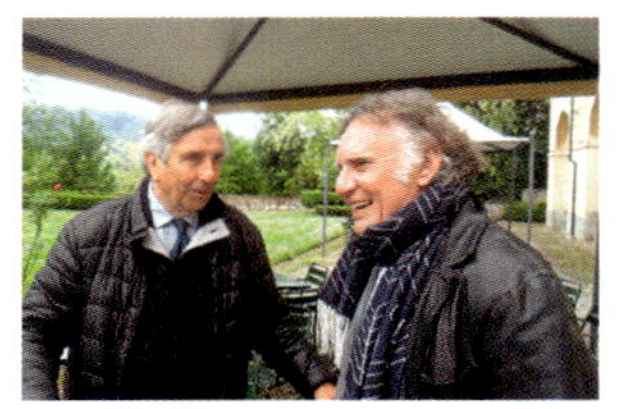

Franz Paludetto and Julien
Friedler, Castello di Rivara, Turin,
2017

border, the first edition of this contemporary art festival that brings together 5 curators and 55 artists from different parts of the world.

Sonia Bressler continued to produce documentaries about *Spirit of Boz*, this time in the Brussels studio, and the questionnaires continued to be presented to the participants of the performances.

2016: the exhibition *Mania Boz* presented at the Fondazione Mudima in Milan continued its tour at the Museo Civico di Villa Bassi in Abano Terme, Italy. On this occasion, only the pictorial works and the *Schnarks* were presented, in a more 'sepulchral' setting in the museum's vaulted basement. The very suggestive exhibition sometimes frightened a somewhat bewildered public.

The works then moved on to Spoleto where, in summer, the Museo delle Arti Visive in Palazzo Collicola presented a complete retrospective of Julien Friedler's work, curated by Gianluca Marziani, under the title *Retro Boz*. The 1500-square metres exhibition presented the successive stages of the artist's production from his first paintings in 1998 to the most recent, dated 22 March 2016, which Friedler painted on the day of the Zaventem airport bombings in Brussels. The bloody aspect of the painting, which uses dripping as a technique, communicates the fear we all suffer in a world ravaged by anger. It is this world that Julien Friedler continues to paint. Marking this exhibition, the Sunday supplement of the newspaper *Corriere della Sera* published the work *Totems* (2014) full page on its cover.

La Forêt des âmes continued on its journey, its nine columns being presented at the Museoteatro della Commenda di Pré in Genoa in concomitance with a meeting on peace. A conference-cum-exhibition was held on the subject of some of the installation's paintings, held at the Alliance française, Casino Venier, in Venice. 'Through his work, Julien Friedler outlines the foundations of a contemporary mythology', announced the press release, inviting each participant to fill in the *Forêt des âmes* questionnaire. Julien Friedler answered questions posed by a large and curious public.

The year was also marked by participation in three group exhibitions: International Art Project 2016 on Cap-d'Ail; at the Spazio Testoni Gallery as part of the Bologna Fair; and at the inauguration of the Fondazione Casa della Divina Bellezza in Forza d'Agrò, Sicily, which had purchased Friedler's painting *Gilgamesh* at the Bologna Fair and was exhibiting it.

Painting was occupying a large part of the artist's life. Using a turbulent technique in a masterful combination of graffiti and dripping, he executed two large works each measuring 300 x 200 cm, *Le Phoenix* (2016) and *Crucifixion* (2016), which represented the focal point of a particularly intense production.

2017: the installation *La Forêt des âmes* continued its travels: in spring it was shown in the exhibition *Boz Legend* held at the Castello di Rivara-Museo d'Arte Contemporanea in Rivara (Turin), and in the Church of Santi Giovanni e Paolo in Spoleto for the entire summer. An encounter between Julien Friedler and Franz Paludetto, a famous figure in the contemporary art world, was an opportunity for lively exchanges.

A performance and conference were held in Genoa: the event *Face to Face* was presented at the city's Museo Villa Croce and UniMediaModern gallery. At the museum, the audience of a *Give up* performance was invited to give an object and a *Spirit of Boz* presentation based on videos told the story of the *Boz* adventure, while at the UniMediaModern gallery Julien Friedler met the public and presented them with questionnaires of the *Tour du Boz en 80 ans*.

In September, in Knokke at the 'Manoir', headquarters of the *Spirit of Boz* association in Belgium, Julien Friedler begins an annual conference cycle with the title 'Les grandes conférences de *Spirit of Boz*'. Luc Ferry, the former French Minister of Culture, discussed with the artist the theme 'The Vices and Weaknesses of our Democracies'. The aim was to question our democracies, to measure their transformation and to evoke the hypothesis of an art able to restore hope. The event was

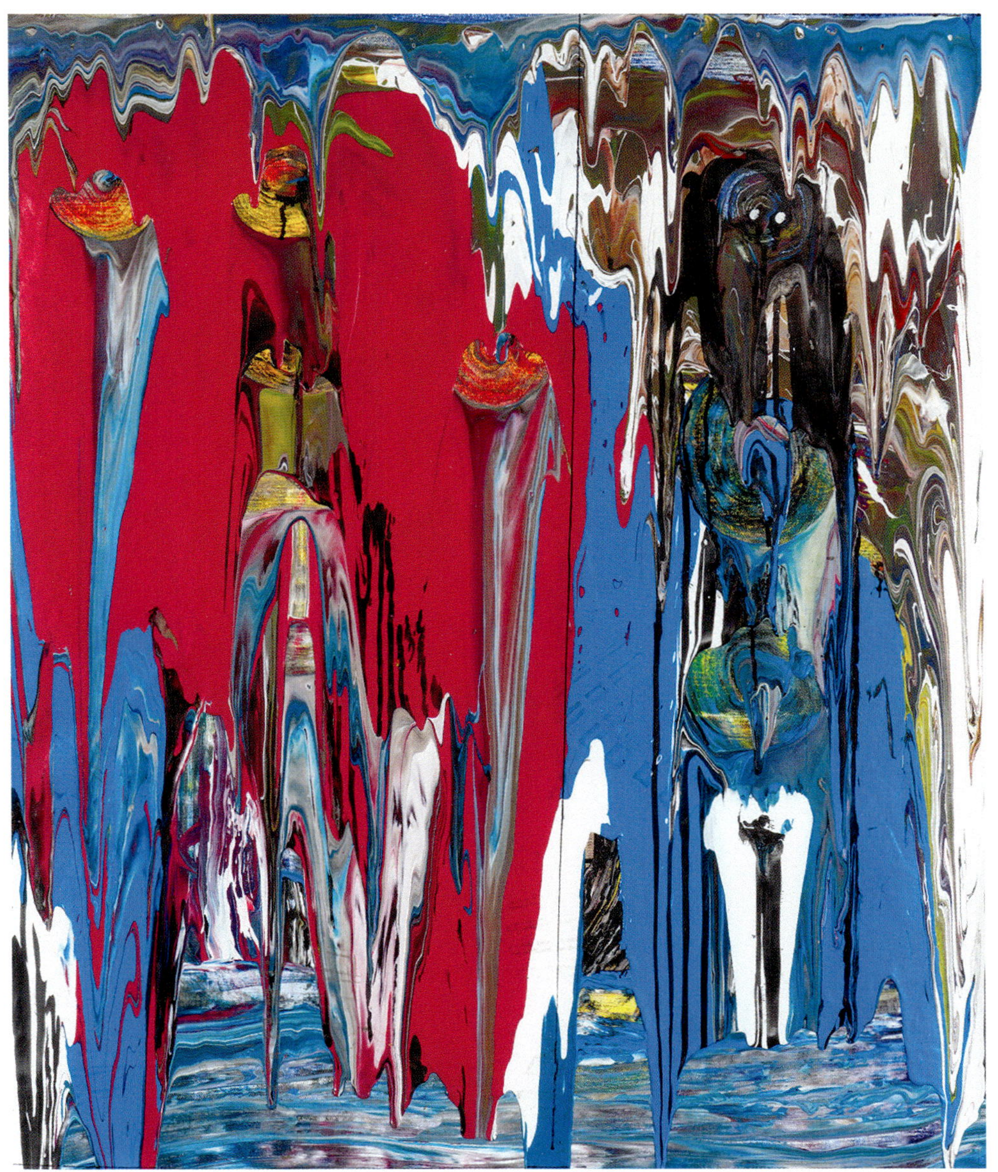

Totems, 2014
Acrylic on canvas, 110 x 90 cm

accompanied by an exhibition of Friedler's major works, including his most recent, *Le Maître des couleurs* (2017), a monumental painting featuring dripping and barely suggested images. A series of wax works by the Italian artist Francesco Sena was presented alongside the event in one of the rooms of the 'Manoir'.

2017: release of the book *La Vérité du Labyrinthe* by Julien Friedler, published by Jacques Flament Éditions. Friedler commented that 'This book is an invitation to embark on an inward journey, to engage in a search for serenity. The world around us is exploding while also merging in all manner of ways. It is therefore particularly urgent to find a way to reconnect with one's inner peace and thus restore harmony and balance to the world'. The book helps to explain the artist's labyrinthine thinking from which he draws the energy of his painted works.

2018: this was a year rich in exhibitions in Belgium and Italy. The first, called *Spirit of Boz Paintings*, was held at the Berlaymont Building at the European Commission in Brussels, under the patronage of Carlos Moedas, European Commissioner of Research, Science and Innovation, who began the opening with a moving speech (https://www.julienfriedler.com/exposition/spirit-of-boz-paintings/). On this

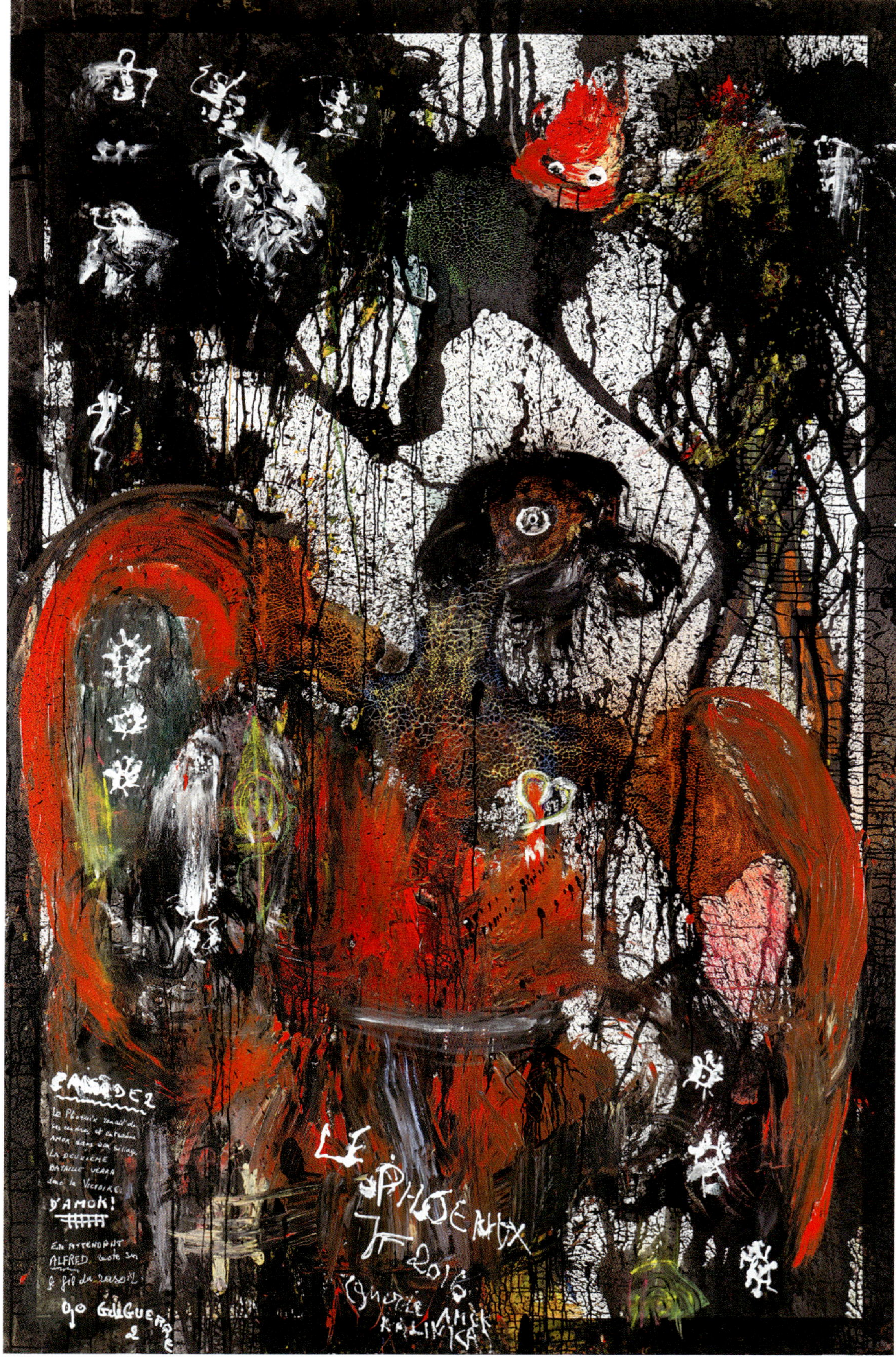

Le Phoenix, 2016
Acrylic on canvas, 300 x 200 cm

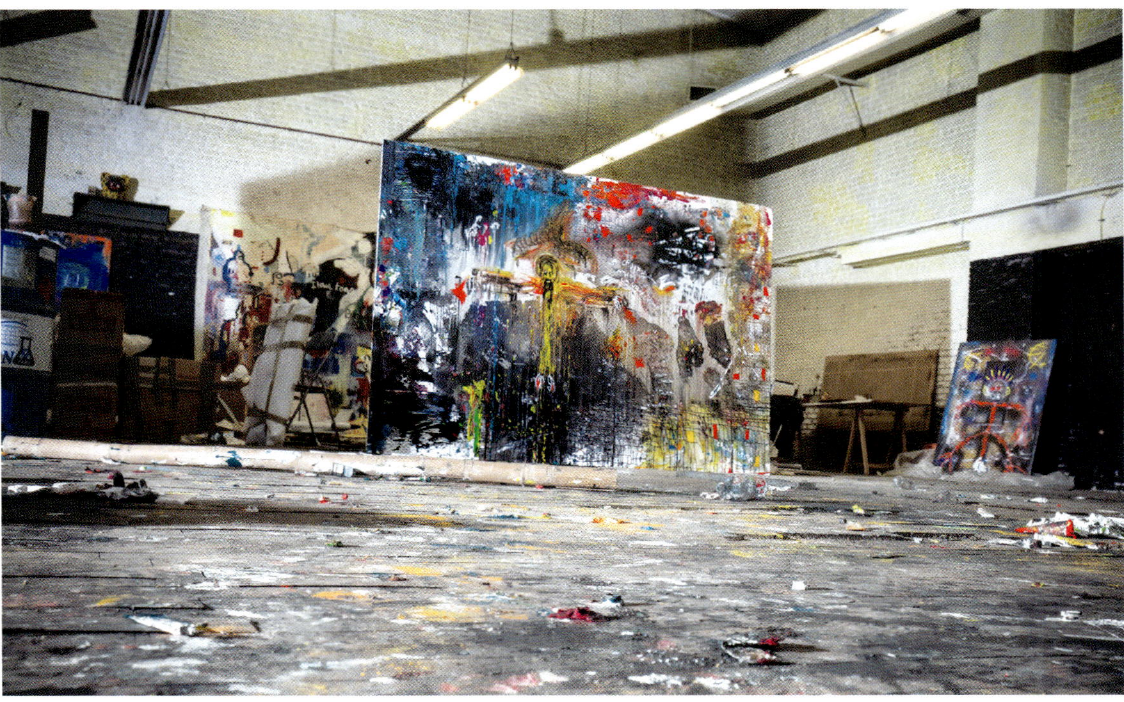

occasion, some twenty large-format paintings from the years 2012 to 2018 were shown. Julien Friedler gave a presentation of his participative project *Boz* with the ambition that it could be integrated into a programme of cultural actions of the European Union.

In February and March, some of Friedler's works were shown alongside the presentation of the *Be Boz Be Art* collection (*Be Boz Be Art and Friedler's Paintings*) at the Galleria Gliacrobati in Turin. The objects, drawings and paintings collected in Togo, Argentina, Indonesia, China, and other places were exhibited to illustrate the objectives of the *Boz* project, and each participant at the vernissage and viewer of the exhibition was invited to fill in the questionnaire of *La Forêt des âmes*. Julien Friedler's lecture at the opening was attended by many members of the public.

The cycle *La Parole des Anges* was shown twice in 2018. The first time at the SRValverde Gallery in Brussels and the second on a museum scale, therefore with larger formats, at La Cité Miroir in Liège. The space of the swimming pool that used to occupy this building was a spectacular setting for Friedler's monumental works. The press release stated: 'In cryptic language, this group of paintings develops a whole symbolism of signs from which emanate works charged by the artist with a meditative value, creating a real path to an inner peace that is intended to be a force for life and sharing'.

The installation *La Forêt des âmes* was included in Arezzo (Italy) at the exhibition *Vibrations* in the Church of the Madonna del Duomo Vecchio alongside *All Over II – La Parole des Anges* (2002), *Ecce Homo* (2009), *Le Maître des couleurs* (2017) and *Crucifixion* (2016), demonstrating that in spite of their rather different pictorial approaches, Friedler's paintings create a harmony and balance that emphasises the sense of the artist's thought.

The final solo exhibition of the year was *Behind the world* at the Complesso del Vittoriano in Rome. This exhibition space lies inside the Monument to Vittorio Emanuele at the very centre of Rome and offered the public the chance to contrast Friedler's works with those of two twentieth-century masters — Andy Warhol and Jackson Pollock — which were also being shown in the building. *Behind the world* was the opportunity for Friedler to show his three most recent paintings, all in large formats, executed during 2018: *Ode Satanique* (2018), *L'Autre* (2018) and *Corps et Artifices* (2018). *Corps et Artifices* uses dripping, while in the other two the painter adopts a rougher, more

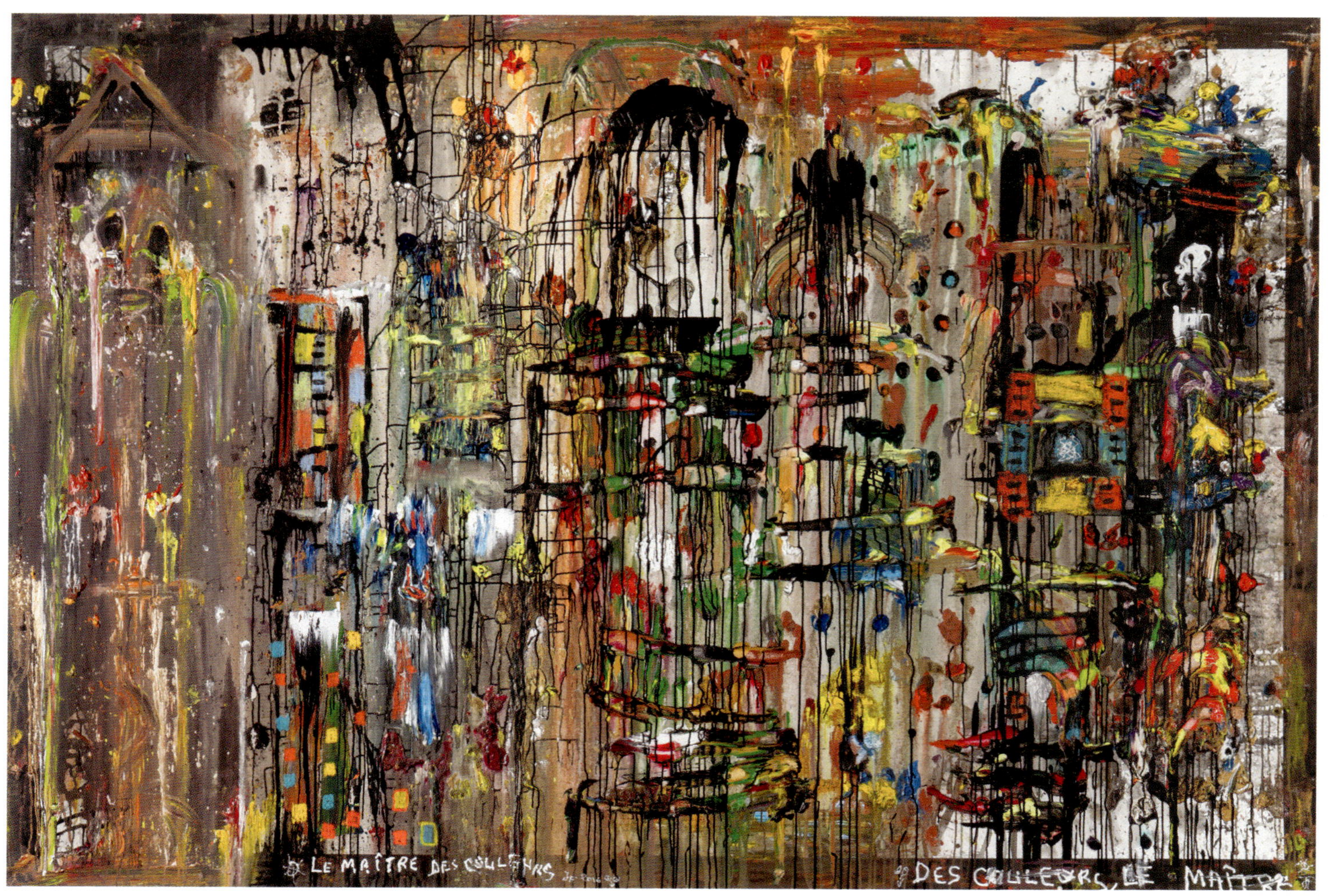

Le Maître des couleurs, 2017
Acrylic on canvas, 200 x 300 cm

flayed matter, like a return to the techniques of the 2010s. The exhibition as a whole showed a huge group of works, including at its centre the nine columns of *La Forêt des âmes*. Several periods of pictorial production were represented, demonstrating Friedler's faithfulness to the subject of his research. He is never content to stick to one style and his art evolves constantly, but his inspiration remains unaltered. Each painting is a facet of his body of work, whose unity is given by reference to the artist's philosophy of life and thought that he summarises in the *Boz*. During the exhibition, the questionnaires left available to the visitors were filled in, each person thus leaving a trace of their passage. The uptake was impressive. Of the approximately 3000 visitors, 672 answered the six questions in the *Boz* survey.

Two group exhibitions in 2018, in Italy, on *La Vérité du Labyrinthe: Labrys, The Truth of the Labyrinth*, at Parco Basaglia and other places in the city of Gorizia, and *Labrys, The Truth of the Labyrinth* at Spazio Testoni, Bologna, both in collaboration with Maria Rebecca Ballestra who in her formal work illustrated a labyrinth traced out with letters and sentences taken from Friedler's book.

In Paris, Friedler was included in the Outsider Art Fair with the Galleria Gliacrobati of Turin, in which he presented a wall of works on paper from the series *Voyages*.

In September another meeting was held in Knokke on 'Les grandes conférences de *Spirit of Boz*', with the participation of Pascal Bruckner and Eric Sadin discussing the theme 'Identity and Citizenship, Before and After the Internet'. This was recorded on video: https://vimeo.com/307944894.

In the continuation of his pictorial work, Friedler adopted an important modification to the works'

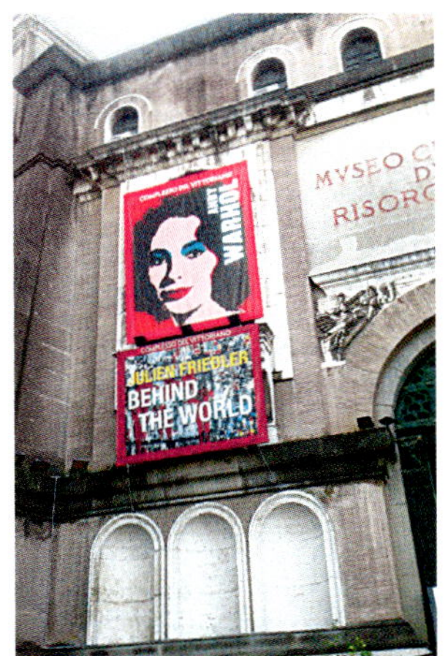

Entrance to the exhibition
Behind the world, Complesso
del Vittoriano, Rome, 2018

themes and style. The year 2018 marked the start of a new cycle of paintings called *Mapping* and was when the artist met Carlo Silvestrin, who would produce the exhibition *È finita la Commedia* in Venice (2022), Church of San Samuele, at the time of the Biennale.

2019–21: obliged by the pandemic to remain in lockdown, Friedler never left the studio. That place of reclusion allowed him to meditate on his work and influenced him. He realizes *Les Pierrots*. His art began to lose its violence while keeping the spirit of mystery and legend built up in the constant oscillation between dramatic art and vital explosion. In the *Mapping* series, the visual expression transcends any graphic or aesthetic solution, embracing research that is certainly philosophical and spiritual, but above all pictorial. Friedler's world is intuitive and his art, which is essentially linked to a mental outlook, is the expression of inward contemplation and life experience, transfigured by the experience of painting. His production is truly painting: matter that is sometimes harsh, sometimes radiant, conveying visible or invisible flows, intense energies that pulsate and arise out of colour.
In abstract impressions, lights and colours emerge from the canvas in an explosive or soothed atmosphere, contingent on contrasts that emerge as a breath stretched towards the mystery of Life.
It was during this period that certain exhibition projects were conceived. In 2019 *Les Innocents* was presented at Forte Santa Tecla in San Remo. The installation occupied the central courtyard of this disused prison, creating a striking effect. It was a great success, with more than 3000 people visiting the exhibition during the month of May. A comments book was made available to the public, allowing visitors to articulate their emotions and reflections.
2020: *La Forêt des âmes* was presented in the Belfry of St-Germain l'Auxerrois church – Mairie in the 1st *arrondissement* in Paris. Facing the Perrault Colonnade in the Louvre, the doors of the Belfry stood open to reveal the nine columns. Visitors were invited to fill in the *Forêt des âmes* questionnaire. By this time, the installation had been travelling for more than ten years and the number of questionnaires collected worldwide came to more than 75,000. Catalogued and duplicated, the questionnaires are now ready to be sent to their intended destination and fill the body of monumental columns erected in different parts of the world. We suggest Venice as the starting point for this new project.

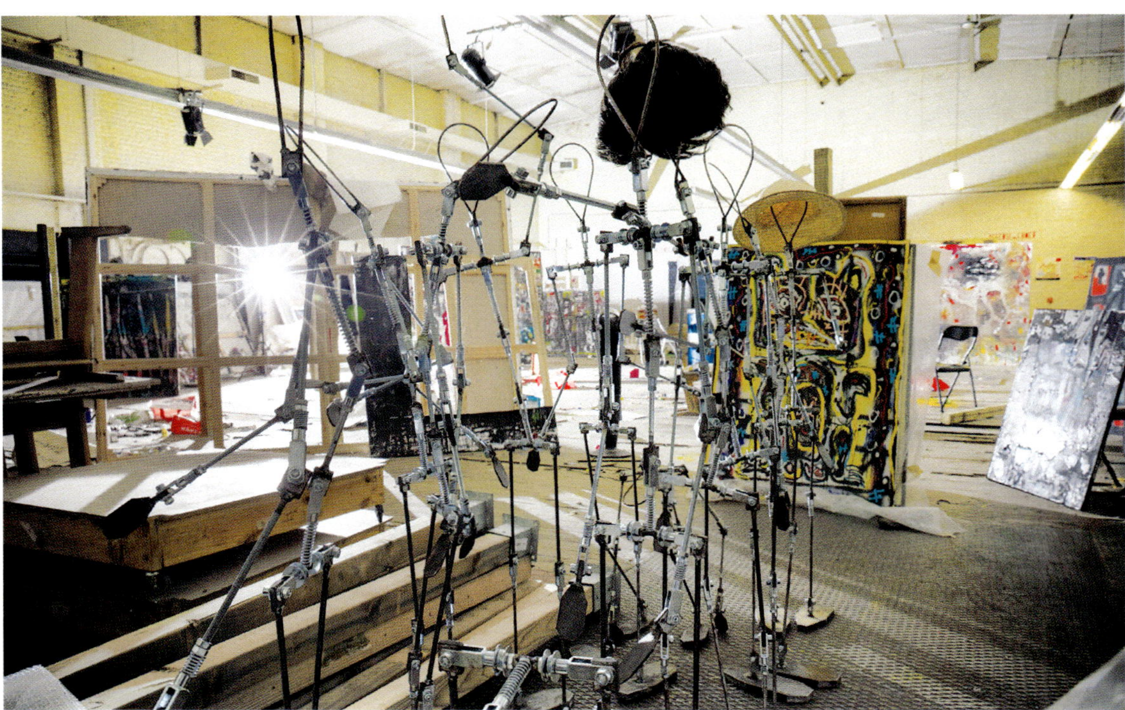

The installation *Les Pierrots*, work
in progress, in the studio, 2018

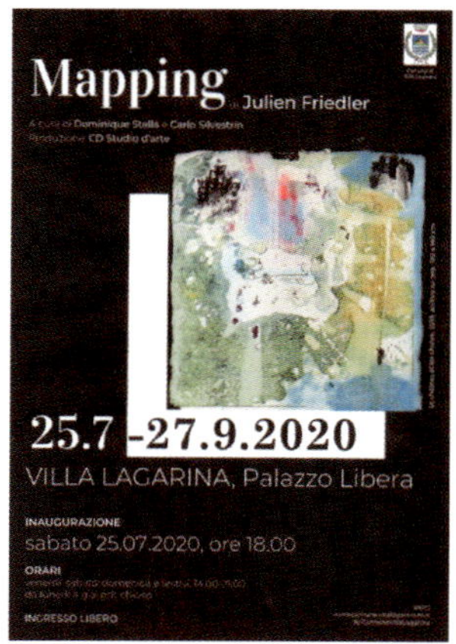

Mapping, exhibition 2020–21
(Palazzo Libera, Villa Lagarina,
Rovereto; Fondazione Sant'Elia,
Palermo; Galleria Civica Cavour,
Padua)

Les Innocents in Forte Santa
Tecla, San Remo, 2019

Two *Mapping* exhibitions were held in the middle of the pandemic and lockdown: one at Palazzo Libera, Villa Lagarina (Rovereto, Italy) and the other at the Fondazione Sant'Elia, Loggiato di San Bartolomeo in Palermo (Sicily). The exhibition in Palermo was also curated by Gianluca Marziani. He wrote: 'As a title, *Mapping* is perfectly suited to Friedler's "chromosomal" geography. The hundreds of paintings are arranged like random particles without a perspectival centre, imaginary nucleic acids (the elements that make up DNA's double helix) that create multiple nuclei, every one different, confirming this inclusive dimension of the corpus, of a single gigantic work out of which emerge the epiphanic energy of Babylon and the cathartic power of Shiva'. Following the lockdown, *Mapping* was the first museum exhibition to be organised in Palermo and even in Sicily. Crowds of visitors flocked to the exhibition in small groups of fifteen people to follow Marziani's impassioned explanations. The press enthusiastically commented on the event. On 18 September 2020, at the Palazzo Barolo in Turin, Julien Friedler took part in a tribute to Maria Rebecca Ballestra, who had died earlier that year. He described their friendship and the closeness of their work, on this occasion the video *La guaritrice* was shown, in which Friedler takes part and in which in three performances Maria Rebecca Ballestra refers to her struggle against illness and suffering. 'Existing is not only something that is easy to do, it is also difficult to understand. You come into the world without having asked for it, and you are almost always forced to leave it against your will', she wrote.

At the Galleria Civica in Padova in 2021, for two summer months, the exhibition *Legends-Mapping II* presented a new selection of works from the *Mapping* cycle (https://www.7goldtelepadova. tv/2021/07/22/friedler-in-mostra/). The artist, forced into confinement by the pandemic, painted relentlessly. The *Mapping* paintings are the expression of his reflection in the material form of colour, which appears as the generating soul, a womb that fuses everything into a living spirit. Life is pulsation, respiration, damnation, salvation. In *La Vérité du Labyrinthe* Friedler describes his work as 'a conjunction of opposites, a paradoxical text, an inscription of the flows that pass through the Spirit'.

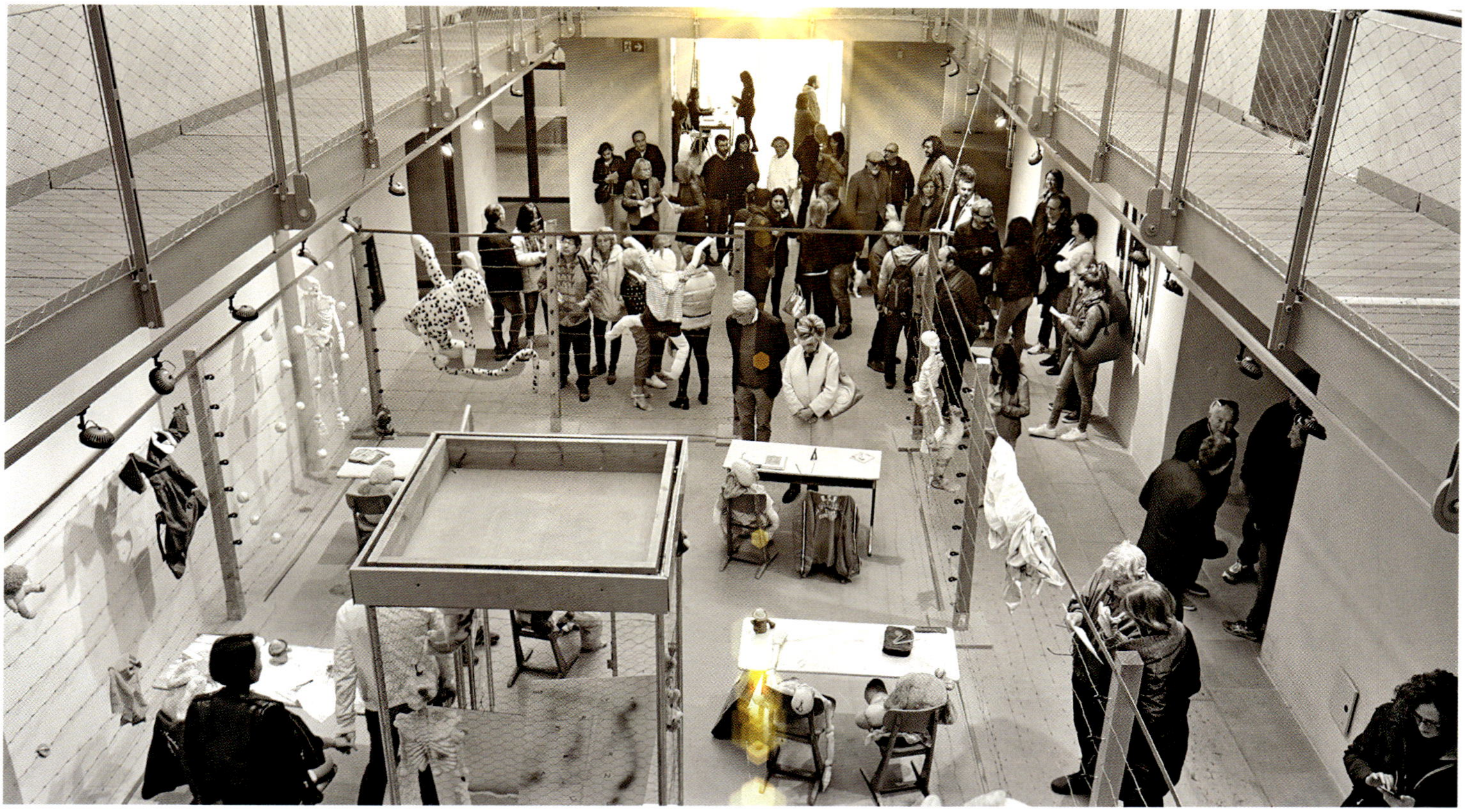

Appendix

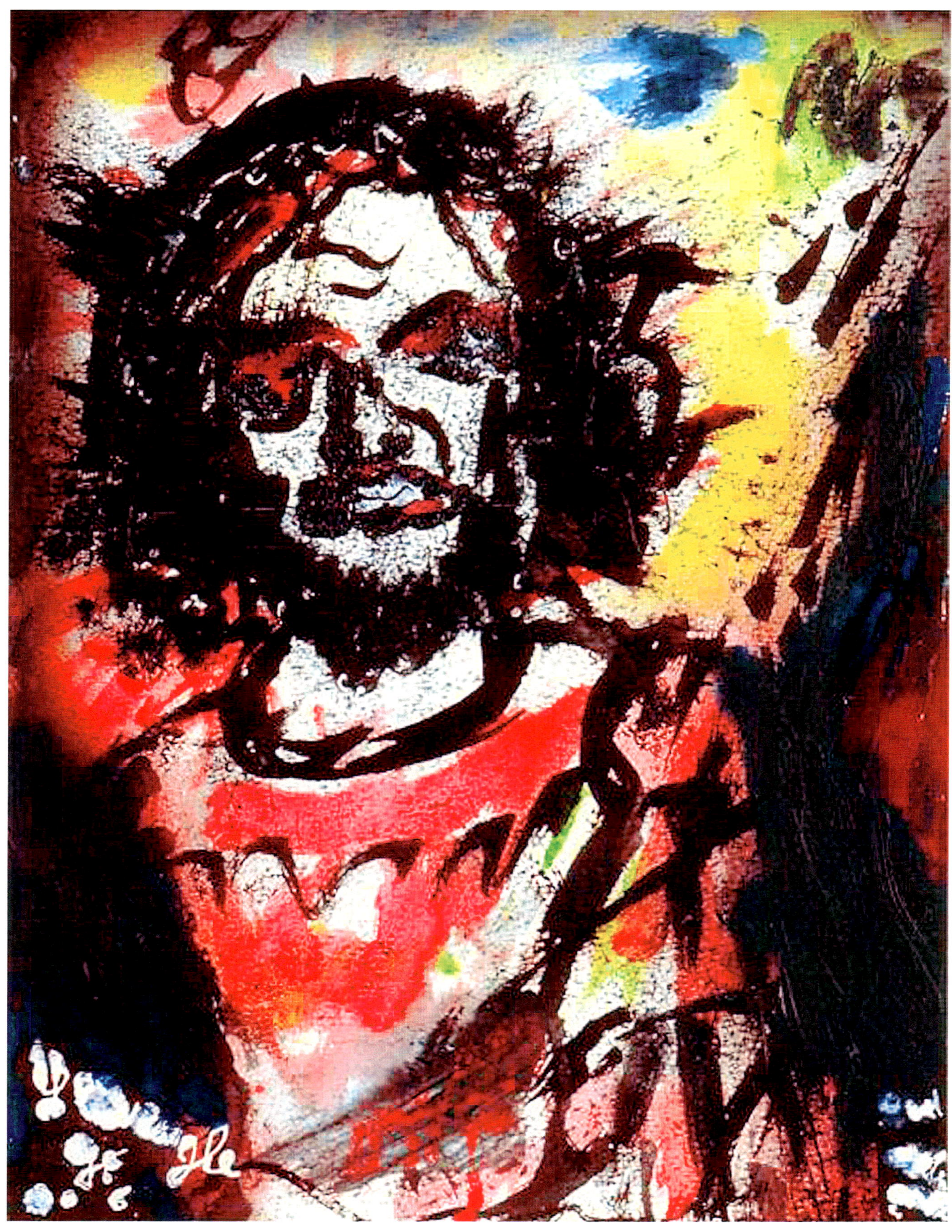

Anthology

Sonia Bressler
Julien Friedler, Witness of the Century (extracts)
My first encounter with Julien Friedler took place in February 2006. In a huge room, his studio in the heart of Brussels, I went back and forth between his installations *Les Innocents* and his paintings in progress. His immense, moving, changing, perpetual work. A perfect balance of inaccuracies, coincidences, intersecting studies of history, time, the surpassing of oneself and others. Understanding that art must be made in spite of rain, wars, atrocities, religions, rights. In spite of oneself, and of others. Human, all too human, art hides, revolts, denounces, theorises. I have had the chance to discover and question Julien Friedler's work over two years. It is this encounter that I describe here in a few snapshots.

Are we still able to talk about innocence?
That Sunday in Brussels, February 2006. Doesn't history have a solution of continuity? I played on the boards in Julien Friedler's studio. Colours, explosions. At first sight, you have to play with the codes, the unexpected. Then, step by step, the work takes a greater, more monumental hold. Something in our chemistry shifts. But what? Step by step, photograph after photograph, two years passed at the rhythm of creation, the rhythm of thought. A thought in the making, taking nourishment from a past and devouring a future. Combining mysticism and (in)human passions. Centuries pass with their monstrosities and destructions… We drift from one end of civilisation to another. Today, the end of American hegemony, the break-up of the blocs, and yet in the midst of our drifting, a voice breaks through, an eye looks down, a hand draws and lets loose. Julien Friedler amidst humanity in disarray. He mocks the codes, he invents, perpetuates reflection, spreads disorder, plays with our sensibilities. His production is unique, sometimes dark, and sometimes luminous. With the same certainty: light that lingers becomes the shadow of another light. We are in his studios in Brussels. We could be here, there, or anywhere. A fragile pendulum of space and time. I play. You play.

We play. But are they playing? Those deprived of everything, those whose nothingness is everything. Those whose gaze has been caught somewhere in a pile of dust. Who are they? Is it you, is it me if we look now, in the present? But if we look back in the past, they are those who were exiled, killed, abandoned on the side of a road during the war. Which war? The Second World War. Without a doubt, if we look at Julien Friedler's installation *Les Innocents*. A photograph of a family. Eternal smiles. The dust of exile. Old buried dreams? Time is distended in this barbed wire space.

The need to bear witness
We are searching for the light, for truth. But is there just one? Or many? The uncertain waltz of things, the little noises of everyday life. The cries of children in the playground. The breath of a sleeping child. The chirping of birds in the early morning. The first mist. The first rains of spring. A door slams. Blood spreads. A stain of colour. Life flees. A heart stops. A monster is born. Now, at the beginning of the twenty-first century, it is essential that someone bears witness, with conviction, but above all with heart and soul, with sensitivity, and lays their experiences bare. Julien Friedler's work is deeply moving, it views the world through its lucidity, its road to ruin, its race to the destruction of itself and others. Each canvas, each installation is an eye open on closed eyes. A fictive eye that scours the extant to make it articulate its being. Each of Julien Friedler's creations is an observant witness, charged with the inquisition whose goal is to lead to the certainty of an impossible identity, an eye pointed towards the inside, towards the underside, but also towards the outside, to the heart of the whole adventure. An attentive journey towards oneself, others and the world. We have to risk distancing ourselves from ourselves so that we may find ourselves again and bear witness with strength.

L'Aveugle (autoportrait), 2006
Mixed media on paper,
52 x 42 cm

Gino Di Maggio
Julien Friedler and the Spark of Life

How many times have I repeated the reply that
Robert Filliou gave to the question 'What is art?' It is
pithy, paradoxical and brilliant: 'Art is the thing that
makes life more interesting than art itself'. Thus, the
heart of the matter is life itself, and it is from life
that we start and to life that we return, taking art as
a fundamental medium, a bridge built between two
shores to connect and exchange emotions and hopes,
revolt and awareness, dialogue and possibility. In all
this, art thus becomes one of the most important
components of life, and therefore that thing, or series
of things and so-called creative activities whose
outcome we conventionally call art. This idea is in
many ways disconcerting, especially for those with
an idealistic and romantic vision of the artist almost
as an omnipotent demiurge capable of creating
autonomously, embalmed in his ivory tower and
detached from his relationship with his fellow-beings
and the world.

However, with his work, Julien Friedler offers living
proof that an artist is inescapably in contact with the
world and, despite his viewpoint being individual and
inextricably bound up with his very personal capacity
for observation and personal experiences, an artist's
production transcends his or her self and is directed
at the Other, presenting itself as a fundamental life
experience.

After all, an artist is truly an artist not only because he
declares himself to be and defines himself as such, but
because he feels the almost obsessive urge to do, to
create incessantly. And it is precisely this that is one
of the principal characteristics of what I have called —
with Giacomo Leopardi in mind — the immensity of the
energy that in infinite forms pervades existence and
makes it monstrously alive, and that I find today not
only in Friedler's installations and paintings but above
all in his visionary outlook that succeeds in making
distant worlds and parallel lives converge, contrast and
come closer together. I have the impression that all this
occurs because those who feel and call themselves
artists, or those who feel an innate predisposition and
call themselves scientists, are the very ones who have
best preserved the biological memory of what we are
and where we came from, a form of biological memory
that clearly the vast majority of us have lost, but which,
thanks to art, is once more developed into a spark of
energy that becomes visible.

(from the catalogue *Mania Boz* [Milan: Mudima,
2015])

Norbert Hillaire
Fragments

Modernity and postmodernity: a clarification
Friedler is a man of salvation, but of what? Is he
modern or postmodern? What is at work here is
a regression that announces itself as such: not a
narcissistic regression, but the experience of a double
disappointment: disappointment in modernity and
disappointment in postmodernity. Clearly, at first sight
Friedler is a postmodern painter, so numerous are the
signs, references and techniques that associate him
a priori with the postmodern territory: bad painting,
graffiti, etc. However, even if his borrowings from
Basquiat and Penk are obvious (as well as certain
reminders of Cobra) and they substantiate this
aesthetic of the 'diversal' rather than the universal that
is the foundation of postmodernity, it is paradoxically
on the side of certain moderns that the key to his
work is to be found (though it has rightly been
said that Basquiat was the last of the moderns).
Regression, in the sense of Paul Klee, for example
towards a childhood that questions history and its
involution, which culminates in the postmodern. But
this is by no means an infantilism: 'The fable of the
childlike nature of my drawing must have its origin in
the linear productions in which I try to combine the
idea of the object — for example, a man — with the
pure representation of the line element. To show the
man as he is, I would need an alarming confusion of
lines. The result is not a pure representation of the
element, but such a blur that it would be impossible
to make out what it is. Apart from that, it is certainly
not my intention to show the man as he is, but as he
could be too. In this way, I can combine my vision of
the world with the pure exercise of art.'

Yet postmodern
Yet postmodern in the sense that Friedler replaces
(for example, in paintings made by others and
integrated into the work) the binary order of the
opposition of the Other and the self with the
complexity of the rhizome that weaves together
differences, and this 'intimate otherness', as Marc
Augé still calls it, makes the very idea of 'absolute
individuality' unthinkable.

(in *Double Vue, 50 fragments pour Julien Friedler*
[Paris: Somogy Éditions d'Art, 2012])

Gianluca Marziani
Retro Boz

Julien Friedler is an artist who defies all categories and systems. I was given confirmation of this when I visited his studio in Brussels last February. Before, he was a nuclear individual, one of those titans of the daily flow able to control the entropic chaos, to fly over the confusion of the world and give order to things on the basis of immensely powerful theoretical methods. Friedler is a supreme intellectual who, following philosophical catharsis, decided to enter the dirty world of real, actual life. His ideational approach of course remained central but within an organic system of artistic work. His choice of art as a field was uncompromising: his purpose to better understand mankind, our burning needs, the potential of individuals, their scope for growth and exchange. His withdrawal from the summit of academia meant looking beyond writing and its accompanying narcissism, beyond the individual and individual work. It meant harmonising with the assorted voices of the world, isolated communities, African cultures, minority groups, remoteness and divergence. His subject was, in the end, the globe, the real world of the life we all experience, support and share.

When I say organic, I mean a creative process that resembles the activities of the human body: eating, chewing, digesting, expelling and regenerating in the endless biological cycle. The body is a complex machine that demands nourishment which it constantly regenerates: similarly, Friedler's art is a mechanism that requires a participative and humanised process in which the principle of order and cleanliness — typical of artificial control — disappears, leaving room for the natural effects of reality. The result entails an apparent confusion in which objects and materials contribute to the noise of the world, becoming soiled with the colours we find in the paintings, to the point of expanding beyond their original nature and altering the sensation of the spaces and the very vibration of the canvases. The painting and objects enter into a close and unified dialogue in which the exchange is generative, and where the attraction between the painting, colours and forms produces and protractedly emits energy. In this sense the word 'organic' implies continual germination, the production of sense (and dissent) that raises the figurative temperature and leaves the project structure open as if there were no epilogue, as if every end were a momentary pause in the cycle of the world. Given the pulsating magma in his paintings, the density of their signs and codes, and the fluid dispersal of the colours, I would call it iconic metabolism. His production recreates an aesthetic that is dynamic, defined and at the same time indefinable, simple and cryptic, transformable and adaptable, direct and at the same time metaphoric. It is a metabolism that resembles a chemical laboratory in the hands of an enlightened visionary in the heart of a sacred mountain.

If I had to illustrate the concept of catharsis through an artist, Julien Friedler would provide the perfect example. His art is a systemic purification that operates within the miasma of the world, a continual act of regeneration that metabolizes chaos through the alchemy of his handling of materials, colours, fragments, citations and so on. It is not by chance that he was a pupil of Jacques Lacan with years of academic and intellectual empathy, until one day Friedler turned his back on that world, adopting visual art as his chosen vehicle for research and achieving his purposes, as his new academy of life and revelation.

The important turning points in Friedler's progress have always been accompanied by catharsis but so have the individual paths that his work takes. Each time you feel that pathos is mounting, that the dramaturgical tone is reaching implosion point, the point that defines the true nature of a radical vision. This Belgian artist explodes feelings and adopts an unbridled passion for life and beauty, searching for well-being through extreme provocation that accepts no intercession. He sets his sights on the fullness of an idea, on his circular design, thereby creating a heritage that can be handed on to others, detaching his vision from the biological life of the individual, and infusing value in an artistic patrimony to be shared: beyond the artist himself, beyond the individual work, beyond the current cycle of exhibitions.

(from *Retro Boz* [Milan: Mudima, 2016])

Gianluca Ranzi
At a Dancing Pace to Conceive the Future

…Friedler's dance thus leads him on a journey of which aim no longer seems to be the final destination but the voyage itself. He ventures beyond the Pillars of Hercules of his own existence, because Friedler is well aware that attachment to oneself makes life more opaque, if the opacity of life increases and within the opacity of the ego one can only lose sight of art. This is why Friedler — just as his canvases transcend themselves, swarming with animistic vitality with signs and chromatic matter that comes to life with every dripping — doubles and multiplies himself in a genealogy of personalities: *Jack Balance*, *Le Boz*, *Le Scribe, L'Homme Miroir*. All of them bear witness to his desire to transcend himself and the singularity of his story, to instead discover an interdisciplinary multiplicity of viewpoints, contributions, references, inspirations and contradictions, which have led Norbert Hillaire to acutely observe that 'Le Boz, c'est une manière de faire des mondes'.

It is anything but coincidental that myths and mysteries have always been at home in Friedler's work. With a fertile ambiguity the artist thus remains hovering on the threshold between the stories rooted in his own individual experience of encounters with others and a meta-historical level formed by a resort to myths, in which the negative aspects of everyday life may take on significance and cultural integration or, as Friedler would say, produce a supplement of soul where misfortune reigns. Friedler's paintings and installations thus create thresholds that may be crossed, back and forth; it is as if the artist wants to stress that barriers are only there in order to be crossed again and again; to become connections, bridges, ships, networks. These works — some of which represent large-scale operative projects — are based on collaborations and enrichments (as in *Le Clochard Céleste* project, which features a collection of drawings by disadvantaged social groups) on doublings and superimpositions (in *Give up* the assemblages are the products of a dialogue between the artist and certain communities, as the Tevogan village in Togo or a number of young Belgian artists) or on inspirations which have been externalized, which then return to base like a boomerang (as the aforementioned *La Forêt des âmes* project). All these thresholds have ceased to represent barriers or obstacles, to become a transitional space which, to quote Benjamin 'contains changes, transitions, tides, significance'.

(from *Mania Boz* [Milan: Mudima, 2015])

Erno Vroonen
The World of Boz

What is art, and what purpose does it serve in our society? The discussion is not new and it has been argued recurrently from various different perspectives. It is the unrestricted privilege of democratic society, but also the prerogative of art itself, to react against any unconditional doctrine or restrictive point of view. Friedler, as author and writer and subsequently as one of the clowns, affirms in his *Livre du Boz* that art, more than any other discipline, holds the capacity to comprehend the true nature of things and in consequence the essence of life itself. This characterisation can be interpreted as being too restraining, or too authoritative, particularly in the art field; Friedler, however, does not regard himself as part of the scene. He feels like a kind of outsider and has the ambition to hold a mirror to the system in which the market price of the artwork has become more important that the true intrinsic value of the creation. Can Art be reduced to being nothing more than a symbol of financial power? Or can art have a different significance? Friedler tries to determinate the full value of art through his work. He broadens the platform on which he operates and in doing so, he makes art accessible for a wide audience. This explains why he presents artworks where they are least expected, or similarly displays a type of art where it is entirely out of place. Who determines what is the right — or wrong — context for art after all? The artist leaves the question open. However, Friedler demands more from art and subsequently from himself.

If art is to have greater cultural significance than it does at present, it must act beyond the restrictive limitations currently established, take up the challenges before it and develop new meanings that could have new meaning for a future society. The realisation of this ambition is inseparable from the realisation that there is a great emptiness at the heart of today's society that aspires to find a new meaning to its raison d'être. Julien Friedler's work invites contemplation and meditation. He paints shamanic figures, primitive or ancient civilizations, and familiar as well as extraterrestrial signs, in order to probe new paths of consciousness.

(from *Julien Friedler Be Boz, Part III*, éditions du Chaman: 2008)

I Fondamentali: la totalizzazione del sacro
Julien Friedler

Non si dirà mai abbastanza: il cuore di *Spirit of Boz* resterà sempre la vita interiore e il suo rapporto con un Creatore enigmatico, inafferrabile, le cui sembianze hanno attraversato la storia. Un Creatore dai molteplici volti, sorto ai margini, e il cui pensiero resta onnipresente nell'uomo, malgrado i cambiamenti di forma. Dall'età della pietra al New Age corre uno stesso ritornello: un'espressione del sacro senza questa riattivazione, rielaborata, ed evidenziata in modo da produrre un mito fondatore. Qui si affrontano due posizioni: un vuoto teologico, che aderisce alla pelle, e condanna all'abietto: di essere un pezzo di carne abbandonato nell'Universo. E l'opzione contraria, ipotizzante un soggetto, al di fuori della materia, responsabile di sé stesso. Un soggetto, ricalcato a immagine di un Altro ipotetico, ma imprescindibile. Si immaginerà quindi una traversata dello specchio, fatta di un incontro, un appello, un sentimento di estraneità, seguito da una ricerca instancabile. Perché, alla fine, come pensare una spiritualità moderna, nata dal presente? Su quale base edificarla? Come definirla? Ce lo eravamo detto: qui, bisogna ingaggiare una battaglia, che non sempre sarà delicata. In definitiva, la nostra intuizione sarà stata la seguente: un ritorno massiccio del religioso, sufficientemente ampio, potente e penetrante da scuotere le nostre certezze e permettere una redistribuzione delle carte. Con l'orizzonte che segue: una totalizzazione del sacro, dall'intento pacificante (pacificante perché unificato) e una mondializzazione dello spirito, aperta a tutti (non dogmatica, ma rigorosa). In quest'ottica, si dovranno costruire dei ponti teologici, consolidati da una critica sufficientemente abrasiva, corrosiva e agguerrita, per rispolverare gli antichi riflessi. Si dovrà individuare altre prassi, al fine di contrastare il male che ci consuma (l'odio di sé, dei tre monoteismi). Insomma, dovremo inventare, creare e immaginare approcci differenti, altri modi di pensare, alternative inaspettate, al fine di ridisegnare una nuova mappa delle "spiritualità", decisamente attuale e adatta ai nostri stili di vita. Si capirà quindi meglio la nostra posizione: di primo germoglio, di tentativo, do bozza per il futuro. A mille miglia da un pio desiderio. O da un'utopia. Spaventati dal furore di alcuni, inquieti per la freddezza degli altri, avremo agito procedendo per sbalzi, inversioni e fughe in avanti, prima di rallentare il passo per affinare i nostri argomenti. E senza mai perdere di vista il nostro progetto: l'iscrizione del divino in un microcosmo – *Spirit of Boz* – dalle istanze universali. Un microcosmo concepito come una matrice di idee, un nuovo modo di vedere, sentire e agire. Tanto è vero che si può credere nel dubbio, e avere fede senza saperlo.

Si parlerà allora di una leggenda. Si alluderà a una ricerca ispirata. Quando i più acuti penseranno a una Visione intangibile. Una Visione di cui siamo i depositari. Una Visione che ci avrà dettato un'opera atipica, destinata a muoversi, a trasformarsi e a modificarsi nel corso del tempo. Ne conosciamo le principali risorse: un libro vicino all'ebraismo (*Le Livre du Boz*) e *La Forêt des âmes*, dalle connotazioni cristiane (universalità, egualitarismo, cura per il prossimo). Senza dimenticare un'installazione in corso di realizzazione: *La Vache rousse* (o *Jihad*). Questa muterà dall'islam il suo "modus operandi" – un passo alla volta verso l'Eterno. Senza soprattutto dimenticare tutto un mondo di immagini arcaiche e allucinate, che evocano la trance e il suo medium: lo sciamano. Senza dimenticare, infine, lo scopo di tutta l'operazione: generare un "supplemento d'anima" la cui amplificazione, elaborazione e vissuto perseguiranno la sola cosa che valga: una pacificazione interiore, attraverso una messa a distanza delle passioni. Il nostro vero ideale.

È finita la Commedia
Dominique Stella

Il progetto di Julien Friedler intitolato *È finita la Commedia* rimanda alle drammatiche realtà che dominano le nostre vite; esso mette in scena la commedia umana in tre atti (tre installazioni) in un'evocazione – più che una critica – delle finzioni del mondo, delle erranze della storia e del cinismo che governano le nostre società, invitandoci a meditare. Non a caso è presentato nella cornice della chiesa di San Samuele. La chiesa è luogo di meditazione, di preghiera, di incontro, celebrazione e mistero, ed è anche il luogo di una ricerca interiore, che ci conduce sulla via di una messa in discussione più elevata. Le opere di Julien Friedler trattano queste tematiche profonde in una ricerca che si rivolge a ognuno di noi, invitandoci alla scoperta di noi stessi, ma anche alla presa di coscienza dell'altro. L'artista intende toccare gli animi nel loro intimo, nel loro interrogarsi sulla sacralità, sul senso della vita, sulla loro appartenenza alla comunità umana con i loro dubbi, gioie e pene, raggiungendo in questo alcuni insegnamenti della Chiesa. Ecco perché questo luogo sacro è indispensabile al progetto dell'artista e ne è un elemento determinante. Entrare a San Samuele porta naturalmente all'introspezione meditativa, al raccoglimento e all'elevazione spirituale, indotta dalla verticalità dell'architettura che le opere concorrono a sottolineare in un percorso che accompagna lo sviluppo spaziale della chiesa. In questo senso, San Samuele fa parte integrante del concetto che l'artista ha costruito attorno alle tre installazioni, inserite in un cammino che riprende l'architettura del luogo. Il titolo stesso indica la solennità del momento che viviamo e ci invita a ricorrere a precetti più atemporali rispetto a quelli promossi dalla nostra epoca. La Chiesa è lo spazio ideale per condurci a riflettere sul nostro mondo, al di là di una fede religiosa, ma nella certezza che qualcosa deve essere salvato e Friedler ci accompagna in questa convinzione attraverso le sue opere. *È finita la Commedia…*

Le realtà contemporanee viaggiano in un immaginario che sottolinea gli aspetti più oscuri dell'animo umano senza per questo condannarlo alla dannazione, ma interrogando ognuno, invitandolo a trarre dalla contemplazione e dalla meditazione le forze necessarie alla rigenerazione. Non vi è alcuna leggerezza in queste opere di Friedler, il titolo dell'esposizione lo indica: *È finita la Commedia*, basta ridere e cantare, "passiamo alle cose serie", sembra dire l'artista, "riflettiamo sul nostro destino".

È in questo pensiero che risiede il cuore del lavoro dell'artista, la cui preoccupazione principale resta sempre "la vita interiore e il suo rapporto con un'espressione del sacro, il suo rapporto con l'enigmatico Creatore dai molteplici volti, che nasce dall'inizio dei tempi, e il cui pensiero resta onnipresente nell'uomo, malgrado i cambiamenti di forma". Vi è dunque una meditazione spirituale rilevante ma anche il rapporto malinconico con l'esistenza, e nei tre tempi dell'esposizione l'artista mette l'Uomo a confronto con le tre esperienze di vita: il Dolore, la Malinconia e la Speranza, fonti di riflessione sul mondo. Tre installazioni illustrano questa meditazione.

La scenografia si sviluppa nella chiesa, riprendendo le tre componenti maggiori della pianta basilicale: la navata centrale, le due navate laterali. Ognuna delle tre tematiche è complementare alle altre; l'insieme propone un tempo di sospensione meditativa sul senso della vita, della morte e di una possibile redenzione. Innanzitutto la violenza, messa in scena nell'installazione *Les Innocents*, che illustra il dolore dell'innocenza violata, ma anche la reclusione, l'isolamento e la ribellione. L'installazione ricorda la dignità incomparabile di ogni bambino, mentre ogni giorno si rinnova il massacro degli Innocenti. La loro sofferenza colpisce la nostra coscienza insensibile, se non anestetizzata. Non si tratta di compiangerli ma di rimettersi in causa con un atteggiamento di conversione di mentalità e di impegno. L'artista suggerisce la lacerazione, la tortura, la fragilità, la morte, sotto una forma simbolica di un'intensità

sconfortante, che malgrado la sua radicalità vuole essere fonte di sollievo e di vita. L'installazione coniuga memoria individuale (quella dell'artista e dei suoi ricordi d'infanzia) e memoria collettiva, invitando a una riflessione approfondita sulla nostra cultura, le sue illusioni, i suoi disincanti ma anche la possibilità di sopravvivenza.

La Malinconia dei *Pierrots* risponde all'innocenza dell'infanzia. Figura ingenua e sognante, Friedler la evoca sotto l'aspetto triste e nostalgico del Pierrot di Verlaine:

"Non è più il sognatore lunare della vecchia aria
che rideva agli avi da sopra gli stipiti:
la sua allegria, come la sua candela, ahimè! è morta,
e oggi il suo spettro ci ossessiona, sottile e chiaro."

Il poeta e l'artista fanno entrambi rivivere il personaggio, un tempo allegro e stravagante, sotto una forma spettrale. Questa figura di commedia, con il suo costume tradizionale, il suo viso lunare che ci incantava, grandi e piccini, ha ormai un triste aspetto. Friedler ci offre l'immagine di un essere scarno, un redivivo che si è disumanizzato sotto forma di uno scheletro robotizzato. A questo corpo senza vita non resta che un piccolo barlume triste e disincantato negli occhi, che esprime come un rimpianto dei tempi passati, un sogno di felicità perduto. Questa evocazione agghiacciante della nostra epoca suggerisce la mutazione che si opera nella nostra società, influenzando la nostra visione del mondo e del nostro corpo, che l'artista illustra attraverso l'erranza di queste anime incorporee, vaganti ai margini del regno di Ade, come ombre in cerca della salvezza. Sono una moltitudine, tutte simili, una riduzione dell'umano allo stato di massa controllata e intorpidita. Queste sculture ci rimandano all'opera *Efficiency Men* di Thomas Schütte.

La Forêt des âmes è un'opera ascensionale che evoca l'elevazione dello spirito. L'artista vi trasmette un messaggio di speranza e di rinnovamento. Evocazione di anime luminose che non incarna il Divino, ma una Coscienza energetica positiva che invita ognuno di noi a un momento di raccoglimento e di riflessione, quest'opera contribuisce a trasmettere ciò che l'artista chiama "un supplemento d'anima", un momento di condivisione e di oblio di sé, per unirsi a un processo collettivo. Friedler definisce questa installazione "di ispirazione cristiana", poiché essa veicola i principi di "universalità, egualitarismo e attenzione al prossimo". Il suo obiettivo è di andare al di là dei dati materiali e visivi per trarne le connessioni più sottili e invisibili, raggiungendo così un'interrogazione di natura psichica, filosofica e anche religiosa.

Le tre installazioni convergono nel creare un unico

racconto tra drammaturgia e salvazione. La scenografia
occupa lo spazio della chiesa in tre atti dello sviluppo
del suo percorso, che verrà arricchito da qualche opera
pittorica e fotografica.

- navata laterale destra: *Les Innocents* (2000)
- navata laterale sinistra: *Les Pierrots* (2019)
- navata centrale: *La Forêt des âmes* (2009)

Le opere pittoriche che accompagnano le installazioni
accentuano ulteriormente il carattere drammatico della
scenografia. Si tratta di: *L'Autre* (2018), *Ode Satanique*
(2018) e *Crucifixion* (2016). A queste opere pittoriche
si aggiungono due fotografie intitolate *Les Ombres,
barbelés* (2002), indissociabili dall'installazione *Les
Innocents* (2000).
Queste sequenze, installazioni e dipinti, che costellano
il percorso della chiesa, sono legate dalla medesima
filosofia creativa che presiede all'insieme dell'opera
dell'artista. Infatti ogni produzione, ogni installazione,
ogni dipinto, ogni performance costituisce la trama di
una storia più vasta, di una "leggenda", dice Friedler,
che comprende la totalità delle azioni artistiche che
egli ha condotto e continua a condurre – un mondo
in espansione che egli chiama *Spirit of Boz*. In questo
universo, Friedler ha inventato personaggi come Jack
Balance, ma ha anche messo in opera programmi di
azione, tutta una gestione dell'immaginario che i dipinti,
le installazioni, le performance e gli incontri animano.
Les Innocents illustrano le premesse di questo pensiero
rigoglioso che permea fortemente gli animi. *La Forêt
des âmes* ne è il veicolo, che permette di andare verso
gli altri, *Les Pierrots* ne sono l'immagine malinconica,
riflessione sul destino dell'umanità.
L'artista belga si fa portatore di una visione umanista,
delineata tramite le opere ma anche con un'attività
di condivisione che porta avanti attraverso *Spirit of
Boz*, associazione nata per instaurare – praticando
l'espressione orale, letteraria, pittorica e creativa
in generale – scambi e legami, costituendo così
una comunità di pensieri e testimonianze su realtà
individuali e collettive, provenienti da svariati luoghi
del mondo. Tale realtà esprime l'urgenza di riconciliare
azione e contemplazione, nell'intento di promuovere
un pensiero umanista e catartico. Il suo universo,
in evoluzione permanente, comporta sfaccettature
contrapposte, le une d'ispirazione collettiva (*La
Forêt des âmes*), le altre (*Les Pierrots* e i dipinti) di
meditazione individuale.
L'arte di Friedler mette in moto sensazioni, relazioni,
analisi, ed è concepita come azione inclusiva di tutte le
espressioni vitali, derivino esse dalla propria esperienza
o da quella altrui. La sua azione, di conseguenza,
riveste molteplici aspetti e abbraccia vari campi,

dalla letteratura alla filosofia, dall'analisi sociologica
alle arti plastiche (pittura, scultura, installazioni).
L'aspetto pittorico della sua produzione è generato
dalla necessità creatrice, dal desiderio di trasmissione
spontanea e viscerale, derivante dal "tentativo di
scoprire ciò che costituisce l'essenza passionale delle
persone". Friedler procede secondo modalità quasi
ipnotiche, senza vincolo di soggetti, di materiali messi in
opera, definendo così un ritmo, un modo d'espressione
informale. La sua energia in espansione deriva dalla
capacità di dissociazione e introspezione che applica
a sé stesso prima di interessarsi agli altri, scoprendo
nell'altro le motivazioni più intime: un viaggio per
esplorare l'animo umano nella sua complessità atavica
e universale.

Opere

Les Innocents, 2000
Filo spinato, peluches, legno e tecnica mista,
dimensioni originali 9 x 11 m

L'installazione *Les Innocents* è una rappresentazione
metaforica della ferita intima del mondo, nata
dall'infanzia soggiogata, imprigionata, come scrive
il filosofo Pierre Bourdieu, in "una scuola terribile
di realismo sociale, in cui tutto è già presente,
attraverso le necessità della lotta per la vita:
l'opportunismo, il servilismo, la delazione": essa
testimonia l'origine sanguinosa della vita. Nel corso
della sua elaborazione, l'opera dalle dimensioni
monumentali ha acquisito le caratteristiche di
un campo di concentramento in cui il simbolo
dell'infanzia violata e maltrattata raggiunge
l'evocazione del martirio del popolo ebraico. A
differenza dei quadri, derivanti da un'espressione
immediata e divampante, il lavoro dell'installazione si
svolge nel corso di diversi mesi, vi entra dunque una
consapevolezza più ampia, un'elaborazione e una
volontà creatrice più determinata rispetto ai dipinti,
segnati dal carattere della spontaneità. Tuttavia
Julien Friedler non vi coglie il lavoro di una volontà
consapevole, nessun desiderio di commentare,
nessuna volontà di ricordare il destino del popolo
ebraico… Egli vi vede un'universalità della sofferenza
che in qualsiasi epoca si riproduce e si ripete nella
follia e nella violenza degli uomini. Si tratta qui di un
gesto espiatorio nel quale l'artista investe le proprie
forze di redenzione. "Ci sono il filo spinato, i peluche, i
banchi di scuola, una messa in scena certo tragica ma
anche ludica, ho utilizzato il linguaggio degli estremi:
l'infanzia e la morte, è la Shoah, naturalmente, ma
anche una metafora dell'infanzia imprigionata… di tutti

i bambini del mondo uccisi e feriti nella loro innocenza."
L'installazione evoca le tematiche della sofferenza: il
dolore, la chiusura, l'isolamento, la ribellione.
Jack Balance occupa il centro dell'installazione *Les
Innocents,* ed è un personaggio speciale nell'universo
creativo di Friedler. È come il gemello dell'artista, una
forma duplicata di sé stesso, un simbolo della difficoltà
a essere e a liberarsi dalle contingenze umane. Jack
Balance è rinchiuso in una gabbia, da cui fugge,
per compiere un giro del mondo. Per esistere, deve
costantemente protestare, ribellarsi. La gabbia illustra
il suo caso specifico, ma fa ugualmente emergere
un simbolismo universale. Jack Balance è un clown
frustrato ma pieno di humour e d'impertinenza, il cui
rimpianto è quello di essere un personaggio e non
un essere umano. Egli sostiene una lotta che l'artista
non potrebbe affrontare senza la finzione di questa
maschera, tuttavia la presenza del personaggio è
virtuale. La sua esistenza è materializzata da una
foto. Una sedia, dei peluche sparsi, uno scheletro
di plastica, dei cellulari che lo collegano con il suo
Creatore, una sorta di lacci invisibili che lo mantengono
in una condizione di dipendenza. Un cartello dice: "Mi
chiamano Jack Balance".
L'opera evoca anche il percorso intimo dell'artista, la
sua difficoltà a vivere, la sua aspirazione a trascendere
i limiti imposti dalla natura, e l'interrogarsi fondamentale
di fronte all'enigma della vita e del divino. È anche
un'opera catartica, di purificazione emotiva; Julien
Friedler opera attraverso il racconto della propria storia,
del proprio vissuto, che si offrono nella genesi di questa
opera, a cui egli attribuisce un carattere universale.
L'interrogarsi sul mondo è qui onnipresente. Così come
Friedler lo evoca nella *Vérité du Labyrinthe* (Texte #22):
"Un mondo spesso impregnato di sangue e di odio.
Il divino frammentato, frantumato, sofferente. Una
guerra, senza sosta, ripresa e riprodotta. Perché tutti i
divini sono in Dio, il surrogato dei nostri sogni. Nessuno
è migliore o più giusto. O più vero. O più bello. O più
umano. O più potente. Nella migliore delle ipotesi, ci
daranno l'idea di un altro affresco generato dall'uomo
per consolarsi.
Un affresco che converge, si riduce, si concentra
in un punto. Un punto chiamato a superarsi. Non
avevamo già evocato un puro Spirito, un al di là, un
vuoto inconcepibile? In tal caso, l'estetica non può non
interpellarci. Si tratta forse di un primo indizio? Perché
un simile dimostrativo richiede uno sguardo non umano
che non dovrebbe nulla agli alieni o altri extraterrestri.
Del resto, non sono sin da ora presi nelle nostre reti:
una leggenda del divino creata dalle nostre fantasie?".
Fotografie: le foto che accompagnano l'installazione
sono le ombre di questa umanità martire, in ogni luogo,
in ogni tempo.

La Forêt des âmes, 2009
Nove colonne di legno, maschere di resina, luce led,
altezza circa 2 m ciascuna

Luce della speranza e condivisione del messaggio
artistico tramite il concetto della *Foresta delle anime*.

L'associazione *Spirit of Boz – Julien Friedler* è il
supporto di un'azione che Julien Friedler intende
condurre in un tempo continuato, che lo supera e
che proseguirà il suo lavoro per ottant'anni e oltre.
L'associazione sviluppa un programma intitolato *Be
Boz Be Art*, che comporta diversi settori di intervento
e che contribuisce a divulgare, in tutto il mondo, nuove
pratiche artistiche allo scopo di dar loro visibilità.
Spirit of Boz di Friedler veicola un ideale di scambio
e di interazioni vantaggiose per tutti, che ha già
trovato eco nelle comunità più lontane. Il progetto *Be
Boz Be Art* poggia su tre programmi che implicano
la ricerca attiva di complicità dai talenti multipli, e
l'incontro con realtà quotidiane molto lontane dalle
nostre, la cui scoperta e approccio in un rispetto
reciproco contribuiscono ad arricchire un'eterogeneità
di espressione e di trasmissione, facendo nascere
opportunità di scambi. A volte dalla più grande
indigenza, dall'apparente ignoranza sorgono così i
segni di un sapere nascosto, l'espressione di alcune
parole che raggiungono la poesia più pura, l'esecuzione
di alcuni tratti, la mescolanza di colori che lasciano
pensare che l'arte sia una forza conduttrice, che porta
all'incontro e alla rivelazione delle possibilità. È in
questa consapevolezza e in questa convinzione che
l'associazione *Spirit of Boz* conduce azioni partecipative
che implicano l'impegno di persone dalle origini sociali
più diverse, dalle provenienze geografiche più lontane.
Queste azioni rispondono ad alcuni criteri definiti dal
programma *Give up*, che raccoglie opere spontanee
in occasione di viaggi (Ruanda, Togo, Messico…) nel
corso dei quali l'équipe del *Boz* va incontro a culture e
tradizioni che spesso gli sono totalmente sconosciute.
Con le persone che lo desiderano, l'équipe raccoglie
oggetti di uso comune, realizzazioni creative spesso a
carattere tribale.
Friedler, attraverso il suo progetto artistico, intende
raccogliere i fremiti emersi dall'inconscio delle
persone, che egli ama esplorare e di cui segue i
meandri attraverso il terzo programma di *Be Boz Be
Art* intitolato *La Forêt des âmes*. Questa genera delle
risposte a un questionario stampato su un foglietto.
Le risposte raccolte, preziosamente conservate,
costituiranno la sostanza stessa dell'opera. Tutti i
questionari saranno infatti racchiusi in casse che
saranno poi impilate in colonne; ogni colonna dà corpo
a un albero. Dalla moltiplicazione degli alberi emergerà

una foresta. Una foresta di anime. L'opera in mostra (9 colonne) è la prefigurazione di questa foresta.

Questionario *La Forêt des âmes - Le Tour du Boz en 80 ans*
La Foresta delle anime origina delle risposte a un questionario, espressione di sei domande:

1. Dio esiste?
2. Come possiamo caratterizzare questa epoca?
3. Come vede l'avvenire?
4. Lei è felice?
5. La sessualità è importante?
6. Chi sono io?

Domande che possono sembrare banali, ma che sono al cuore della nostra costruzione sociale; esse sono al centro di preoccupazioni esistenziali che costituiscono il motore dello sviluppo delle nostre culture. L'équipe di *Spirit of Boz* viaggia in tutto il mondo per distribuire e raccogliere questi questionari. Dal Togo all'Amazzonia, passando per gli Stati Uniti, l'Indonesia, il Ruanda, l'Argentina, il Belgio, il Tibet. Intrapresa nel 2006, si presenta all'inverso della nostra concezione del tempo: lo svolgimento del *Tour du Boz* è previsto in ottant'anni. Il questionario ha lo scopo di privilegiare l'incontro. Sono già state raccolte più di 75.000 risposte. A ogni presentazione dell'installazione si chiede al pubblico di compilare il questionario.

Les Pierrots, 2019
12 strutture in metallo laccato di nero, con maschera dipinta (altezza variabile fino a 1,6 m),
spazio occupato variabile circa 3,5 x 5 m

Les Pierrots è un'installazione estremamente recente, risalente alla fine del 2019. È il culmine di una riflessione sul destino dell'uomo contemporaneo e la proiezione dell'immagine di una società disincarnata, persa e nostalgica. Il *Pierrot* è qui uno strumento necessario per l'artista, che sottolinea il valore archetipico di questa grande figura della Commedia dell'arte, questa commedia umana la cui maschera simboleggia il candore e l'ingenuità che lo rendono vulnerabile. La vulnerabilità ci appare come quella dell'artista (e di noi stessi), che si nasconde dietro questa apparizione per comunicarci meglio l'intensità di un dramma che si svolge nel profondo del nostro essere. Il dispositivo di questo simulacro appartiene strettamente alla mitologia di Friedler che già nel personaggio di Jack Balance, il suo doppio, si era inventato un'incarnazione mascherata che gli consentiva di aggiornare i problemi esistenziali che lo abitano.

I Pierrots sono robot, prefigurazione di un'umanità meccanizzata e disincarnata, quasi realtà del nostro mondo la cui volontà sempre più forte consiste nel codificare ulteriormente l'esistenza, mettendo a repentaglio le nostre capacità. Questa è una minaccia esistenziale, suggerisce Friedler. L'opera è una parabola dell'alienazione acconsentita, della nostra sottomissione a un mondo connesso e decerebrante, che comprime l'individuo nella massa informe e anonima degli uomini ultradipendente dagli strumenti informatici che ha inventato, racchiudendosi così in una cultura di massa che allontana il pensiero, sterilizza l'iniziativa e standardizza tutti i riflessi. La schematizzazione robotica dei corpi enfatizza la standardizzazione e la meccanizzazione che cancellano l'individualità, una realtà che l'artista accentua attraverso la ripetizione. La riduzione dell'aspetto dei Pierrots a uno scheletro di metallo illustra l'annientamento della vita; l'esistenza viene persa in quanto neutralizzata e ridotta a una sostanza spettrale, emaciata, ma comunque animata da uno sguardo triste. Solo le anime vagano ancora nella nostalgia sottolineata da Friedler con le lacrime di questi Pierrots che ricordano ancora la loro luminosa umanità. Il lavoro è commovente quanto inquietante, altamente espressionista, mette in discussione i principi di metamorfosi e mutazione offerti da una cyber-società che fantastica sul dominio dell'ego e sulla demoltiplicazione delle nostre capacità. Possiamo sfuggire al tragico destino che l'artista disegna per noi? Gli occhi tristi dei suoi Pierrots ci fanno vedere una disperazione più umana… un pentimento.

I dipinti

La sequenza dei *Pierrots* è accompagnata da tre quadri che suggeriscono il buio esistenziale che abita gli esseri.

- *L'Autre*, 2018, acrilico e collage su tela, 150 x 200 cm
- *Ode Satanique*, 2018, acrilico su tela, 150 x 200 cm
- *Crucifixion*, 2016, acrilico su tela, 200 x 300 cm
(presentata sul retro della parete della *Forêt des âmes*)

Questi tre quadri sono emblematici del periodo pittorico 2016-2018. Dopo tutta una serie di opere solari legate alla natura, alla luce, che Julien Friedler ha dipinto negli anni 2012-2016, la sua ispirazione torna più cupa e primitiva. La materia è ruvida e i colori oscuri evocano le tenebre. In queste opere monumentali, rappresentative dell'atteggiamento dell'artista che esplora il mondo al di là delle evidenze percepibili e intelligibili, s'impone un'inquietante realtà che fa

nascere connessioni segrete con l'invisibile, nascoste
nelle profondità dell'inconscio. È a questo che arriva
l'artista, a questa introspezione lenta e viscerale che
accompagna il gesto, oppure che è accompagnata
dal gesto e che elimina tutta la fiducia cartesiana
nella ragione umana lasciando spazio al mistero.
L'immersione nell'irrazionale esplora le profondità
dell'infinito e del divenire. È così che potremmo
descrivere la pittura di Julien Friedler, che nasce da una
pratica psicanalitica di indagine sull'inconscio; una volta
abbandonato qualsiasi carattere dogmatico, tuttavia,
egli si abbandona alla meditazione che si oppone al
mondo delle forme, delle abitudini e dei comportamenti,
arrivando così allo splendore degli abissi. È qui che
scopriamo la profondità dell'anima che, riflettendosi, si
proietta sulle tele e diventa dipinto.
Friedler scrive: "A cosa mirano i nostri dipinti, le nostre
sculture e le nostre installazioni? Se non a questo: una
combinazione di opposti, una scrittura paradossale,
un inserimento dei flussi che attraversano lo *Spirit of
Boz*. Qui, l'universo si espanderà fino a raggiungere
un punto di interruzione: una pura sincronia, nascosta
sotto la massa delle creazioni, in cui si confondono
tutti i mezzi. Perché, fondamentalmente, ogni opera
disgiunta, separata, visibile da tutti e da ciascuno, non
sarà che un dettaglio, un'immagine, la manifestazione
isolata di un fenomeno globale: un solo e unico
quadro, visto da diverse angolazioni. Un quadro in
grado di ricomporsi nella mente di tutti coloro che vi
si dedicheranno. Non vi è differenza di natura tra il
microcosmo soggettivo e il macrocosmo universale."
Friedler è mosso da un'aspirazione superiore che
illustra la dimensione infinita dell'arte e mette in scena
la sua capacità di reinventare il mondo.

Biografia
Dominique Stella

L'opera: "L'inscrizione del Divino in un microcosmo
(*Spirit of Boz*) dalle istanze universali" J.F.

Figlio di genitori ebrei, entrambi originari della
Transilvania, Julien Friedler nasce a Bruxelles nel 1950.
Attualmente vive a Montecarlo. Riceve un'educazione
religiosa attenta, rispettosa dei precetti dell'ebraismo.
Dopo gli studi di filosofia ed etnologia, frequenta corsi
di psicanalisi a Parigi; aderisce allora alle teorie post-
strutturaliste di Jacques Lacan, intraprendendo insieme
a quest'ultimo una psicanalisi personale.
Julien Friedler è un personaggio complesso e la
costruzione della sua arte poggia su alcune ferite
sempre dolorose che tormentano da tempo la memoria
familiare. La guerra, ancora così vicina, ha lasciato
tracce indelebili nella sua famiglia, segnata dal destino
tragico dei deportati e dispersi nei campi nazisti. Sua
madre non se ne riavrà mai, vivendo nel dolore e nel
ricordo, trasmettendo così a suo figlio il fermento di
un'inquietudine profonda che sarà per sempre il segno
di un carattere tormentato.
Lacan muore nel 1981, senza che una frequentazione
quotidiana con l'illustre psicanalista abbia permesso a
Julien Friedler di attenuare il proprio malessere.

Nel corso degli anni ottanta cerca la sua strada,
viaggia, scopre, grazie a suo padre gioielliere, il mondo
degli affari al quale prende parte anche Lutty de
Geest, la sua compagna, che sposa nel 1984. Durante
questo periodo, dedica nondimeno una grande parte
del proprio tempo alla scrittura. Nel 1982 pubblica il
suo primo libro, *Mosaïque*, racconto poetico che mette
in scena una molteplicità di storie inventate destinate
a far smarrire il lettore nel labirinto del pensiero. Il
libro *L'Ombre du rabbin,* pubblicato nel 1985 dalla
casa editrice Lieu Commun, Parigi, affronta, invece,
il problema della Shoah attraverso personaggi il cui
interrogarsi sul destino tragico del popolo martire
raggiunge quello dell'artista. La parola "Ricerca", mitica
ed epica al tempo stesso, illustra il percorso degli
eroi del libro, figure emblematiche della problematica
friedleriana.
1988: nascita della figlia Tatiana.

Negli anni novanta, l'esplorazione dell'ambito
psicanalitico costituisce la base della sua ricerca. Ma
il tormento essenziale che lo abita non trova alcuna
tregua e apre la via a una ricerca estenuante del
Senso che si afferma negli interrogativi fondamentali,
che egli pone e tenta di chiarire nei suoi scritti e nelle
sue opere plastiche. Infatti, il lavoro artistico che egli

intraprende verso il 1996 prolunga il suo interrogarsi sull'Inconscio, e l'epopea artistica che egli sviluppa, denominata genericamente *Spirit of Boz*, ingloba così la totalità degli aspetti del suo racconto personale, che unito alle sue opere definisce una ricerca il cui cuore, come ricorda l'artista, "resterà per sempre la vita interiore e il suo rapporto con un Creatore enigmatico, inafferrabile".

Malgrado l'emergere della pittura nel suo lavoro, Friedler continua a scrivere. Gli anni novanta vedono la pubblicazione di tre libri. Nel 1995 esce *Psychanalyse et neurosciences: la légende du boiteux* (PUF, Paris). L'autore vi riprende l'interrogativo posto dallo *Schizzo per una psicologia scientifica* di Sigmund Freud, dedicandosi a un'analisi comparativa alla luce delle conoscenze attuali sviluppate dalle neuroscienze. Il libro, apprezzato dal pubblico, gli vale diversi elogi. Poi, nel 1998, escono successivamente *Tirésias*, dramma poetico (Caractères, Paris) e *L'ivrogne* pubblicato dalle Éditions de Janus, la cui copertina è illustrata con uno dei primi quadri del pittore, *Le Petit homme jaune*.

Nella seconda metà degli anni novanta, la pittura invade definitivamente il lavoro di Julien Friedler. L'arte diventa per lui la fonte "di una verità sopportabile" che attraverso la sua forza espressiva consente "la raffigurazione dei miti dell'umanità". Le prime opere costituiscono la testimonianza, a volte maldestra, di un lavoro spontaneo e già dominato dalla brillantezza del colore, che molto rapidamente trova un'espressione personale in una serie di dipinti come *Le Petit homme jaune*, *Le Miroir de la Princesse*, o *Le Cheval fou*. La volontà pittorica dell'artista vi s'impone con una forza espressiva talvolta ingenua, paragonabile a un'arte del graffito in cui il segno impone molto rapidamente la sua presenza tormentosa.

Anni duemila, la pittura è sempre più presente. *Le Shaman* (2000), lo sciamano, sarà l'immagine simbolica del processo di mutazione di Friedler che tuttavia non dimentica da dove proviene. L'arte appare allora come una sintesi, e gli scritti poetici che ricoprono le sue prime tele illustrano il passaggio dal pittorico al segno, che ben presto diventa linguaggio criptato attraverso la serie delle opere intitolate *La Parole des Anges*. Questo ciclo di dipinti, realizzato tra il 2000 e il 2002, riveste una dimensione concettuale nel contenuto ed estetica nella forma. In questa serie di opere, Friedler mette a punto un linguaggio criptato, esoterico, primordiale, basato su una simbologia del segno. "*La Parole des Anges*", dice Friedler, "è una mistica, una lingua fondamentale soggiacente alla proliferazione dei discorsi, ogni segno, se non la totalità del dipinto, potrebbe costituire l'oggetto di

una meditazione". Attraverso l'elaborazione di questo linguaggio, Julien Friedler stabilisce una cartografia dei concetti che interrogano l'uomo sull'idea del Sacro, di cui egli cerca di interpretare i misteri tramite una scrittura quasi religiosa. Una retrospettiva di questo ciclo di dipinti avrà luogo più tardi, nel 2018, alla Cité Miroir di Liegi, con l'edizione di un catalogo che riprende le opere maggiori della *Parole des Anges*.

Nel 2000, *Les Innocents* occupano l'atelier. Un recinto di 11 x 9 m, fatto di filo spinato, racchiude peluche, banchi di scuola, in una messa in scena, certo, tragica ma anche ludica. L'installazione è monumentale. Friedler precisa: "Ho utilizzato un linguaggio degli estremi: l'infanzia e la morte, è la Shoah, certo, ma anche una metafora dell'infanzia imprigionata… di tutti i bambini del mondo uccisi e feriti nella loro innocenza." L'installazione diventa presto un punto di riferimento nell'opera dell'artista, veicolando l'idea di un'arte di condivisione, invitando a interrogarsi. Lo spettatore, percorrendo l'esposizione, è portato a confrontarsi sulle domande fondamentali del mondo. Versioni successive degli *Innocents* viaggeranno da allora in numerose esposizioni dedicate all'artista.

È in questo periodo (2000) che nasce Jack Balance (http://rebelle.blogspirit.com/archive/2021/04/29/julien-friedler-dealer-d-utopies-3251717.html). Altro personaggio importante della mitologia friedleriana, egli esprime il superamento di sé; è il sosia, il volto pubblico dell'artista, alcolizzato, libertino, consapevole di ciò che lo circonda e lo opprime. Occupa la gabbia situata al centro dell'installazione *Les Innocents*. "Jack Balance mi è necessario", dice Julien Friedler, "probabilmente perché amo essere in disparte dal mondo. Sono timido e solitario, ho dunque inventato una maschera che mi permette di dire e di fare ciò che io non sarei mai in grado di dire e di fare." Jack Balance simboleggia la lotta che l'uomo conduce per esistere nella terribile dipendenza dal suo Creatore. Egli cerca di proclamarsi "soggetto" e per questo deve superare i limiti che gli sono stati imposti, come il mutismo dal quale è colpito. I suoi sistemi di comunicazione sono dunque molteplici: la scrittura, il dipinto, ma anche infrangere la legge del mutismo quando il suo creatore è disattento. Anche Jack Balance è chiuso in una gabbia, dalla quale scappa per fare il giro del mondo. Per esistere, deve costantemente imbrogliare, protestare, ribellarsi. Jack Balance è un clown frustrato che si pone domande esistenziali, percorrendo il pianeta in una ricerca mistica. Egli incarna la Coscienza.

Nel 2003, Friedler si è trasformato in clown faceto, l'atelier comincia a popolarsi di personaggi fantomatici, i muri si coprono di scrittura e questo luogo immenso, in pieno centro di Bruxelles, diventa l'antro che vede nascere l'universo in espansione di Julien Friedler, che dal 2003 egli chiamerà *Le Boz.* È qui che, dal 2006, si costruisce *Spirit of Boz*, che nella sua definizione rappresenta una ricerca metafisica, un invito a prolungare l'avventura dell'arte nel campo della vita, un'opera unica che ci obbliga a uscire da noi stessi, a dissolverci in essa. Perché, infatti, al di là di un'opera prolifica, radiosa e a volte inquietante, Friedler ci invita a modificare la nostra consapevolezza di essere. L'arte è fonte di rivelazione di sé, un luogo di condivisione e di scambio, un invito al sogno, una ricerca di senso, una via d'uscita dalle mediocri realtà del quotidiano, una via verso l'inaccessibile verità della vita. Un'avventura metafisica, "l'espressione dell'indicibile", dice Sonia Bressler[1]. "La forza di Julien Friedler", dice, "consiste nell'avere i suoi gesti creativi nel proprio spazio e *Spirit of Boz* come estensione di questi ultimi nello spazio mondo."[2]

È tutto questo che Friedler intuisce, attraverso le sue azioni, performance, installazioni, dipinti. Il suo interrogarsi si fa sempre più intenso e necessita di un'indispensabile apertura sul mondo. L'artista, e più spesso il suo doppio, esce dall'atelier ed entra in scena. Noi siamo gli spettatori e siamo invitati a diventare anche gli attori. Il mondo del *Boz* inizia a organizzarsi. Jeanne Zeler entra nell'avventura, al fine di coordinarne lo sviluppo.

Inizio della scrittura del *Livre du Boz*, che accompagna la messa a punto della filosofia del *Boz*. Questo libro è una rincorsa, una ricerca, un'epopea, un'opera meditativa ed epica, la cui redazione occupa gli anni successivi e che Julien Friedler definisce nei *Fondamentaux*: "Tre clown – Jack Balance, lo Scriba e l'Uomo specchio – saranno presi nella propria trappola: una visione che scorre e scivola tra le loro dita. A vederli evolvere, si avrà la sensazione di un sogno a occhi aperti. Il racconto è non lineare, aperto a tutto e sapientemente deflagrato. Si svolge su diversi piani – simultanei – inserendo le storie le une nelle altre, come in un gioco di matrioske. La temporalità è fluttuante, ampiamente imprevedibile. Lo spazio è indistinto. L'intrigo è sfuggente…"

2003: prime esposizioni. "L'infanzia dell'arte", esposizione personale alla Fondazione Mudima, Milano. Dipinti della serie *La Parole des Anges* e installazione *Les Innocents* – recensione su Rai 3 di Philippe Daverio, che si entusiasma per l'opera. Arturo Schwarz prende la parola in occasione del vernissage per elogiare la forza del lavoro di Friedler e più in particolare degli *Innocents*. Il catalogo riprende numerose vedute dell'atelier di Bruxelles.

Due partecipazioni a fiere: Art Brussels con la Galleria

Damasquine, e Fiera di Basilea con la galleria Pailhas di Marsiglia.

Realizzazione delle prime opere-installazioni che mettono in scena questo personaggio al tempo stesso burlesco e drammatico che è Jack Balance, che comincia a conquistare la propria autonomia nell'universo di Friedler: *BB Jack Balance, Jack Balance dans son transat*. Il mondo del *Boz* si sviluppa e l'atelier, a poco a poco, diventa un luogo che l'artista vuole in espansione verso il mondo esterno.

2004, la scrittura è sempre presente, pubblicazione di *L'Œil d'Œdipe*, edizioni PUF. Decostruire il mito per farne un'illusione, questo è l'obiettivo di Friedler, che nel volume denuncia l'ipertrofia dell'inconscio e invoca la necessità di procedere in senso inverso: dall'illusione verso il mito, il che presuppone l'elaborazione di nuovi "mitemi". Riconosciamo in questo le inquietudini dell'artista, costruttore di una mitologia leggendaria che sviluppa attraverso un universo mitico, ancorato simultaneamente al reale e all'inconscio.

Nel 2004 al suo percorso si aggiungono due esposizioni personali: *Paroles et Paraboles ou le Mythe en question* al Passage de Retz, Parigi, e *Memories* alla Galleria David Di Maggio, Berlino. Friedler partecipa anche a due esposizioni collettive: *De leur Temps – Collections privées françaises*, Musée des Beaux-Arts, Tourcoing. *Vanitas, Eitelkeit der Eitelkeiten*, IKOB, Eupen.

2000-2009, dopo *La Parole des Anges*, questo periodo è dominato dalla pittura. Dalla nascita di *Spirit of Boz* scaturisce una forza creatrice che trascende l'opera pittorica in un'irruzione spontanea e conquistatrice, che impone la pittura come fonte di energia introspettiva e al contempo prorompente. *La Parole des Anges* conteneva già tutti gli aspetti della meditazione che ispirerà in seguito il lavoro dell'artista. La complessità della sua opera vi è tracciata in modo profetico, attivando così tutte le sfaccettature che compongono la diversità del personaggio Julien Friedler: lo psicanalista, lo scrittore, il poeta, l'artista. Tutti tendono verso uno stesso scopo, quello di riattivare i miti in una società in equilibrio instabile, al fine di trovarvi un senso. È in questo spirito di ricorso alle grandi mitologie fondatrici che Friedler dipinge una serie di figure emblematiche e leggendarie, dei giganti favolosi, ammalianti, personificazioni immaginarie delle nostre paure inconsce: *Le Foudroyer* (2004), *Ecce Homo* (2009), *Le Cavalier de l'Apocalypse* (2009), *Le Clown androgyne, Le Guerrier* (2010) e innanzitutto *Le Shaman* (2000), figura potente dell'universo friedleriano, particolarmente significativa dell'opera dell'artista. Questa rappresentazione potrebbe essere

---

[1] In Sonia Bressler, *Julien Friedler. De la Métaphysique de l'errance*, Jacques Flament Éditions, Mariac 2013, p. 75.
[2] *Ibidem*, p. 76.

il suo stesso autoritratto. Lo sciamano è, in effetti, nella tradizione, il poeta, l'erudito, lo stregone che consegna ai viventi un messaggio dall'aldilà.

In questi stessi anni, produce tre opere importanti: *Les Demoiselles revisitées* (2005), installazione di tre sculture in resina liberamente ispirate alle *Demoiselles d'Avignon* di Picasso, che saranno esposte nel 2007 alla Francis Naumann Gallery, New York. Realizza anche due sculture iperrealiste, la scultura *Le Juif errant* (2004), immagine archetipica di un personaggio inquietante e al contempo malinconico. E infine una rappresentazione di *Arafat* (2004), che è venduta da Phillips de Pury & Company, a Londra nel 2005. Queste opere testimoniano un realismo critico verso la società, ricordando che Friedler cerca di ritrascrivere delle immagini suggestive e significative.

2005: *Les Innocents* vengono presentati in una messa in scena originale, intitolata *La Fin des temps*, prodotta in occasione del Festival delle Fiandre nel 2005 e costruita attorno alla musica di Olivier Messiaen (*Quatuor pour la fin des temps*) e alle parole di Primo Levi. Questo momento toccante invita lo spettatore a rivisitare la seconda guerra mondiale e a ripensare il presente.
Sempre nel 2005, il ciclo di dipinti *La Parole des Anges* è esposto alla Galleria Philippe Cazeau - La Béraudière, a Parigi.
Infine non bisogna dimenticare, in questi ultimi mesi del 2005, la nascita della matrice madre dell'intera idea dell'artista che è *Spirit of Boz*, concetto indispensabile all'ampliamento del discorso sull'arte alla totalità degli individui in cerca di sé stessi e degli altri. *Spirit of Boz* è il crogiolo in cui si analizza il nostro ambiente e in cui si elabora la presa di coscienza delle turbolenze che agitano il nostro mondo, è anche il luogo dell'azione e del pensiero proliferante che si alimenta con i pettegolezzi delle nostre società, perché tutti insieme noi li combattiamo, in difesa di un'utopia fondatrice di una società in cui l'arte sarebbe salvifica.
2006: parallelamente alla pittura Julien Friedler porta avanti e sviluppa l'epopea leggendaria del *Boz*. Creazione dell'Associazione *Sprit of Boz*. Cercando di proiettare il campo dell'arte nel campo sociale (e non l'inverso), Julien Friedler ha creato *Be Boz Be Art*. Un programma completo: artistico, umanistico e filosofico, il cui obiettivo principale consiste nel creare o generare flussi creativi. In questo universo, immaginario ma al contempo anche molto reale, egli costruisce un'opera labirintica, ipertestuale e multimediale che mette in relazione un sistema di energie destinate a far emergere connivenze recondite tra gli individui più disparati e più distanti geograficamente, grazie all'azione che egli conduce attraverso *Spirit of Boz*.

Sonia Bressler ne parla così: "L'opera più complessa di Julien Friedler non è quella che si dà a vedere… La sua opera è un gesto globale, vi è un inizio, un impulso, poi vi è il suo slancio, il suo meccanismo, poi vi è la sua spazialità e infine il suo prolungamento. Egli ama parlare di lavoro in rizoma. L'opera di Julien Friedler è *Spirit of Boz*."[3]

Il 2 dicembre 2006 ha luogo *La Nuit du Boz*, happening che si svolge presso il Canale di Bruxelles (http://rebelle.blogspirit.com/archive/2021/04/29/julien-friedler-dealer-d-utopies-3251717.html). Affissione nelle strade di Bruxelles, in un happening; la serata si annuncia animata. Sonia Bressler racconta: "Tutti si divertono, giocando con la musica e le bollicine di champagne, una dolce e poetica ebbrezza si impossessa dei ballerini per una notte su uno sfondo di musica elettronica. Proiezione della vita che passa o allegoria contemporanea della caverna? Qui inizia la *Forêt des âmes*". L'evento, momento disturbante nella banalità quotidiana, introduce all'insieme dei progetti che alimenteranno la macchina per pensare il mondo secondo la logica dell'arte, secondo la logica di un tempo arrestato sulla meditazione, sull'altra riva del nostro essere, lontano dalle contingenze e dai precetti materialisti delle nostre società. Friedler invita ognuno a essere "Be Boz Be Art". *Be Boz Be Art* è un programma contemplativo, apolitico. Si tratta di un movimento di cercatori d'arte. Gli interventi permettono di far nascere l'espressione artistica là dove sembrava mancare. Il programma si sviluppa secondo tre direttrici di lavoro: *La Forêt des âmes*, *Le Clochard Céleste* e *Give up*. Questa parte dell'opera di Friedler, pluridisciplinare e collegiale, costituisce un tentativo di fusione tra diverse forme di espressione. L'arte è qui il supporto di scambio e di comunicazione, incarna la fine delle certezze e l'inizio di un'era creativa, invitando ognuno a prendervi parte…

Dal 2006 al 2009, elaborazione dei concetti fondatori di *Spirit of Boz* (https://docplayer.fr/200236625-La-foret-des-ames-de-julien-friedler.html). *La Forêt des âmes - Le Tour du Boz en 80 ans* è la prima azione che porta alla costruzione di *Spirit of Boz*. Si tratta di un questionario, distribuito nel corso di eventi e happening del *Boz*, al quale ognuno è invitato a rispondere. Sei domande che introducono al percorso del pensiero profondo, slancio collettivo e interrogazione su sé stessi: 1. Dio esiste? 2. Come possiamo caratterizzare questa epoca? 3. Come vede l'avvenire? 4. Lei è felice? 5. La sessualità è importante? 6. Chi sono io?
Il questionario viene presentato per la prima volta al pubblico il 2 dicembre 2006. Nell'intenzione di Friedler, l'esperienza proseguirà per ottant'anni e si concluderà

quindi nel 2086, "oltre le nostre vite", precisa l'artista come una forma di vanità, lo scopo essendo quello di raccogliere le risposte a questi sei interrogativi. Dal 2007 e ancora oggi, gli attori di questa avventura hanno percorso innumerevoli territori per raccogliere, nei luoghi più insoliti del pianeta, i pensieri ponderati o fugaci di migliaia di partecipanti che hanno accettato di rispondere a queste sei domande fondamentali, invariabili indipendentemente dalle società. Dal Togo a Santiago del Cile passando per New York, Milano, Roma, Parigi, Londra, Mosca, Katmandu, Lhassa, Pechino, la *Forêt des âmes* propone a ognuno di fermarsi.

2007: arrivano questionari dal Ruanda e dal Marocco, dalla Bulgaria, dal Brasile. Detenuti, malati, allievi di scuole, studenti, permettono, attraverso la scrittura, o il disegno, di condividere questo momento di eternità. Perché si tratta proprio di questo. I questionari così raccolti saranno sigillati in colonne la cui molteplicità creerà questa *Foresta di anime.* Settembre 2007, Carmen Ferreyra percorre l'America del Sud. Insieme ai suoi team, raccoglie risposte da Buenos Aires, Córdoba, Rosario, Loncopué (provincia di Neuquén), Gualeguaychú, Santiago del Cile, Montevideo, dalle favelas di Belém in Brasile.
Realizzazione di *Give up* e primi oggetti ricevuti in condivisione: *Give up* è un programma di scambio che si sviluppa nel corso di dieci anni, è anche un'opera che si costruisce attorno al dono, al "lasciare andare". Il dono di un oggetto qualunque, un oggetto del quotidiano o anche un'opera d'arte. Questo programma è stato inizialmente sviluppato nel Togo, in Argentina, poi in Indonesia e in Europa… Una delle azioni più significative di questo "viaggio" *Give up* fu condotta a Loncopué, in Argentina, dove la popolazione di questa piccola cittadina di 6000 abitanti, completamente estranea alle preoccupazioni artistiche, fu invitata a compilare il questionario della *Forêt des âmes*, e a condividere la propria realtà quotidiana attraverso la realizzazione di disegni, dipinti o il dono di alcuni oggetti. Un concorso selezionò venticinque tra le centinaia di opere raccolte, formando un *corpus* omogeneo di testimonianze che furono poi integrate alla collezione del *Boz*, costituendo la prova più eloquente dell'impatto di una riflessione sull'arte, in individui privi di ogni riferimento in questo ambito. Degni di nota sono i disegni eseguiti da Ida Leandro. Sempre nel 2007, il programma di *Spirit of Boz* propone un principio di scambio e un dialogo con gli individui più dimenticati della nostra società. Si tratta del programma *Le Clochard Céleste*: "Dalle strade di Bruxelles, alle periferie di Jakarta o ancora con i bambini delle strade del Ruanda, il programma

Clochard Céleste consiste nel donare i mezzi di espressione artistica a persone in situazione di disagio o precarietà. È l'espressione artistica così come può nascere ovunque."
Mostra "In Quest", alla galleria Philippe Seghers di Ostenda (a cura di Michael Dewilde). La mostra è accompagnata da una performance di Jack Balance sulla diga di Ostenda (https://www.paperblog. fr/209641/la-cabine-du-boz-performance-a-ostende/ – https://www.youtube.com/watch?v=xshbcF0DZLI). "Verso le 14, un'armata di sosia di Jack Balance si è dispiegata attorno alla cabina. Berretto nero, occhiali, naso finto, baffi folti, maglietta rossa e questionario del *Tour du Boz* alla mano, vanno incontro agli spettatori, ai quali propongono di compilare il questionario di cui sopra".
Torniamo a Julien Friedler, che mette a punto questa macchina del *Boz* in un periodo in cui s'interroga sui fondamentali della sua azione artistica. Sebbene dipinga già da alcuni anni, egli torna ad attingere alle origini più lontane della nostra civiltà, dalle fonti meno alterate da idee preconcette, per trarre le risposte al suo interrogarsi: "Di cosa si tratta?", chiede Friedler. "Anziché dare una definizione astratta, sempre riduttiva, ci sforzeremo qui di illustrare un luogo di emersione: un conglomerato di affetti, di pensieri e di sensazioni, nati da un concatenamento di atti che interrogano lo statuto dell'artista."[4] È questo statuto che gli interessa, che legittima la sua opera e quella di tanti altri. Malgrado tutto il fermento prodotto da questo mondo del *Boz*, Julien Friedler porta avanti la sua opera personale. Dipinti e sculture, installazioni, continuano a invadere lo spazio dell'atelier. La sua pittura nata dalle lettere e dai segni (*La Forêt des âmes*) continua a sviluppare le sue tematiche rituali, vicine a esperienze di trance e di ipnosi. L'artista scruta, setaccia la materia, al fine di estrarne la linfa vitale. La forma pittorica è vicina ai graffiti. Sono opere primitive, dalla materia magmatica e ruvida.

2008: l'avventura di *Spirit of Boz* prosegue. Dai primi elementi raccolti da questa ricerca condotta ai quattro angoli del mondo, emergono perle che avvalorano la convinzione dell'artista, di come l'arte sia fermento delle nostre vite, generatrice di una forza di luce e di verità. 18 giugno 2008, le opere realizzate a Loncopué, piccolo villaggio della Patagonia, sono presentate da Sotheby's a Monaco, in occasione di una mostra in cui disegni, dipinti, sculture e questionari sono mostrati a collezionisti abituati alle opere quotate di artisti affermati. L'evento suscita interrogativi. Friedler risponde che si tratta "di cercare l'arte dove non ce la si aspetta." Parallelamente all'esposizione presentata da Sotheby's, una performance *Be Boz* si svolge nella

[4] Julien Friedler, *Les Fondamentaux*, La Route de la Soie - Éditions, Paris 2020, p. 7.

Heilig-Kreuz-Kirche di Monaco di Baviera. Durante la cerimonia religiosa, il parroco invita ognuno a riflettere sul questionario della *Forêt des âmes*. Nella sua omelia, sottolinea: "Le domande dell'essere e del divenire, dell'apparenza e della verità non sono estranee al progetto *Be Boz.* Si tratta di un interrogarsi in cui la risposta forse importa meno della domanda". Le sei domande sono inscritte al di sopra del presbiterio della chiesa, mentre all'apice della navata si dispiega l'installazione *L'Envol* (2008) dove i questionari si avvolgono in un movimento a spirale.

Un evento *Give up* intitolato *Out There in the Middle of Nowhere* organizzato alla Galerie der Künstler di Monaco di Baviera, esorta gli spettatori a offrire un oggetto simboleggiante il proprio desiderio intimo, posandolo all'interno di un cerchio di cenere. La trilogia monacense segna un momento importante nella storia nascente di *Spirit of Boz*. Di questa avventura si conserva un video: https://www.dailymotion.com/video/x4pj56

2008: Friedler crea l'installazione *La Forêt des âmes*. Nove colonne di legno sormontate da maschere d'ispirazione africana, realizzate in resina trasparente che una luce a led illumina dall'interno. L'effetto è sorprendente, la musica che l'accompagna invita alla meditazione. Questa installazione è la prefigurazione di un insieme di colonne nelle quali saranno sigillati i questionari raccolti nel mondo.

Nel 2008 prosegue l'azione *Give up Togo*. Agnès Mukarubayiza, incaricata del programma del *Boz* in questo paese, raccoglie numerosi oggetti simbolici tra cui la *Statuette des jumeaux* che servirà da punto di partenza per una performance di artisti belgi presso l'atelier del *Boz* a Bruxelles nel 2010.

2009: un anno importante per Jack Balance. La Christopher Henry Gallery di New York presenta la prima esposizione personale di Julien Friedler, a cura di Gabrielle Bryer, "Who is Jack Balance?". Il comunicato stampa precisa: "Sui due piani della galleria, l'esposizione ci porta alla scoperta di Jack Balance e del Mondo del *Boz*. Attraverso i suoi scritti, dipinti, sculture e happening il progetto concettuale di Friedler ci conduce nell'avventura di un mondo parallelo in cui l'artista ci porta a confrontarci con interrogativi non risolti, che ossessionano il nostro animo … Vi è spiritualità nel mondo imperfetto di Friedler: egli ci aiuta a vedere, comprendere e accettare l'inaccettabile imperfezione della nostra condizione umana. Per fare ciò, inventa una figura allegorica di sé stesso, Jack Balance, le cui avventure permettono all'artista di distillare il proprio messaggio".

Altre due esposizioni si svolgono questo stesso anno, la prima al MUBE (Museu Brasileiro da Escultura), San Paolo, Brasile nell'ottobre 2009 (https://www.julienfriedler.com/exposition/mube/). Questa vasta retrospettiva mette in scena il lavoro di Friedler. Impregnata di concetti filosofici o di riferimenti alla storia dell'arte e alla Pop Art, l'esposizione mette in luce la coesistenza di diverse mitologie. Alla maniera del termine *Boz*, costrutto senza vero e proprio significato, tutto il progetto possiede una dimensione ludica, caotica e umoristica, ma anche un aspetto psicologico. L'esposizione propone una trentina di opere, attinenti a diversi ambiti artistici: dipinti, sculture, letteratura, video, fotografie, installazioni e performance.

La presenza di Julien Friedler in Brasile è anche l'occasione di performance di strada durante le quali ognuno è invitato a compilare un questionario, donare un oggetto, proporre un disegno. La collezione del *Boz* si arricchisce.

L'altra esposizione del 2009 si svolge alla National Gallery for Foreign Art a Sofia, in Bulgaria, da maggio a giugno. La mostra, intitolata "Dialogues" (https://www.spiritofboz.com/julien-friedler/julien-friedler-artwork/sofia/), mette a confronto le opere di Julien Friedler con il progetto *Be Boz Be Art*. In questa esposizione concettuale e atipica Friedler fa dialogare il singolare con l'universale, il sogno e l'ideale con la realtà, la modernità con le tradizioni, lo scritto con il visivo, nel proposito di far reagire e partecipare i visitatori, invitati a rispondere alle sei domande del *Tour du Boz en 80 ans*.

Il 2009 è anche l'anno in cui è esposta per la prima volta l'installazione *La Forêt des âmes*. Isolde Brielmaier la propone in una mostra collettiva alla Jack Shainman Gallery di New York. L'esposizione, presentata nel quadro del progetto *Spirit of Boz*, illustra il ruolo significativo degli artisti africani o dell'influenza africana sulla scena mondiale.

Malgrado i continui viaggi, Julien Friedler prosegue la sua opera pittorica: nell'atelier di Bruxelles nascono *Ecce Homo* (2009), *Le Cavalier de l'Apocalypse* (2009) e molte altre opere rappresentative del potere introspettivo dell'artista. Friedler afferma ormai il suo gesto pittorico. È un esempio notevole di questo approccio, illustrato in uno stile apertamente soggettivo che da Appel passa per De Kooning e arriva a Basquiat, ma il cui oggetto non è più il tormento dell'io e l'estasi dell'artista ("tragedy, ecstasy and doom", proclamava la generazione dell'Espressionismo Astratto) bensì le forme fluide ed erranti, gli idoli e i totem, le costellazioni e gli animali, gli abissi e le battaglie.

2010: esposizione: "Spirit of Boz, the Truth of the Labyrinth", CW Gallery, New York, attorno alla leggenda del Boz e alla sua proiezione nella realtà letteraria del *Livre du Boz*. Questo volume a sviluppi multipli dà luogo qui a un'interpretazione sotto forma di fumetto, che mette in scena i nostri tre clown in cerca del divino. Vi è un po' di burlesco, un po' di tragico in queste avventure che di eco in eco, di associazione in associazione, creano una trama trasversale, obliqua, al di sotto dell'intrigo che esso sviluppa. Una trama propizia all'inconscio e al mito che esso sottintende.

Friedler sviluppa il suo testo *La Vérité du Labyrinthe*, che in seguito darà luogo ad alcuni dibattiti e sarà pubblicato nel 2017.

Conferenza-dibattito, Montecarlo, luglio 2010, sulla tematica *Spirit of Boz*.

Give up Togo continua la sua avventura. Dopo i suoi viaggi in Ruanda, Agnès Mukarubayiza è di ritorno in Africa nel quadro del *Tour du Boz en 80 ans* (https://www.spiritofboz.com/be-boz-be-art/the-program-around-the-world/togo/). Gli abitanti della contea di Tovegan propongono di ribattezzare un villaggio come "il villaggio del *Boz*". Numerosi questionari e oggetti raccolti.

10 ottobre 2010: all'atelier del *Boz* si svolge un'importante performance: *Give up Togo/Bruxelles – La performance des Jumeaux*. Un gruppo di artisti belgi, ispirati dagli oggetti riportati dal Togo, entrano in dialogo artistico in particolare con la statuetta dei gemelli, piccola scultura simbolica togolese, e dipingono tre opere, in un'azione che partecipa dell'illusione e della trance (https://www.spiritofboz.com/be-boz-be-art/the-program-around-the-world/togo/).

Il 2010 vede anche il ritorno di Julien Friedler all'atelier. La sua produzione pittorica s'intensifica: dipinge *La Chute du Joker*, opera importante che segna una tecnica pittorica prossima a un'astrazione drammatica. Prosegue la stesura del *Livre du Boz*.

Julien Friedler partecipa a un'esposizione collettiva alla galleria Gourvennec Ogor di Marsiglia. Per la sua inaugurazione, la galleria riunisce artisti di generazioni diverse. Poetica e magica, talvolta sconcertante, la mostra propone di riscoprire un panorama di scelte estetiche eterogenee e di ripensare temi eterogenei quali le relazioni umane, la politica, il reale e le sue metamorfosi, ma anche la storia dell'arte, lo spazio e l'illusione.

Dal 2011 al 2015 le azioni *Give up* e *La Forêt des âmes* si moltiplicano in Togo, ma anche a Bruxelles e a New York (2012). Sonia Bressler, filosofa e scrittrice, intraprende un periplo attraverso l'Asia, da cui riporta opere dipinte, oggetti simbolici e questionari. Si reca dapprima a Giakarta nel 2011, poi a Lhassa, in Tibet, nel 2012. È in India, a Bombay, a Katmandu, in Nepal, nel 2013, e nuovi fogli, disegni, collage, oggetti singolari vengono ad aggiungersi alla raccolta del *Boz*. Si reca nel Gansù, in Cina, nel 2015 e più di recente presso gli uiguri (2017). Questi viaggi alimentano il suo lavoro di etno-filosofa: "Osservo le metamorfosi dell'umanità", dice, "per meglio comprendere e trasmettere". Grazie al suo impegno, gli scambi e i dialoghi si diversificano: l'arte serve da vettore di comunicazione secondo la teoria del *Boz*. Questo percorso è costellato di interviste, reportage, in un programma di ascolto, di scoperta degli altri e di scambi che Bressler chiama *The Wall of Humanity*. È una ricerca specifica all'interno dell'universo del *Boz* che la filosofa conduce in Francia così come in Indonesia, in Tibet, in Cina, e che porta avanti nel 2012.

In questi anni vengono pubblicati due libri dedicati all'universo di Julien Friedler. Nel 2012, Norbert Hillaire pubblica *Double vue, 50 fragments pour Julien Friedler*, presso le Éditions Somogy. "Di fronte all'universo di Julien Friedler", scrive, "alla frontiera del sociale, dell'estetica e delle scienze del sogno, abbiamo voluto condividerne la sfida".

1° settembre 2012: esposizione personale "Les Disparus" alla Galleria Gourvennec Ogor di Marsiglia (https://www.julienfriedler.com/exposition/les-disparus/). Mettendo lo spettatore a confronto con una serie di fotografie scattate nella primavera 2012 nel suo atelier di Bruxelles, l'artista ci porta ai confini intimi della sua opera, nel cerchio privato della sua memoria d'uomo e d'artista. Rivelando le impronte di un processo creativo incandescente, irradiante lo spazio di materiali e pigmenti, di corpi e di segni, l'artista ci svela il suo campo di battaglia interiore. Sulle fotografie non appare alcun dipinto reale. Sono visibili solo tracce della loro esistenza, come vestigia di un'opera di cui non si sa se sia realmente conclusa o non ancora terminata. Al centro dell'esposizione, la bambola con la stella di Davide, testimone delle atrocità e delle persone scomparse per sempre, che solo la memoria salva. Non compare neanche l'artista, presente solo attraverso la propria assenza.

La sera del vernissage Julien Friedler, o piuttosto Jack Balance, esegue la *Performance des allumettes*: fiammiferi, alcol, un paio di forbici, una tela e un recipiente per raccogliere i pezzi tagliati. La tela è tagliata in piccoli pezzi. Si accende un fiammifero, poi un altro, la tela prende fuoco, è ridotta in cenere. Allegoria di una soppressione programmata, interrogativo sulla vanità delle cose. L'artista continua il suo percorso di traghettatore.

2013: pubblicazione del *Livre du Boz* da Jacques Flament Éditions. Così lo definisce Julien Friedler: "Il *Livre du Boz* non è né un romanzo, né un poema, né un racconto, ancor meno un dramma o un saggio. Non è nulla, se non lo stile che lo ispira e lo ossessiona. Qui, nessun riferimento. Nessun faro. Si naviga seguendo il vento. Le storie si tessono, finiscono, rinascono sul filo della corrente, prima che si levi una tempesta per portarci lontano, alle soglie di una nuova visione. Perché questo è il *Livre du Boz*: un'opera fuori dal comune, inclassificabile, creata da un errante per altri erranti".

Nello stesso anno Sonia Bressler dedica un libro all'opera di Julien Friedler: *Julien Friedler, De la Métaphysique de l'errance*, Jacques Flament Éditions: "Né il tempo né lo spazio così come li conosciamo", scrive, "bastano a cogliere la forma, la materia del pensiero e della creazione di Julien Friedler… Con lui bisogna accettare di porre l'arte (nel senso di creatività) al cuore della vita, della costruzione sociale ed economica. Il suo lavoro è ascoltare la misura del movimento del mondo, è definire un'alternativa". Sonia Bressler si reca in Nepal, dove organizza l'atelier coreografico *La Forêt des âmes*, messo in scena da Marylin Alasset. Si reca anche in India a Bombay (conferenza + questionari / video e incontri con alcuni artisti).

2012-2015, la pittura: in questo periodo ricco di avvenimenti "dall'esterno", Friedler dipinge opere importanti. S'impone un ripiegamento, bisogna lavorare, dipingere, inventare anche nell'atelier: tele, targhe di metallo, scatole, oggetti di utilizzo comune diventano i contenitori di microcosmi che scaturiscono in modo sporadico e inquietante, capaci di captare i sussulti, i ritmi sincopati, gli stati febbrili e le opacità di un universo meticcio nel quale si animano aggregazioni di piccoli spiriti e di figure serpentine (*Saturnins*, 2012), lemuri e paesaggi incantati (*Le Parapet*, 2012), colori graffiati e grida soffocate (*La Chute du Joker*, 2010), fuochi d'artificio e cosmogonie (*Planète Alpha*, 2012), una bestialità trasudante e un decoro raffinato (*Maou*, 2011). Lo spazio onnipresente della pittura di Friedler mette così in scena un mondo in ebollizione le cui minuscole cellule, sottomesse a un movimento ondeggiante, sono impegnate in una danza di forme e di segni sinuosi che suggeriscono le palpitazioni della natura. È un mondo proliferante, intenso, drammatico ma anche gioioso. Dai paesaggi, dalla luce, dai lustrini, il gesto di Friedler libera un'energia creatrice che esplode in fuochi variopinti sulla tela.

Il 2012 annuncia il periodo nomade dell'artista. Tra il 2012 e il 2018 Julien Friedler abbandona la vita sedentaria e intraprende diversi viaggi che lo portano a soggiornare spesso in hotel. In queste occasioni, proseguendo la sua meditazione pittorica, produce in sei anni un insieme di oltre trecento opere su carta. Piccoli formati facili da produrre e trasportare, scaturiscono da un'ispirazione meditativa e variopinta che oscilla tra figurazione e astrazione, in cui i fantasmi erranti abitano universi incerti. Queste piccole opere sono collegate alle grandi tele dell'atelier dello stesso periodo; esse veicolano la stessa forza, la stessa energia, lo stesso mistero.

2014: "Voyage", esposizione al Museo Civico Archeologico Girolamo Rossi, Forte dell'Annunziata, Ventimiglia, Italia. In questa occasione Jacques Flament Éditions pubblica il catalogo della mostra. Sono esposte alcune grandi opere archetipiche e primitive della serie delle figure emblematiche degli anni 2008-2011, alcune opere della serie dei paesaggi, pianeti e universi incantati (2010-2014), e infine una serie di opere su carta eseguite durante i viaggi dell'artista. "Voyage" riflette gli aspetti di una meditazione interiore, viaggio intimo che Friedler restituisce in un'opera suggestiva e poetica. I dipinti dialogano con le installazioni permanenti del Museo Archeologico, in un'evocazione atemporale che risale alle origini dell'arte.

I viaggi continuano, alternandosi a presenze in atelier. A Bruxelles vengono organizzati alcuni incontri attorno al testo *La Vérité du Labyrinthe*.

Performance di Carmen Ferreira attorno al tema della *Vérité du Labyrinthe*, una all'Armory Show di New York e l'altra alla fiera Untitled Art di Miami.

Dal 2014, vengono alla luce nuove opere, eseguite secondo una tecnica nuova che potremmo qualificare "pittura liquida", espressione mutuata dal critico italiano Gianluigi Colin, che la utilizza in un articolo del 2016, nel "Corriere della Sera". *Totem* (2014), *Le Patriarche* (2014), *Ecstasy* (2014), *Le Totem et les deux Chevaliers* (2014), *La Grotte aux résurrections* (2015) e numerose altre opere sono altrettanti segni della fervente attività del pittore.

Dal 2012 e fino al 2015 alcuni personaggi spettrali, gli *Schnarks*, popolano l'atelier dell'artista a Bruxelles; grotteschi giullari, sono la personificazione deformata o fantastica dei sogni più inquietanti, ma anche eroi favolosi, esseri leggendari che abitano mondi sconosciuti. *L'Homme poubelle* (2014), *Démon* (2014), *Le Noir Chevalier* (2014) … sono elaborati a partire da stoffe e materiali recuperati; nati dall'oggetto, s'identificano in una storia ordinaria ma anche eccezionale, che Julien Friedler ci racconta; sono anche i personaggi delle leggende che l'artista costruisce, esposti insieme ai dipinti.

Il 2015 è segnato da tre mostre personali e tre partecipazioni a esposizioni collettive. *Amok & Kalinka* alla Riflemaker Gallery di Londra, mostra personale che riunisce "pitture liquide", dipinti degli anni 2012-2014 e installazioni *Schnarks*. Un'altra esposizione personale, "Mania Boz", alla Fondazione Mudima, Milano, accompagnata dalla pubblicazione di un catalogo con un testo di Dominique Stella e Gianluca

Ranzi. Vi troviamo il lavoro di Julien Friedler, dalla *Forêt des âmes* ai dipinti più recenti, agli *Schnarks*. Tre opere della serie dei paesaggi (2012-2014) e *La Chute du Joker* occupano la scena dell'ex Chiesa Anglicana di Bordighera, mentre, commentando queste opere, Philippe Daverio e Julien Friedler dialogano sul tema dell'*artista sciamano* (https://www.bordighera. tv/2016/06/spoleto-julien-friedler-%E2%80%9C-retro-boz%E2%80%9D/).

Sempre nel 2015, a Bologna, il racconto di Friedler *La Vérité du Labyrinthe* funge da punto di riferimento per un'esposizione-dialogo tra Friedler e Maria Rebecca Ballestra alla galleria Spazio Testoni. "Gli obiettivi della *Vérité du Labyrinthe* sono quelli di ogni onest'uomo in cerca di una spiritualità moderna", scrive Friedler. "Attraverso le mie esperienze, le mie ricerche, ho cercato di tessere un cammino per raggiungere la pace e la serenità. Per uscire dal caos dobbiamo, tappa dopo tappa, comprendere di quale materia tutti noi siamo fatti. Nel corso del tempo, il rumore e la collera si allontanano". *La Parole des Anges* è esposta in occasione della Biennale di Venezia 2015 a Palazzo Molin. Questa mostra riunisce di nuovo Julien Friedler e Maria Rebecca Ballestra, organizzatrice dell'evento, che vi espone il proprio ciclo di ricerca *Journey into Fragility.*

Il lavoro di Julien Friedler è presente anche alla Bienal de las Fronteras Tamaulipas, alla frontiera tra Messico e Stati Uniti, prima edizione di questo festival d'arte contemporanea che riunisce cinque curatori e cinquantacinque artisti di diverse parti del mondo. Sonia Bressler prosegue la produzione di documentari attorno a *Spirit of Boz*, questa volta all'atelier di Bruxelles. E i questionari continuano a essere proposti alla riflessione dei partecipanti alle performance.

2016: l'esposizione itinerante "Mania Boz" prosegue il suo cammino, giungendo dalla Fondazione Mudima di Milano al Museo Civico di Villa Bassi ad Abano Terme. Una scenografia più "sepolcrale" presenta unicamente le opere pittoriche e gli *Schnarks*, nel seminterrato con soffitto a volta del museo. La mostra, assai suggestiva, è talvolta risultata inquietante per un pubblico un po' sconcertato.

Le opere partiranno poi alla volta di Spoleto, dove nell'estate del 2016 vengono presentate al Museo delle Arti Visive, Palazzo Collicola, con il titolo "Retro Boz", una retrospettiva completa del lavoro di Julien Friedler, a cura di Gianluca Marziani. Millecinquecento metri quadri di esposizione raccontano le tappe successive della produzione dell'artista, dai primi dipinti del 1998 fino all'ultimo quadro *22 mars 2016*, realizzato il giorno degli attentati all'aeroporto di Zaventem, a Bruxelles. L'aspetto sanguinolento del quadro, realizzato secondo la tecnica delle "colature", comunica il terrore che ci coglie tutti, in un mondo dominato dalla rabbia. Questo mondo è ciò che Julien Friedler continua a dipingere. In occasione di questa mostra, il supplemento domenicale del "Corriere della Sera" pubblica in copertina l'opera *Totems* (2014).

La Forêt des âmes prosegue il suo cammino: le nove colonne sono presentate al Museoteatro della Commenda di Pré a Genova in occasione di un incontro sulla pace. E una conferenza-esposizione attorno ad alcuni dipinti, intitolata *La Forêt des âmes*, ha luogo all'Alliance française, Casino Venier, a Venezia. "Attraverso la sua opera, Julien Friedler disegna i fondamenti di una mitologia contemporanea", annuncia il comunicato stampa, invitando ogni partecipante a compilare il questionario della *Forêt des âmes*. Julien Friedler risponde alle domande di un pubblico numeroso e curioso. Il 2016 è anche costellato dalla partecipazione a tre esposizioni collettive, e dall'International Art Project 2016, Cap d'Ail. Julien Friedler partecipa alla Fiera di Bologna con la galleria Spazio Testoni. In questa occasione la Fondazione Casa della Divina Bellezza a Forza d'Agrò, in Sicilia, acquisisce la tela *Gilgamesh* e Julien Friedler è accolto in occasione dell'inaugurazione della fondazione, dove la tela viene esposta.

La pittura occupa in maniera preponderante la vita dell'artista. Egli esegue con una tecnica selvaggia, tra graffiti e colature, due grandi formati di 300 x 200 cm, esempi magistrali di una tecnica ormai padroneggiata. *Le Phoenix* (2016) e *Crucifixion* (2016) costituiscono il centro di una produzione particolarmente intensa.

2017: l'installazione *La Forêt des âmes* prosegue il suo viaggio: è presentata a Spoleto alla chiesa Santi Giovanni e Paolo durante tutta l'estate, mentre in primavera figurava in un'esposizione intitolata "Boz Legend" al Castello di Rivara-Museo d'Arte Contemporanea, Rivara (Torino). L'incontro con Franz Paludetto, padrone di casa e personaggio mitico del mondo dell'arte contemporanea, è occasione di scambi intensi.

Performance e conferenza a Genova: l'evento *Face to Face* viene presentato al Museo Villa Croce di Genova e alla galleria UniMediaModern. Al museo, una performance *Give up* invita gli spettatori a donare un oggetto mentre una presentazione di *Spirit of Boz*, a partire da un video, ripercorre l'avventura del *Boz*. Alla galleria UniMediaModern, invece, Julien Friedler incontra il pubblico e propone questionari del *Tour du Boz en 80 ans*.

In settembre, al "Manoir" di Knokke, sede dell'associazione *Spirit of Boz* in Belgio, Julien Friedler avvia un ciclo di conferenze annuali: "Le grandi

conferenze di *Spirit of Boz*". Luc Ferry, ex ministro
francese della Cultura, dialoga con l'artista sul tema
Vizi e debolezze delle nostre democrazie. Si tratta qui
d'interrogare le nostre democrazie, di misurare la loro
trasformazione e di evocare l'ipotesi di un'arte del re-
incanto? Un'installazione delle opere maggiori di Julien
Friedler accompagna questo momento, permettendo di
scoprirvi anche l'ultima produzione dell'artista, *Le Maître
des couleurs* (2018), quadro monumentale tutto dripping
e immagini sfuggenti. In una delle sale del "Manoir" è
presentata una serie di opere di cera dell'artista italiano
Francesco Sena congiuntamente all'evento.
Il 2017 è anche l'anno della pubblicazione di *La Vérité
du Labyrinthe*, presso da Jacques Flament Éditions
(collana Philosophies). "Questo libro", afferma l'autore,
"è un invito al viaggio interiore, alla ricerca della
serenità. Il mondo attorno a noi si scioglie, fonde in
tutti i sensi. Quindi è più urgente trovare un mezzo per
rinnovare la pace interiore e ristabilire così l'armonia
e l'equilibrio del mondo". Il libro serve da sostegno al
pensiero labirintico dell'artista, che vi attinge anche
l'energia delle sue opere dipinte.

Il 2018 è un anno ricco di esposizioni tra il Belgio
e l'Italia. La prima esposizione, intitolata "Spirit of
Boz paintings" si svolge al Berlaymont Building,
Commission Européenne de Bruxelles, sotto il
patrocinio di Carlos Moedas, Commissario europeo
alla Ricerca, Scienza e Innovazione, che introduce il
vernissage con un discorso emozionante (https://www.
julienfriedler.com/exposition/spirit-of-boz-paintings/).
In questa occasione viene esposta una ventina di
dipinti di grande formato degli anni compresi tra il
2012 e il 2018. Julien Friedler presenta il suo progetto
partecipativo del *Boz* con l'ambizione che possa
rientrare in un programma di azioni culturali dell'Unione
Europea.
Da febbraio a marzo alcune opere dell'artista
accompagnano la presentazione della collezione *Be
Boz Be Art* (*Be Boz Be Art and Friedler's Paintings)*, alla
galleria Gliacrobati di Torino. Gli oggetti, disegni e pitture
raccolti in Togo, in Argentina, in Indonesia, in Cina e
altri luoghi sono esposti al fine di illustrare gli obiettivi
del progetto del *Boz*; ogni partecipante al vernissage,
ogni visitatore, è invitato a compilare il questionario
della *Forêt des âmes*. Conferenza di Julien Friedler in
occasione del vernissage – numerose partecipazioni.
Nel corso dell'anno, il ciclo *La Parole des Anges* è
mostrato a due riprese. La prima volta alla SRValverde
Gallery a Bruxelles e la seconda, a livello museale e
quindi con formati di più grande dimensione, alla Cité
Miroir di Liegi. La piscina che un tempo occupava
lo spazio centrale di questo museo offre alle opere
monumentali di Friedler una scenografia che si

snoda intorno al perimetro. Il comunicato stampa
riporta: "Questo insieme di quadri sviluppa, in un
linguaggio criptato, tutta una simbologia di segni da
cui scaturiscono opere che l'artista carica di un valore
meditativo, vero e proprio cammino che conduce a una
pace interiore che si vuole forza di vita e condivisione".
L'installazione *La Forêt des âmes* è presente ad Arezzo
nell'esposizione "Vibrations", che si svolge nella chiesa
della Madonna del Duomo Vecchio, ad Arezzo (Italia);
insieme all'installazione, sono esposte *All Over II –
La Parole des Anges* (2002), *Ecce Homo* (2009),
Crucifixion (2016) e *Le Maître des couleurs* (2017),
a dimostrazione che, malgrado i loro approcci pittorici
assai lontani, i quadri di Friedler creano un'armonia
e un equilibrio che sottolinea il senso del pensiero
dell'artista.
Ultima esposizione personale dell'anno: "Behind
the world", che si tiene al Complesso del Vittoriano
a Roma. Questo spazio espositivo, situato nel
Monumento a Vittorio Emanuele, si trova nel cuore
della città romana. Esso offre all'artista un'opportunità
eccezionale di confrontarsi con due maestri del XX
secolo, presentati nello stesso momento al museo
con un'esposizione dedicata a Andy Warhol e un'altra
a Jackson Pollock. "Behind the world" è l'occasione
di mostrare gli ultimi quadri dipinti nel corso del
2018: *Ode Satanique*, *L'Autre* e *Corps et Artifices*, tre
quadri di grande formato. *Corps et Artifices* è dipinto
secondo la tecnica delle colature, mentre negli altri
due quadri il pittore adotta una materia più aspra, più
graffiata, una sorta di ritorno alle tecniche del periodo
degli anni 2010. L'esposizione offre un vasto insieme
di opere e nella sua parte centrale sono installate le
nove colonne della *Forêt des âmes*. Vi si mescolano
diversi periodi di produzione pittorica, che dimostrano
l'ostinazione di Friedler nel condurre la propria ricerca.
Egli non si ferma mai a uno stile, non mantiene mai
alcuna abitudine pittorica. La sua arte evolve senza
sosta, la sua ispirazione rimane intatta. Ogni quadro
entra nell'insieme della sua produzione, la cui unità
è il riferimento a una filosofia di vita e di pensiero
che l'artista riassume nel *Boz*. Per tutta la durata
dell'esposizione, i visitatori compilano i questionari
messi a loro disposizione, lasciando così una traccia
del proprio passaggio. Il raccolto è abbondante. Dei
tremila visitatori circa, seicentosettantadue rispondono
alle domande del sondaggio del *Boz*. Sempre nel 2018
si tengono due esposizioni collettive attorno alla *Vérité
du Labyrinthe*: *Labrys*, *The Truth of the Labyrinth*, presso
il Parco Basaglia e altri luoghi della città di Gorizia, e
Labrys, *The Truth of the Labyrinth*, allo Spazio Testoni di
Bologna, sempre in collaborazione con Maria Rebecca
Ballestra, che illustra nel suo lavoro formale un labirinto
tracciato con le lettere e frasi del libro di Friedler.

A Parigi, Julien Friedler partecipa all'Outsider Art Fair con la Galleria Gliacrobati di Torino, proponendo un muro di opere su carta delle serie dei *Voyages*.
In settembre nuovo incontro a Knokke per "Le grandi conferenze di *Spirit of Boz*", con la partecipazione di Pascal Bruckner ed Eric Sadin sul tema *Identità e Cittadinanza, prima e dopo Internet,* documentato da un video (https://vimeo.com/307944894).
Julien Friedler prosegue il suo lavoro pittorico. Nelle tematiche e nello stile dei quadri avviene un importante cambiamento. In effetti, il 2018 segna l'inizio di un nuovo ciclo di dipinti che Friedler intitola *Mapping*.
È anche l'anno in cui Julien Friedler incontra Carlo Silvestrin, che sarà il produttore dell'esposizione "È finita la Commedia", a Venezia, nella chiesa di San Samuele, durante il periodo della Biennale 2022.

2019-2021: l'artista non lascia più l'atelier, ritiro d'obbligo, a causa delle condizioni sanitarie. Questo luogo di reclusione porta alla meditazione e ne influenza il corso. Realizza l'installazione *Les Pierrots*. La sua arte si placa, conservando al contempo lo spirito del mistero e della leggenda che egli costruisce in questa oscillazione costante tra drammaturgia ed esplosione vitale. Nella serie *Mapping* l'espressione visiva segue un progetto che supera ogni soluzione grafica o estetica; raggiunge una ricerca che si ricollega a problematiche certo filosofiche e spirituali, ma soprattutto pittoriche. Il mondo di Friedler è intuitivo e la sua arte, essenzialmente legata a un atteggiamento mentale, è la forma espressa da una contemplazione interiore e da un'esperienza di vita, trasfigurata dall'esperienza della pittura. Perché qui si tratta davvero di pittura: una materia a volte aspra, a volte luminosa, conduttrice di flussi visibili o invisibili, di energie vive che palpitano e nascono dal colore. Luci e colori emergono dalla tela in una sensazione esplosiva o pacificata secondo contrasti che rappresentano un soffio, una respirazione tesa verso il mistero della Vita. Si tratta qui di impressioni astratte.
In questo periodo particolare, vedono la luce alcuni progetti di esposizioni.
Nel 2019 Friedler presenta *Les Innocents* al Forte Santa Tecla a San Remo. L'installazione occupa la corte centrale di questa prigione dismessa, con un effetto sorprendente. È un successo, con più di tremila visitatori nel corso del mese di maggio. Il quaderno messo a disposizione del pubblico permette di raccoglierne le riflessioni commosse.
2020: *La Forêt des âmes* è al Beffroi de l'église Saint-Germain-l'Auxerrois, Mairie du 1er Arrondissement, a Parigi. Davanti al colonnato del Louvre, le porte del campanile si aprono sull'installazione delle nove colonne. I visitatori sono invitati a compilare il questionario della *Forêt des âmes*. L'installazione viaggia ormai da più di dieci anni. Il numero di questionari raccolti nel mondo nel corso di questi anni supera i settantacinquemila. catalogati e duplicati, potranno ormai raggiungere la destinazione che è riservata loro, e costituire il cuore di colonne monumentali erette in diversi luoghi del mondo. Suggeriamo Venezia come punto di partenza di questo nuovo progetto…
In pieno periodo di pandemia e confinamento si tengono due esposizioni "Mapping": una a Palazzo Libera, Villa Lagarina (Rovereto) e l'altra alla Fondazione Sant'Elia, Loggiato di San Bartolomeo di Palermo. A Palermo la mostra è nuovamente a cura di Gianluca Marziani, che scrive: "'Mapping' è un titolo perfettamente adattato alla geografia 'cromosomica' di Friedler. Centinaia di quadri che sono disposti come particelle aleatorie senza centro di prospettiva; acidi nucleici ideali (gli elementi che compongono la doppia elica del DNA) che creano molteplici nuclei ogni volta diseguali, confermando questa dimensione inclusiva del *corpus*, di un'opera unica gigantesca da cui emerge l'energia epifanica di Babilonia e la potenza catartica di Shiva." Nella città, e in Sicilia, "Mapping" è la prima esposizione museale organizzata dopo il confinamento. La moltitudine di visitatori vi si accalca in piccoli gruppi di quindici persone, al fine di seguire le spiegazioni infervorate di Marziani. La stampa si fa eco entusiastica dell'evento. Il 18 settembre 2020 a Torino, a Palazzo Barolo, Julien Friedler partecipa all'omaggio reso a Maria Rebecca Ballestra, deceduta durante l'anno, ricordando la loro amicizia e la loro complicità nel lavoro. In questa occasione viene proiettato un video, *La guaritrice*, al quale Friedler partecipa e nel quale attraverso tre performance Maria Rebecca Ballestra rievoca la propria lotta contro la malattia e la sofferenza. "Esistere non è solo una cosa facile da fare, ma è anche una cosa difficile da comprendere. Veniamo al mondo senza averlo chiesto, e siamo quasi sempre obbligati a lasciarlo contro la nostra volontà…", scrive.
Nel 2021, alla Galleria Civica Cavour di Padova, durante i due mesi estivi, "Legends-Mapping II" propone una nuova selezione di opere del ciclo *Mapping* (https://www.7goldtelepadova.tv/2021/07/22/friedler-in-mostra/). L'artista, costretto al confinamento a causa della pandemia, dipinge con determinazione. I quadri *Mapping* sono l'espressione di una meditazione che si materializza nel colore, che appare come l'anima generatrice, vera e propria matrice madre che fonde tutto in uno spirito vivo. La vita è pulsazione, respiro, dannazione, salvezza. Così è l'opera, "una congiunzione di contrari, una scrittura paradossale, un'inscrizione dei flussi che attraversano lo Spirito", scrive Friedler nella *Vérité du Labyrinthe*.

Sonia Bressler
Julien Friedler, témoin du siècle (estratti)

Il mio primo incontro con Julien Friedler risale al febbraio 2006. Una stanza enorme, il suo atelier in pieno centro a Bruxelles, andavo e venivo tra le sue installazioni, *Les Innocents*, e le sue tele in via di realizzazione. La sua opera immensa, mobile, mutevole, perpetua. Un perfetto equilibrio di inesattezze, coincidenze, sguardi trasversali sulla storia, il tempo, il superamento di sé e degli altri. Comprendere che l'arte deve farsi malgrado la pioggia, le guerre, le atrocità, le religioni, i diritti. Malgrado sé, malgrado gli altri. Umana, troppo umana, l'arte si nasconde, si ribella, denuncia, teorizza. L'opera di Julien Friedler, ho la fortuna di scoprirla in due anni, d'interrogarla. È questo incontro che consegno in qualche immagine.

Siamo ancora capaci di parlare d'innocenza?
Quella domenica a Bruxelles. Febbraio 2006. La Storia non avrebbe soluzione di continuità? Ho giocato sulle assi, nell'atelier di Julien Friedler. Colori, frammentazioni. Di primo acchito, bisogna prendersi gioco dei codici, degli imprevisti. Poi, passo dopo passo, l'influsso dell'opera si fa più grande. Qualcosa della nostra chimica vi si muove. Ma cosa? Passo dopo passo, immagine dopo immagine, due anni sono trascorsi al ritmo della creazione, al ritmo del pensiero. Un pensiero che si fa, che si nutre di uno ieri divorando un domani. Tra misticismo e passioni (dis)umane. I secoli passano con le loro mostruosità, le distruzioni… Noi erriamo tra la fine di una civiltà a un'altra. Fine dell'egemonia americana di oggi, crollo dei blocchi eppure, nel mezzo della nostra erranza, una voce indica, uno sguardo s'inclina, una mano disegna e scatena. Julien Friedler nel caos dell'umanità. Si beffa dei codici, inventa, perpetua la riflessione, propaga il disordine, smuove le nostre sensibilità. Un'opera unica, talvolta cupa, talvolta luminosa. Con questa stessa certezza: la luce che indugia, diviene l'ombra di un'altra luce. Siamo a Bruxelles nei suoi atelier. Potremmo essere qui, là, altrove. Pendolo fragile dello spazio e del tempo. Io gioco. Tu giochi. Voi giocate. Noi giochiamo. Ma loro, giocano? Coloro che sono privati di tutto, coloro il cui niente fa un grande tutto. Loro, il cui sguardo è stato attirato da qualche parte, in un ammasso di polvere(i). Loro, chi sono? Siete voi, sono io se guardiamo il presente? Ma se guardiamo il passato, sono quegli esiliati, uccisi, abbandonati all'angolo di una strada durante una guerra. Quale? La seconda guerra mondiale. Senza alcun dubbio, se guardiamo l'installazione degli *Innocents* di Julien

Friedler. Fotografia di una famiglia. Sorrisi eterni. Vecchi sogni nascosti? Il tempo è dilatato in questo spazio di filo spinato.

La necessità di testimoniare
Siamo alla ricerca della luce, della verità. Ma è una? Molteplice? Walzer incerto delle cose, dei piccoli rumori del quotidiano. Le grida dei bambini nel cortile della ricreazione. Il respiro di un bambino addormentato. I pigolii degli uccelli nelle prime ore del mattino. La prima nebbia. Le prime piogge di primavera. Una porta sbatte. Il sangue si spande. Macchia di colore. Fuga della vita. Un cuore si ferma. Un mostro nasce. Bisogna che in questo inizio del XXI secolo, un personaggio testimoni, con convinzione, ma soprattutto con il suo istinto, con la sua sensibilità, e che illustri il suo vissuto. Julien Friedler redige un'opera perturbante che vede il mondo attraverso la sua lucidità, la sua corsa alla rovina, alla distruzione di sé e degli altri. Ogni tela, ogni installazione, trovata qui, è un occhio aperto sugli occhi chiusi. Occhio fittizio, che scruta l'esistente per fargli dire il suo essere. Ogni creazione di Julien Friedler è un'attenzione testimoniante, carica dell'inquisizione che vorrebbe giungere alla certezza dell'identità irrealizzabile, occhio puntato verso l'interno, verso il sottostante, ma anche verso l'esterno, al corrente di tutta l'avventura. Viaggio attento verso sé stesso, gli altri, il mondo. Bisogna rischiare la distanza dell'altrove per incontrarsi e testimoniare con forza.

Gino Di Maggio
Julien Friedler e la scintilla della vita

Quante e quante volte ho raccontato della risposta che Robert Filliou diede alla domanda "Che cos'è l'arte?". È una risposta sintetica, paradossale, geniale: "L'arte è la cosa che rende la vita più interessante dell'arte stessa". Dunque è la vita stessa a costituire il fulcro della questione ed è dalla vita che si parte e nella vita che si ritorna, assumendo l'arte come un fondamentale vettore, un ponte gettato tra due sponde per connettere e scambiare emozioni e speranze, rivolta e consapevolezza, dialogo e possibilità. In tutto questo l'arte diviene perciò una delle componenti più importanti della vita, e quindi quella cosa, o quella serie di cose, e di attività cosiddette creative il cui risultato noi chiamiamo per convenzione arte. È questa un'idea per molti versi spiazzante, soprattutto nei confronti di una visione idealista e romantica dell'artista concepito quasi come demiurgo onnipotente capace di creare autonomamente, imbalsamato nella sua torre d'avorio e svincolato dalla relazione con i suoi simili e col mondo. Con il suo lavoro, Julien Friedler è invece la prova

vivente che l'artista opera costantemente a contatto
col mondo e, per quanto il suo punto d'osservazione
sia individuale e abbia a che fare con la sua
personalissima capacità d'osservazione e con il suo
vissuto d'esperienza, la sua proposta si espande oltre
il sé e si dirige verso l'altro, presentandosi come una
fondamentale esperienza di vita.
Dopotutto l'artista è tale autenticamente non solo
perché si dichiara e si autodefinisce artista, ma perché
sente l'urgenza quasi ossessiva di fare, di creare
sempre incessantemente. E questa è proprio una delle
caratteristiche principali di quella che ho chiamato,
ricordandomi di Giacomo Leopardi, l'immensità
dell'energia che in forme particolari pervade l'esistenza
e la rende mostruosamente vivente e che oggi ritrovo
non solo nelle installazioni e nella pittura di Friedler
ma soprattutto nella sua visionarietà progettuale che
riesce ad far convergere, confrontare e ravvicinare
mondi lontani e vite parallele. Ho l'impressione che
tutto questo avvenga perché quelli che si sentono e
si autodefiniscono artisti o quelli che sentono l'innata
predisposizione e si autodefiniscono scienziati sono
quelli stessi che hanno meglio di altri conservato la
memoria biologica di quello che siamo e del luogo delle
origini, una forma di memoria biologica che in modo
evidente la grande maggioranza di noi ha perduto ma
che grazie all'arte torna a essere una scintilla d'energia
che ritorna a farsi visibile.
(tratto da *Mania Boz*, Mudima, Milano 2015)

Norbert Hillaire
Frammenti

Modernità e postmodernità: puntualizzazione
Friedler è un uomo della salvezza, ma di cosa? È
moderno o postmoderno?
Ciò che qui è all'opera è una regressione che si
annuncia come tale: non una regressione narcisistica,
ma la prova di una duplice delusione, delusione della
modernità e delusione della postmodernità. Certo
Friedler è di primo acchito un pittore postmoderno,
tanto sono numerosi i segni, i riferimenti, le tecniche
che lo identificano a priori con il territorio della
postmodernità: *bad painting,* graffiti e così via Eppure,
anche se il suo attingere a Basquiat, a Penk è
evidente (così come sono evidenti certi richiami a
Cobra) e testimonia l'estetica del "diversale" e non
più dell'universale che fonda la postmodernità, è
paradossalmente dalla parte di certi moderni che si
troverebbe piuttosto la chiave di questa opera (ma si
è potuto dire a giusto titolo che Basquiat era l'ultimo
dei moderni). Regressione nel senso di Paul Klee,
ad esempio, verso un'infanzia che viene a mettere in

dubbio e la storia e la sua involuzione che culmina
nel postmoderno. Ma che non è in alcun modo un
infantilismo: "La favola dell'infantilismo del mio disegno
deve avere la sua origine nelle produzioni lineari in cui
cerco di combinare l'idea dell'oggetto – ad esempio,
un uomo – con la pura rappresentazione dell'elemento
linea. Per mostrare l'uomo come è, mi ci sarebbe
voluto un tale guazzabuglio di linee perfettamente
confusionario. Il risultato non sarebbe stato allora
una rappresentazione pura dell'elemento, ma un
rimescolamento tale che non ci si sarebbe orientati. Al
di là di questo, non è certamente nelle mie intenzioni
mostrare l'uomo così com'è, ma così come potrebbe
anche essere. In questo modo, posso giungere ad
associare la mia visione del mondo al puro esercizio
dell'arte".
Gli accenti moderni di queste linee non hanno nulla
d'ingenuo, di regressivo, e testimoniano al contrario
una grande sofisticazione nella ricerca di una purezza
quasi minimalista dell'opera d'arte (sono in questo
senso, come del resto i peluche, le bambole, gli
orsacchiotti utilizzati da Friedler nelle sue opere, agli
antipodi dell'utilizzo di alcuni fra questi stessi accessori
da parte di altri artisti contemporanei, chiaramente
postmoderni).

Eppure postmoderno
Eppure postmoderno, secondo la definizione, Friedler
sostituisce l'ordine binario dell'opposizione dell'altro
e del sé con la complessità del rizoma che intreccia
le differenze, e questa "alterità intima", come la
chiama Marc Augé, rende impensabile l'idea stessa di
"individualità assoluta" (ad esempio, nei dipinti fatti da
altri e integrati nell'opera).
(tratto da *Double Vue, 50 fragments pour Julien Friedler*,
Somogy Éditions d'Art, Paris 2012)

Gianluca Marziani
Retro Boz

Julien Friedler è un artista che sfugge a categorie e sistemi elementari. Quando lo scorso febbraio sono entrato nel suo studio a Bruxelles, ne ho avuta la conferma: di fronte a me c'era un *personaggio nucleare*, uno di quei titani del flusso quotidiano, capace di gestire il caos entropico, di sorvolare il marasma del mondo per dispensare un ordine successivo alle cose, secondo metodi teorici dal deciso sviluppo muscolare. Friedler è un intellettuale d'eccellenza che a un certo punto, avvenuta la catarsi filosofica, ha scelto il campo sporco della vita reale e globale. L'approccio ideativo sarebbe rimasto centrale, ovvio, ma ormai dentro un *sistema organico* del lavoro artistico. La scelta di campo era per lui senza compromessi: fare arte per capire meglio l'umanità, le necessità impellenti, il potenziale degli individui, i loro spazi di crescita e scambio. Abdicare all'olimpo accademico significava ampliare lo sguardo oltre la scrittura, oltre il narcisismo autoriale, oltre l'individuo e la singola opera. Significava sintonizzarsi sulle voci eterogenee del mondo, sulle comunità isolate, sulle culture africane, sui gruppi minoritari, sulle lontananze e divergenze. Il soggetto era finalmente il globo, quello reale della vita incontrata, vissuta, supportata, condivisa…
Quando parlo di *organico*, intendo un processo creativo che somigli alle attività di sostegno del corpo umano: mangiare, masticare, digerire, espellere e rigenerare nel motore continuo del flusso biologico. Il corpo è una macchina complessa che impone un supporto alimentare e di un ciclo rigenerativo; così l'arte di Friedler è un meccanismo rivelatorio che necessita di un processo partecipativo e umanizzato, dove scompare il principio di ordine e pulizia, tipico del controllo artificiale, lasciando il posto agli effetti naturali del vero. Il risultato implica un apparente marasma in cui oggetti e materiali contribuiscono al rumore del mondo, sporcandosi con gli stessi colori che ritroviamo nei quadri, al punto da espandersi oltre la loro natura originaria, modificando il sentimento degli spazi e la stessa vibrazione delle tele. Il quadro e gli oggetti partecipano a un dialogo serrato, senza scissioni, dove lo scambio è generativo, dove l'attrazione tra pittura, colore e forme produce energie a rilascio prolungato. In tal senso la parola "organico" implica una germinazione continua, una produzione di senso (e dissenso) che alza la temperatura figurativa e lascia aperta la struttura progettuale, come se non esistesse epilogo, come se ogni fine fosse una pausa momentanea nel ciclo del mondo. Lo chiamerei *metabolismo iconico* visto il magma pulsante dei quadri, la densità popolosa di segni e codici, le fluide dispersioni del colore. Una produzione che ricrea un'estetica viva, definita e al contempo indefinibile, semplice e criptica, trasformabile e adattabile, diretta e al contempo metaforica. Un metabolismo che sembra un laboratorio chimico nelle mani di un illuminista visionario nel cuore di una montagna sacra.
Se dovessi raccontare il concetto di *catarsi* attraverso un artista, userei Julien Friedler come esempio virtuoso. La sua arte è una purificazione sistemica dentro il miasma del mondo globale, un continuo atto rigenerativo che metabolizza il caos attraverso la gestione alchemica di materiali, colori, frammenti, citazioni… non è un caso che sia stato allievo di Jacques Lacan, anni e anni di empatia accademica e intellettuale, finché un giorno il nostro amico rifiutò quel mondo, rendendo l'arte visiva un approdo privilegiato di ricerca e finalità, la sua nuova accademia di vita e rivelazione.
La catarsi accompagna da sempre le grandi svolte di Friedler ma anche le singole strade che il lavoro intraprende. Ogni volta senti che il pathos sale verso l'alto, cresce il tono drammaturgico fino al punto implosivo, quel picco che definisce la vera natura di una visione radicale. L'artista belga usa la detonazione dei sentimenti, la passione sfrenata per la vita e la bellezza, cerca un benessere attraverso una sfida estrema che non prevede mediazioni. Ambisce alla pienezza dell'idea, al suo disegno circolare, creando un patrimonio complessivo da trasmettere ad altri, svincolando la visione dalla vita biologica del singolo, instillando valore a un patrimonio artistico che è un bene comune da condividere: oltre lo stesso artista, oltre la singola opera, oltre il ciclo espositivo in corso.
(tratto da *Retro Boz*, Mudima, Milano 2016)

Gianluca Ranzi
A passo di danza per pensare il futuro

…La danza di Friedler lo porta così a navigare intorno in un viaggio il cui scopo sembra essere non più la meta finale ma il viaggio stesso, portato oltre le colonne d'Ercole della propria esistenza perché Friedler sa bene che l'attaccamento a sé aumenta l'opacità della vita e dentro l'opacità dell'io non si può che perdere di vista l'arte. Per questa ragione, così come le sue tele vanno oltre sé stesse brulicando di vitalità animistica con un segno e una materia cromatica che prende vita autonoma in ogni sgocciolatura, anche Friedler stesso si sdoppia e si moltiplica in una genealogia di personaggi, *Jack Balance*, *Le Boz*, *Le Scribe*, *L'Homme Miroir*, che rendono conto del suo voler uscire da se stesso e dalla singolarità del suo racconto per ritrovare invece una molteplicità interdisciplinare di punti di vista, di apporti, di riferimenti, di sollecitazioni, di contraddizioni, quanto ha fatto ben scrivere a Norbert Hillaire che: "Il *Boz* è un modo di costruire mondi".

Non è un caso che mito e mistero abitino da sempre il lavoro di Friedler, che con fertile ambiguità resta in questo modo sospeso sulla soglia tra i racconti che provengono dalla sua storia individuale o dal confronto con gli altri e un piano metastorico dato dal ricorso ai miti nel quale il negativo del quotidiano può trovare senso e reintegrazione culturale o, come direbbe Friedler, produrre un supplemento d'anima là dove regna la sventura. Il lavoro pittorico e installativo di Friedler predispone così delle soglie da attraversare avanti e indietro, come a voler ribadire che le barriere esistono soltanto per essere attraversate di continuo e per divenire connettori, ponti, navi, network. Questi lavori, in alcuni casi dei veri e propri progetti operativi su larga scala, si basano su collaborazioni e integrazioni (come nel progetto *Le Clochard Céleste* che raccoglie i disegni di gruppi sociali in difficoltà), su sdoppiamenti e sovrapposizioni (in *Give up* gli *assemblages* nascono dal dialogo tra l'artista e alcune comunità di riferimento come il villaggio di Tevogan nel Togo o alcuni giovani artisti belgi), o su sollecitazioni portate all'esterno che come un boomerang ritornano poi alla base (è il caso del già citato progetto *La Forêt des âmes*). Tutte queste soglie non sono più barriera e ostacolo, ma uno spazio transizionale in cui, come dice Benjamin, "sono compresi mutamento, passaggio, maree, significato".
(tratto da *Mania Boz*, Mudima, Milano 2015)

Erno Vroonen
Le Monde du Boz

Cos'è l'arte e a cosa serve nella nostra società? La discussione non è nuova ed è stata argomentata in maniera ricorrente numerose volte. È, senza alcun dubbio, privilegio delle nostre società democratiche, ma anche dell'arte stessa, quello di poter insorgere contro una dottrina che si vuole assoluta o contro un punto di vista restrittivo. Friedler, in quanto autore e scrittore poi in quanto clown, afferma nel suo *Livre du Boz* che l'arte, più di ogni disciplina, possiede la capacità di comprendere la vera natura delle cose e di conseguenza l'essenza stessa della vita. Questa dichiarazione può essere considerata troppo restrittiva, o troppo definitiva, soprattutto nell'ambito dell'arte. Friedler, tuttavia, non si considera facente parte del dibattito. Egli si sente come una sorta di outsider la cui ambizione è mettere in evidenza gli eccessi del sistema nel quale il prezzo di mercato di un'opera d'arte è diventato più importante del valore intrinseco dell'opera stessa. L'Arte può ridursi a essere semplicemente un simbolo di potere finanziario? Oppure l'arte può avere un altro significato? Friedler cerca di determinare il pieno valore dell'arte attraverso il suo lavoro. Egli amplia i suoi criteri d'azione e, ciò facendo, rende l'arte accessibile a un pubblico di non "iniziati". Questo spiega perché egli presenta opere là dove meno ci si aspetterebbe, in luoghi insoliti, o espone un tipo di arte totalmente fuori sincronia rispetto alle dottrine generalmente accettate. Chi determina qual è il buono – o il cattivo – contesto per l'arte dopo tutto? L'artista lascia la questione aperta. Nondimeno, Friedler esige di più dall'arte e quindi da sé stesso.

Perché l'arte abbia un significato culturale più ampio di quello che ha attualmente, essa deve agire al di là dei limiti restrittivi attualmente stabiliti, affrontare le sfide che le si offrono e sviluppare nuovi significati che potrebbero avere un senso nuovo per una società futura. La realizzazione di questa ambizione è indissociabile dalla presa di coscienza che un grande vuoto si è installato nel cuore della società attuale, che aspira a trovare un nuovo senso alla propria ragion d'essere. L'opera di Julien Friedler invita alla contemplazione e alla meditazione. Egli dipinge figure sciamaniche, di civiltà primitive o antiche, e segni familiari così come extraterrestri, al fine di sondare nuovi percorsi di consapevolezza.
(tratto da *Julien Friedler Be Boz, Part III*, éditions du Chaman, 2008)

Les Fondamentaux : la totalisation du sacré
Julien Friedler

On ne le dira jamais assez : le cœur de *Spirit of Boz* restera à jamais la vie intérieure et son rapport à un Créateur énigmatique, insaisissable, dont le semblant a traversé l'histoire. Un Créateur, aux multiples visages, surgi dès l'orée, et dont la pensée en l'homme reste omniprésente, malgré les changements de forme. De l'âge des cavernes au New Age court un même refrain : une expression du sacré, sans cette remise sur le fil, retravaillée, et mise en avant, de sorte à produire un mythe fondateur. Ici, deux positions s'affrontent : un vide théologique, qui vous colle à la peau, et vous condamne à l'abject : d'être un bout de viande abandonné dans l'Univers. L'option contraire supposant un sujet, hors matière, responsable de lui-même. Un sujet, calqué à l'image d'un Autre hypothétique, mais incontournable. On imaginera de la sorte une traversée du miroir faite d'une rencontre, d'un appel, d'un sentiment d'étrangeté, suivi d'une recherche inlassable. Car, finalement, comment penser une spiritualité moderne, née du présent ? Sur quelle base l'édifier ? Comment la définir ? On se l'était dit : ici, un combat est à livrer, qui ne sera pas toujours tendre. En définitive, notre intuition aura donc été la suivante : un retour massif du religieux, suffisamment ample, puissant et pénétrant pour ébranler nos certitudes et permettre une redistribution des cartes. Avec, pour horizon : une totalisation du sacré, à l'objectif pacifiant (pacifiant parce qu'unifié) et une mondialisation de l'esprit, ouverte à tous (non dogmatique, mais rigoureuse). Dans cette optique, des ponts théologiques devront être bâtis, consolidés par une critique suffisamment décapante, corrosive et aguerrie, pour dépoussiérer les anciens réflexes. D'autres praxis devront être envisagées, afin de parer au mal qui nous ronge (la haine de soi des trois monothéismes). Bref, il nous faudra inventer, créer et imaginer des approches différentes, d'autres modes de penser, des alternatives inattendues, afin de redessiner une nouvelle carte des « spiritualités » résolument actuelle et adaptée à nos styles de vie. On comprendra dès lors mieux notre position. D'être un premier jet, un essai, une esquisse pour le futur. À mille lieues d'un vœu pieu. Ou, d'une utopie. Effrayé par la fureur de certains, inquiet de la tiédeur des autres, nous aurons agi en procédant par à-coups, revirements, et fuites en avant, avant de ralentir le pas pour peaufiner nos arguments. Cela, sans jamais perdre de vue notre projet : l'inscription du divin dans un microcosme – *Spirit of Boz* – aux ressorts universels. Un microcosme conçu comme une matrice à idées, une nouvelle façon de voir, de sentir et d'agir.

Tant il est vrai qu'on peut croire dans le doute et avoir la foi sans le savoir. On parlera alors d'une légende. On évoquera une quête inspirée. Quand les plus fins songeront à une Vision intangible. Une Vision dont nous sommes les dépositaires. Une Vision qui nous aura dicté une œuvre atypique, destinée à se mouvoir, à se transformer et à se métamorphoser au fil du temps. On en connaît les principales ressources : un livre proche du Judaïsme (*Le Livre du Boz*) et *La Forêt des âmes*, aux connotations chrétiennes (universalité, égalitarisme, souci du prochain). Sans oublier, une installation en cours à venir : *La Vache rousse* (ou *Djihad*). Celle-ci empruntera à l'Islam son « modus operandi » – un pas à pas vers l'Éternel. Sans davantage oublier, tout un monde d'images archaïques et hallucinées, évoquant la transe et son médium : le chaman. Sans oublier, enfin, le but de toute l'opération : générer un « supplément d'âme » dont l'amplification, la perlaboration et le vécu, viseront la seule chose qui vaille : un apaisement intérieur, par une mise à distance des passions. Notre véritable idéal.

È finita la Commedia
Dominique Stella

Le projet de Julien Friedler intitulé *È finita la Commedia* renvoie aux dramatiques réalités qui régissent nos vies ; il met en scène, en trois actes (trois installations), la comédie humaine dans une évocation plutôt qu'une critique des faux-semblants du monde, des errances de l'histoire et du cynisme qui gouvernent notre société, nous invitant à y méditer. Il n'est pas présenté par hasard dans le cadre de l'église San Samuele. L'église est lieu de méditation, de prière, de rassemblement, de célébration et de mystère, c'est aussi le lieu d'une recherche intérieure, qui nous conduit sur la voie d'un questionnement supérieur. Les œuvres de Julien Friedler abordent toutes ces thématiques profondes dans une recherche qui s'adresse à chacun, nous invitant à la découverte de nous-mêmes, mais aussi à la prise de conscience de l'autre. L'artiste entend toucher les êtres dans leur for intérieur, dans leur questionnement sur la sacralité, sur le sens de la vie, sur leur appartenance à la communauté humaine avec leurs doutes, leurs joies et leurs peines, rejoignant en cela certains enseignements de l'Église. C'est pourquoi ce lieu sacré est indispensable au projet de l'artiste et en est un élément déterminant. Pénétrer dans San Samuele conduit naturellement à l'introspection méditative, au recueillement et à l'élévation spirituelle, induite par la verticalité de l'architecture, que les œuvres concourent à souligner dans un cheminement qui accompagne le développement spatial de l'église. Dans ce sens San Samuele fait partie intégrante du concept que l'artiste a construit autour des trois installations insérées dans un parcours qui reprend l'architecture du lieu. Le titre lui-même indique la solennité du moment que nous vivons et nous invite à recourir à des préceptes plus intemporels que ceux promus par notre époque. L'Église est l'espace idéal pour nous conduire à réfléchir sur notre monde, au-delà d'une foi religieuse, mais dans la certitude que quelque chose doit être sauvé et Friedler nous accompagne dans cette conviction à travers ses œuvres. *È finita la Commedia…*

Les réalités contemporaines voyagent dans un imaginaire qui souligne les aspects les plus obscurs de l'âme humaine sans la condamner pour autant à la damnation, mais en interrogeant chacun, l'invitant à puiser dans la contemplation et la méditation les forces nécessaires à la régénérescence. Il n'y a aucune légèreté dans ces œuvres de Friedler, le titre de l'exposition l'indique *È finita la Commedia*, finit de rire et de chanter, « nous passons aux choses sérieuses », semble dire l'artiste, « réfléchissons à notre destin. »

C'est dans cette pensée que réside le cœur du travail de l'artiste dont la préoccupation première reste à jamais « la vie intérieure et son rapport à une expression du sacré, son rapport à l'énigmatique Créateur aux multiples visages, surgit dès l'orée, et dont la pensée en l'homme reste omniprésente, malgré les changements de forme ». Il y a donc une méditation d'ordre spirituel, presque mystique dans ces œuvres mais aussi un rapport mélancolique à l'existence et dans les trois temps de l'exposition, l'artiste, confronte l'Homme aux trois expériences de la vie : la Douleur, la Mélancolie, l'Espérance, sources de réflexion sur le monde. Trois installations illustrent cette méditation.

La scénographie de l'exposition accompagne le plan de l'église en reprenant les trois composantes majeures du plan basilical : la nef, ses bas-côtés et le chœur. Chacune des trois thématiques se complète, l'ensemble proposant un temps d'arrêt méditatif sur le sens de la vie, de la mort et d'une possible rédemption.

D'abord, la violence, mise en scène dans l'installation *Les Innocents* qui illustre la douleur de l'innocence bafouée, mais aussi l'enfermement, l'isolement et la rébellion. L'installation rappelle la dignité incomparable de tout enfant, alors que se renouvelle chaque jour le massacre des Innocents. Leur souffrance frappe notre conscience insensible, voire anesthésiée. Il ne s'agit pas de les plaindre mais de se remettre en cause dans une démarche de conversion de mentalité et d'engagement. L'artiste suggère le déchirement, l'écartèlement, la fragilité, la mort sous une forme symbolique d'une intensité désespérante, qui malgré sa radicalité se veut source d'apaisement et d'espérance. L'installation conjugue mémoire individuelle (celle propre à l'artiste et à ses souvenirs d'enfance) et mémoire collective, invitant à une réflexion approfondie sur notre culture, ses illusions, ses désenchantements mais aussi la possibilité de survie.

La Mélancolie des *Pierrots* répond à l'Innocence de l'enfance. Figure naïve et rêveuse, Friedler nous l'évoque sous l'aspect triste et nostalgique du Pierrot de Verlaine :

« Ce n'est plus le rêveur lunaire du vieil air
Qui riait aux aïeux dans les dessus de porte ;
Sa gaîté, comme sa chandelle, hélas ! est morte.
Et son spectre aujourd'hui nous hante, mince et clair. »

Le poète et l'artiste font, tous deux, revivre le personnage autrefois gai et fantasque sous une forme spectrale. Cette figure de comédie avec son costume traditionnel, son visage lunaire qui nous enchantait petits et grands ont désormais triste allure. Friedler nous en offre l'image d'un être décharné, un revenant qui s'est désincarné sous la forme d'un squelette robotisé. Il ne lui reste plus à ce corps sans vie qu'une petite lueur triste et désenchantée dans les yeux, qui exprime comme un regret de temps révolus, un rêve de bonheur perdu. Cette évocation glaçante de notre époque suggère la mutation qui s'opère dans notre société, affectant notre vision du monde et de notre propre corps et que l'artiste illustre par l'errance de ces âmes désincarnées vaguant aux marges du royaume d'Hadès, telles des ombres en recherche de salut. Elles sont une multitude, toutes semblables, une réduction de l'humain à l'état de masse contrôlée et insensibilisée. Ces sculptures ne sont pas sans rappeler l'œuvre *Efficiency Men* de Thomas Schütte. *La Forêt des âmes* est une œuvre ascensionnelle qui évoque l'élévation de l'esprit. L'artiste y délivre un message d'espérance et de renouveau. Évocation d'âmes lumineuses qui n'incarne pas le Divin, mais une Conscience énergétique positive invitant chacun à un moment de recueillement et de réflexion, cette œuvre contribue à transmettre, ce que l'artiste appelle « un supplément d'âme », un moment de partage et d'oubli de soi, pour s'unir à un processus collectif. Friedler définit cette installation comme étant « d'inspiration chrétienne », car elle véhicule les principes « d'universalité, d'égalitarisme et le souci du prochain ». Son objectif est d'aller au-delà des données matérielles et visuelles pour en extraire les connexions les plus subtiles et invisibles, rejoignant ainsi une interrogation de nature psychique, philosophique et même religieuse.

Les trois installations participent d'un même récit qui se développe entre dramaturgie et salvation. La mise en scènes des trois œuvres occupe l'espace de l'église en trois temps d'un parcours qui est enrichie de quelques œuvres picturales et photographiques.

- Travée latérale droite : *Les Innocents* (2000)
- Travée latérale gauche : *Les Pierrots* (2019)
- Nef centrale : *La Forêt des âmes* (2009)

Les œuvres picturales qui accompagnent les installations accentuent encore davantage le caractère dramatique de la scénographie. Il s'agit de *L'Autre* (2018), d'*Ode Satanique* (2018) et de *Crucifixion* (2016).

À ces peintures s'ajoutent deux photos intitulées *Les Ombres, barbelés* (2002), indissociables de l'installation *Les Innocents* (2000).

È finita la Commedia comprend donc trois installations. Elles appartiennent à l'univers artistique de Julien Friedler et témoignent de la diversité de son inspiration. Toutes trois sont cependant liées par la philosophie créative qui préside à l'ensemble de l'œuvre de l'artiste. En effet chaque production, chaque installation, chaque peinture, chaque performance constitue la trame d'une histoire plus vaste, d'une « légende » dit Friedler, qui englobe la totalité des actions artistiques qu'il a mené et continue de mener – un monde en expansion qu'il appelle *Spirit of Boz*. Dans cet univers Friedler a inventé des êtres comme Jack Balance, mais aussi mis en œuvre des programmes d'action, toute une gestion de l'imaginaire qu'animent les tableaux, les installations, les performances, les rencontres. *Les Innocents* illustrent les prémices de cette pensée foisonnante qui imprègne fortement les esprits. *La Forêt des âmes* en est le véhicule, qui permet d'aller vers les autres, les Pierrots en sont l'image mélancolique, réflexion sur le destin de l'humanité.

L'artiste belge est porteur d'une vision humaniste, qu'il définit à travers ses œuvres mais aussi à travers une action de partage qu'il mène au sein de *Spirit of Boz*, association née pour établir – en pratiquant l'expression orale, littéraire, picturale et créative en général – des échanges et liens, constituant ainsi une communauté de réflexions et de témoignages sur des réalités individuelles et collectives appartenant à des cultures de divers endroits du monde. Cette réalité exprime l'urgence de concilier action et contemplation, dans le but de promouvoir une pensée humaniste et cathartique. Son univers, en évolution permanente, comporte des facettes opposées, l'une d'inspiration collective (*La Forêt des âmes*), l'autre (*Les Pierrots* et les peintures) de méditation personnelle.

L'art de Friedler active des sensations, des relations, des analyses, et est conçu comme une opération conciliant toutes les expressions vitales, qu'elles découlent de sa propre expérience ou de celle des autres. Son action recouvre par conséquent de multiples aspects et embrasse des domaines variés, de la littérature à la philosophie, de l'analyse sociologique aux arts plastiques (peinture, sculpture, installations). L'aspect pictural de sa production est généré par le besoin créatif, le désir de transmission spontanée et viscérale, découlant de la « tentative de découvrir ce qui constitue l'essence passionnelle des êtres ». Friedler procède de manière presque hypnotique, sans contrainte de sujets ni de matériaux, définissant ainsi un rythme, un mode d'expression informel. Son énergie en expansion découle de la capacité de dissociation et d'introspection qu'il applique à lui-même avant de s'intéresser aux autres, de découvrir en l'autre les motivations les plus intimes : un voyage à la découverte de l'âme humaine dans sa complexité atavique et universelle.

Les œuvres

Les Innocents, 2000
Fil de fer barbelé, peluches, bois et technique mixte, dimensions originales 9 x 11 m

L'installation *Les Innocents* est une représentation métaphorique de la blessure intime du monde, née de l'enfance contrainte, enfermée comme le décrit le philosophe Pierre Bourdieu dans « une école terrible de réalisme sociale, où tout est déjà présent, à travers les nécessités de la lutte pour la vie : l'opportunisme, la servilité, la délation », elle témoigne de l'origine sanglante de la vie. Au cours de son élaboration, l'œuvre aux dimensions monumentales a pris les caractéristiques d'un camp de concentration où le symbole de l'enfance violée et maltraitée rejoint l'évocation du martyre du peuple juif. À la différence des tableaux résultants d'une expression immédiate et jaillissante, le travail de l'installation se déroule sur plusieurs mois, y entre donc une conscience plus large, une élaboration et une volonté créatrice plus déterminées que dans les peintures marquées du caractère de la spontanéité. Cependant Julien Friedler n'y voit pas le travail d'une volonté consciente, nul désir de commentaire, nulle volonté de rappel au destin du peuple juif… Il y voit une universalité de la souffrance qui de tout temps se reproduit et se répète dans la folie et la violence des hommes. Il s'agit ici d'un geste expiatoire dans lequel l'artiste investit ses propres forces de rédemption.

«Il y a les barbelés, les peluches, les bancs d'école, mise en scène certes tragique mais aussi ludique, j'ai utilisé un langage des extrêmes : l'enfance et la mort, c'est la Shoah, évidemment, mais aussi une métaphore de l'enfance emprisonnée… de tous les enfants du monde tués et blessés dans leur innocence.» L'installation *Les Innocents* est une évocation puissante des thématiques de la souffrance : douleur, enfermement, isolement, rébellion, que vit le personnage de Jack Balance. Celui-ci occupe le centre de l'installation *Les Innocents* et est un personnage à part dans l'univers de Friedler. Ce serait comme le jumeau de l'artiste, une forme dupliquée de lui-même, symbole d'une difficulté d'être et de s'affranchir des contingences humaines. Jack Balance est enfermé dans une cage d'où il s'échappe pour faire le tour du monde. Pour exister il doit sans cesse frauder, protester, se rebeller. La cage illustre son propre cas, mais relève également d'une symbolique universelle. Jack Balance est un clown frustré mais plein d'humour et d'impertinence, dont le regret est celui d'être un personnage et non un être humain. Il soutient un combat que l'artiste ne pourrait affronter sans la fiction de ce masque, pourtant la présence du personnage est virtuelle. Son existence est matérialisée par une photo. Une chaise, des peluches éparpillées, un squelette en plastique, des téléphones portables qui le relient à son Créateur, des sortes d'entrelacs invisibles qui le maintiennent dans un état d'addiction. Un panneau dit : «On m'appelle Jack Balance». C'est autour de lui qu'est née l'installation *Les Innocents*.

L'œuvre évoque aussi le parcours intime de l'artiste, sa propre difficulté à vivre, son aspiration à transcender les limites imposées par la nature, et le questionnement fondamental face à l'énigme de la vie et du divin. Elle est aussi une œuvre cathartique, de purification émotionnelle, que Julien Friedler opère à travers le récit de sa propre histoire, son propre ressenti, qui s'offrent en genèse de cette œuvre qu'il revêt d'un caractère universel.

L'interrogation sur monde est ici omniprésente. Comme l'évoque Friedler dans *La Vérité du Labyrinthe* (Texte #22) : «Un monde souvent imprégné de sang et de haine. Du divin morcelé, éclaté, en souffrance. Une guerre, sans cesse, reprise et rejouée. Car tous les divins sont en Dieu, l'ersatz de nos rêves. Aucun n'est meilleur ou plus juste. Ou plus vrai. Ou plus beau. Ou plus humain. Ou plus puissant. Au mieux, nous donnerons-ils l'idée d'une autre fresque générée par l'homme pour se consoler.

Une fresque qui converge, se réduit, se concentre en un point. Un point appelé à se surmonter. N'avions-nous pas déjà évoqué un pur Esprit, un en-dehors, un vide inconcevable ? En l'occurrence, l'esthétique ne peut pas ne pas nous interpeller. Peut-être s'agit-il d'un premier indice ? Car, pareille monstration, appelle un regard inhumain qui ne devrait rien aux aliens ou autres extraterrestres. D'ailleurs, ne sont-ils pas d'ores et déjà pris dans nos filets : une légende du divin créée par nos imaginaires ?»

Photographies : les photos qui accompagnent l'installation sont les ombres de cette humanité martyre, en tout lieu, en tout temps.

La Forêt des âmes, 2009
9 colonne de bois, masques de résine et lumière led, hauteur de chaque colonne environ 2 m

Lumière de l'espérance et partage de l'universalité du message artistique à travers le concept de la *Forêt des âmes.*

L'association *Spirit of Boz - Julien Friedler* est le soutien d'une action que l'artiste entend mener dans une continuité de temps qui le dépasse et qui poursuivra son œuvre pendant 80 ans. L'association développe un programme intitulé *Be Boz Be Art*, qui implique différents secteurs d'intervention et qui contribue à diffuser de nouvelles pratiques artistiques à travers le monde afin de leur donner de la visibilité. *La Forêt des âmes* en fait partie.

Spirit of Boz véhicule un idéal d'échange et d'interactions bénéfiques à tous, qui a déjà trouvé un écho dans des communautés les plus éloignées. Le projet *Be Boz Be Art* repose sur trois programmes qui impliquent la complicité de talents multiples ainsi que la rencontre avec des réalités quotidiennes très éloignées des nôtres dont la découverte et l'approche, dans le respect mutuel, contribuent à enrichir une hétérogénéité d'expression et de transmission, donnant lieu à des opportunités d'échanges.

Parfois les signes d'un savoir caché naissent de la plus grande indigence, de l'ignorance apparente, de l'expression de quelques mots qui rejoignent la poésie la plus pure, de l'exécution de quelques traits, du mélange des couleurs qui suggèrent que l'art est une force directrice, qui conduit à la rencontre et à la révélation des possibles. C'est dans cette conscience et cette conviction que l'association *Spirit of Boz* mène des actions participatives qui impliquent l'engagement de personnes d'origines sociales les plus diverses, d'origines géographiques les plus

éloignées. Ces actions répondent à certains critères
définis par le programme *Give up*, qui collecte des
œuvres spontanées à l'occasion de voyages (Rwanda,
Togo, Mexique…) au cours desquels l'équipe *Boz* va
à la rencontre de cultures et de traditions souvent
totalement inconnues. Auprès des personnes qui
souhaitent participer au projet, l'équipe collecte des
objets d'usage courant ou des créations originales
souvent à caractère tribal.
Friedler, à travers son projet artistique, entend ainsi
recueillir ces frémissements issus de l'inconscient,
qu'il aime à explorer et dont il suit les méandres
à travers le troisième programme de *Be Boz Be
Art* intitulé *La Forêt des âmes*. Celui-ci génère des
réponses à un questionnaire imprimé sur un feuillet.
Les réponses obtenues, précieusement recueillies et
conservées, doivent constituer la substance même
de l'œuvre. En effet, tous les questionnaires seront
enfermés dans des caissons, eux-mêmes empilés
dans des colonnes, chaque colonne matérialise un
arbre. De la multiplication des arbres émergera une
forêt. Une forêt d'âmes. La forêt des âmes est avant
tout mouvement. Un élan vers l'autre et vers soi, une
œuvre se faisant, au fil des échanges, un véritable
laboratoire de la rencontre. L'installation constituée de
neuf colonnes est la préfiguration de cette forêt.

Questionnaire de *La Forêt des âmes - Le Tour
du Boz en 80 ans*
La Forêt des âmes génère des réponses à un
questionnaire, expression de six interrogations :

1. Dieu existe-t-il ?
2. Comment caractériser cette époque ?
3. Comment voyez-vous l'avenir ?
4. Êtes-vous heureux ?
5. La sexualité est-elle importante ?
6. Qui suis-je ?

Des questions qui peuvent sembler banales, mais
toutes sont au cœur de notre construction sociale,
elles sont le centre de préoccupations existentielles
moteur du développement de nos cultures. L'équipe
de *Spirit of Boz* se rend aux quatre coins du monde
pour distribuer et recueillir ces questionnaires. Du
Togo à l'Amazonie, en passant par les États-Unis,
l'Indonésie, le Rwanda, l'Argentine, la Belgique,
Indonésie, Tibet, *La Forêt des âmes* s'étoffe de
rencontres et de découvertes inattendues. Initié en
2006, le projet se déroule dans un espace temporel
qui va à l'encontre de notre conception actuelle du
temps : *Le Tour du Boz* est prévu sur 80 ans. Le
questionnaire a pour but de privilégier la rencontre.
Plus de 75.000 questionnaires ont déjà été recueillis.

Et à chaque présentation de l'installation, le public est
invité à le remplir.

Les Pierrots, 2019
12 structures en métal laqué noir, avec masques
peints (hauteur variable jusqu'à 1,60 m), espace
occupé variable, environ 3.5 x 5 m

Les Pierrots sont une installation extrêmement
récente, datant de la fin 2019. C'est l'aboutissement
d'une réflexion sur le destin de l'homme contemporain
et la projection de l'image d'une société désincarnée,
perdue et nostalgique. Le *Pierrot* est ici un
allié nécessaire à l'artiste qui souligne la valeur
archétypale de cette grande figure de la *Commedia
dell'arte*, cette comédie humaine, dans laquelle le
masque du *Pierrot* symbolise à la fois la candeur et la
naïveté qui le rendent vulnérable. La vulnérabilité nous
apparaît comme celle de l'artiste (et de nous-mêmes)
qui se cache derrière cette apparition pour mieux
nous communiquer l'intensité d'un drame qui se
déroule au plus profond de notre être. Le dispositif de
ce simulacre appartient strictement à la mythologie
de Friedler qui déjà, à travers son personnage de
Jack Balance, double de lui-même, avait inventé une
incarnation masquée de lui-même, lui permettant
d'affronter les problèmes existentiels qui l'habitent.
Les Pierrots sont des robots, préfiguration d'une
humanité mécanisée et désincarnée, une réalité
presque actuelle de notre monde dont la volonté
croissante consiste à coder toujours davantage
nos existences, mettant en péril nos capacités
propres. C'est une menace existentielle, suggère
Friedler. L'œuvre est une parabole de l'aliénation
consentie, de notre soumission à un monde connecté
et décérébrant, qui comprime l'individu dans la
mouvance informe et anonyme d'une humanité ultra-
dépendante des outils informatiques qu'il a inventés,
s'enfermant ainsi dans une culture de masse qui
détruit la pensée, stérilise l'initiative et uniformise
tous les réflexes. La schématisation robotique
des corps met l'accent sur la standardisation et la
mécanisation qui annulent l'individualité, une réalité
que l'artiste accentue par la répétition. La réduction
de l'apparence des *Pierrots* à un squelette de métal
illustre l'anéantissement de la vie ; l'existence se
perd, elle est neutralisée et réduite à une substance
fantomatique, émaciée, mais toujours animée
d'un regard triste. Seules les âmes errent encore
dans la nostalgie dont Friedler souligne l'intensité
par les larmes de ces *Pierrots* qui se souviennent
encore de leur humanité lumineuse. L'œuvre est
aussi émouvante que dérangeante, hautement
expressionniste, elle questionne sur les concepts de

métamorphose et de mutation portés par une cyber-
société qui fantasme sur la maîtrise de notre ego et la
démultiplication de nos capacités. Peut-on échapper
au destin tragique que l'artiste nous dessine ?
Les yeux tristes de ses *Pierrots* nous montrent un
désespoir plus humain… un repentir.

Les peintures

La séquence des *Pierrots* est accompagnée de trois
tableaux qui suggèrent la noirceur existentielle qui
habitent les êtres.

- *L'Autre*, 2018, acrylique et collage sur toile,
150 x 200 cm
- *Ode Satanique*, 2018, acrylique sur toile,
150 x 200 cm
- *Crucifixion*, 2016, acrylique sur toile, 200 x 300 cm
(présentée au dos du mur de la *Forêt des âmes*)

Ces trois tableaux sont emblématiques de la période
picturale 2016-2018. Après toute une série d'œuvres
solaires liées à la nature et à la lumière que Julien
Friedler a peintes dans les années 2012-2016, son
inspiration redevient plus sombre et plus primitive. La
matière est rude et les couleurs sombres évoquent
les ténèbres. Une inquiétante réalité s'impose dans
ces œuvres monumentales, représentatives de la
démarche de l'artiste qui explore le monde au-delà
des évidences perceptibles et intelligibles, faisant
naître des connections secrètes avec l'invisibilité des
songes enfouis au plus profond de l'inconscient. C'est
à cela que parvient Friedler, à cette introspection
lente et viscérale qui accompagne le geste, ou qui
s'accompagne du geste et qui efface toute croyance
cartésienne de la raison humaine, laissant place
au mystère. Une immersion dans l'irrationnel qui
explore les profondeurs de l'infini et du devenir. C'est
ainsi que l'on pourrait décrire la peinture de Julien
Friedler qui naît d'une pratique psychanalytique
de l'exploration de l'inconscient, mais une fois
abandonné tout caractère dogmatique, il se livre à la
méditation qui s'oppose au monde des formes, des
habitudes et des comportements, rejoignant ainsi la
splendeur de l'abîme. C'est ici que l'on découvre la
profondeur de l'âme qui, se reflétant, se projette sur la
toile et devient tableau.
Friedler écrit : « A quoi servent nos peintures, nos
sculptures et nos installations ? Sinon à ça : une
combinaison d'opposés, une écriture paradoxale,
une insertion des flux qui traversent *Spirit of Boz*.
Ici, l'univers s'étendra jusqu'à atteindre un point
d'interruption : une pure synchronie, cachée sous la
masse des créations, dans laquelle tous les moyens
se confondent. Car, au fond, toute œuvre disjointe,
séparée, visible de chacun, ne sera qu'un détail,
une image, la manifestation isolée d'un phénomène
global : une seule et même peinture, vue sous
des angles différents. Une peinture capable de
se recomposer dans l'esprit de tous ceux qui s'y
consacrent. Il n'y a pas de différence de nature entre
le microcosme subjectif et le macrocosme universel. »
Friedler est mû par une aspiration supérieure qui
illustre la dimension infinie de l'art et met en scène sa
capacité à réinventer le monde.

Biographie
Dominique Stella

L'œuvre : « L'inscription du Divin dans un microcosme
(*Spirit of Boz*) aux ressorts universels. » J.F.

Fils de parents juifs, tous deux d'origine
transylvanienne, Julien Friedler est né à Bruxelles
en 1950 et réside actuellement à Monaco. Il reçoit
une éducation religieuse attentive, respectueuse
des préceptes du judaïsme. Après des études de
philosophie et d'ethnologie, il suit un cursus de
psychanalyse à Paris ; il adhère alors aux théories
poststructuralistes de Jacques Lacan, tout en
débutant une psychanalyse personnelle avec ce
dernier.
Julien Friedler est un personnage complexe et
la construction de son art s'appuie sur quelques
blessures toujours douloureuses qui hantent depuis
longtemps la mémoire familiale. La guerre, encore
si proche, a laissé des traces indélébiles dans sa
famille marquée par le destin tragique des déportés
et disparus dans les camps nazis. Sa mère ne s'en
remettra jamais, vivant dans la douleur et le souvenir,
transmettant ainsi à son fils le ferment d'une
inquiétude profonde qui sera pour toujours la marque
d'un caractère tourmenté.
Lacan meurt en 1981, sans qu'une fréquentation
quotidienne avec l'illustre psychanalyste n'ait permis à
Julien Friedler d'atténuer son mal-être.

Au cours des années 1980, il cherche sa voie, voyage,
découvre grâce à son père joaillier, le monde des
affaires dans lequel s'implique aussi Lutty de Geest,
sa compagne qu'il épouse en 1984. Durant toute
cette période, il consacre néanmoins une grande
partie de son temps à l'écriture. En 1982, il publie
son premier livre, *Mosaïque*, récit poétique qui met
en scène une multiplicité de fictions destinées à
égarer le lecteur dans le labyrinthe de la pensée. Le

livre *L'Ombre du rabbin*, publié en 1985 à la maison d'édition Lieu Commun, Paris, aborde, quant à lui, le problème de la Shoah à travers des personnages dont le questionnement sur le destin tragique du peuple martyre, rejoint celui de l'artiste. Le mot *Quête*, à la fois mythique et épique, illustre le parcours des héros du livre, figures emblématiques de la problématique friedlérienne.

1988 : naissance de sa fille Tatiana.

Dans les années 1990, l'exploration du champ psychanalytique constitue la base de sa recherche. Mais le tourment essentiel qui l'habite ne trouve aucun répit et ouvre la voie à une quête harassante du Sens qui s'affirme dans les interrogations fondamentales qu'il pose et tente d'éclairer dans ses écrits et ses œuvres plastiques. En effet, le travail artistique qu'il entreprend vers 1996, prolonge son interrogation sur l'Inconscient et l'épopée artistique qu'il mène, qu'il nomme génériquement *Spirit of Boz*, englobant ainsi la totalité des aspects de son récit personnel, qui, uni à ses œuvres, définit une recherche dont le cœur, comme le rappelle l'artiste, « restera à jamais la vie intérieure et son rapport à un Créateur énigmatique, insaisissable ».

Malgré l'émergence de la peinture dans son travail, Friedler continue d'écrire. Les années 1990 voient la parution de trois livres. En 1995 sort *Psychanalyse et neurosciences : la légende du boiteux* (PUF, Paris). L'auteur y reprend la question posée par l'*Esquisse d'une psychologie scientifique* de Sigmund Freud, en se livrant à une analyse comparative, à la lumière des connaissances actuelles développées par les neurosciences. Le livre apprécié du public averti, lui vaut quelques louanges. Puis, en 1998, paraissent successivement, *Tirésias*, drame poétique (Caractères, Paris) et *L'ivrogne* (Éditions de Janus, Paris), dont la couverture est illustrée par un des premiers tableaux du peintre, *Le Petit homme jaune*.

Dans la seconde moitié des années 1990, la peinture envahit définitivement le travail de Julien Friedler. L'art devient pour lui la source « d'une vérité supportable » qui par sa force expressive consent « à la mise en image des mythes de l'humanité ». Les premières œuvres constituent le témoignage, d'un travail spontané, primitif, déjà dominé par l'éclat de la couleur, qui très vite trouve une expression personnelle dans une série de peintures comme *Le Petit homme jaune*, ou le *Miroir de la Princesse*, *Le Cheval fou*. La volonté picturale de l'artiste s'y impose avec une force expressive parfois naïve, s'apparentant à un art du graffiti où le signe écrit impose très vite sa présence lancinante.

Années 2000, la peinture est toujours plus présente. *Le Shaman* (2000) sera l'image symbolique du processus de mutation de Friedler qui n'oublie cependant pas d'où il vient. L'art apparaît alors comme une synthèse et les écrits poétiques qui couvrent ses premières toiles illustrent le passage du pictural au signe qui très vite devient langage crypté à travers la série des œuvres intitulées *La Parole des Anges*. Ce cycle de peintures réalisé entre 2000 et 2002 revêt une dimension conceptuelle dans son contenu et esthétique par sa forme. Dans cette série d'œuvres, Friedler met en place un langage codé, ésotérique, primordial, basé sur une symbolique du signe. « *La Parole des Anges* », dit Friedler, « est une mystique, une langue fondamentale sous-jacente à la prolifération des discours, chaque signe, voire l'entièreté du tableau pourront donc faire l'objet d'une méditation. » À travers la mise en place de ce langage Julien Friedler établit une cartographie des concepts qui interrogent l'homme sur l'idée du Sacré dont il tente d'interpréter les mystères par le biais d'une écriture quasi religieuse. Une rétrospective de ce cycle de peinture aura lieu plus tard en 2018 à La Cité Miroir de Liège avec l'édition d'un catalogue qui reprend les œuvres majeures de *La Parole des Anges*.

En 2000, *Les Innocents* occupent l'atelier. Un enclos de 11 x 9 m, fait de fils barbelés, enferme des peluches, des bancs d'école, dans une mise en scène, certes, tragique mais aussi ludique. L'installation est monumentale. Friedler précise : « J'ai utilisé un langage des extrêmes : l'enfance et la mort, c'est la Shoah, évidemment, mais aussi une métaphore de l'enfance emprisonnée… de tous les enfants du monde tués et blessés dans leur innocence. » L'installation devient vite un point de repère dans l'œuvre de l'artiste, véhiculant l'idée d'un art de partage, invitant au questionnement. Le spectateur parcourant l'installation est amené à se confronter aux interrogations fondamentales du monde. Des versions successives des *Innocents* voyageront dès lors dans de nombreuses expositions dédiées à l'artiste.

C'est à cette époque (2000) que naît Jack Balance (http://rebelle.blogspirit.com/archive/2021/04/29/julien-friedler-dealer-d-utopies-3251717.html). Celui-ci est un autre personnage majeur de la mythologie friedlérienne, il exprime le dépassement de soi, il est le double social de l'artiste, alcoolique, dépravé, conscient de ce qui l'entoure et l'opprime. Il occupe la cage située au centre de l'installation *Les Innocents*. « Jack Balance m'est nécessaire », dit Julien Friedler, « probablement parce que j'aime être en retrait du monde. Je suis timide et solitaire, j'ai donc sécrété une parade qui me permet de dire et de faire ce que moi-même je ne serais jamais en mesure d'exprimer et de faire.» Jack Balance symbolise le combat que mène l'homme pour exister dans la terrible dépendance de son Créateur. Il tente de se proclamer «sujet» et pour cela il doit dépasser les limites qu'on lui a imposées, tel le mutisme dont il est atteint. Ses modes de communication sont donc multiples, l'écriture, le tableau, mais aussi enfreindre la loi du mutisme lorsque son créateur est inattentif. Jack Balance est aussi enfermé dans une cage d'où il s'échappe pour faire le tour du monde. Pour exister il doit sans cesse frauder, protester, se rebeller. Jack Balance est un clown frustré qui se pose des questions existentielles, parcourant la planète dans une quête mystique. Il incarne la Conscience.

2003 : Friedler s'est transmuté en clown facétieux, l'atelier commence à se peupler de personnages fantomatiques, les murs se couvrent d'écriture et ce lieu immense, en plein cœur de Bruxelles, devient l'antre qui voit naître l'univers en expansion de Julien Friedler qu'il nommera dès 2003 *Le Boz*. C'est là que se construit dès 2006 *Spirit of Boz*, qui dans sa définition représente une quête métaphysique, une invitation à prolonger l'aventure de l'art dans le champ de la vie, une œuvre unique qui nous force à sortir de nous-même, à nous dissoudre en elle. Car, en effet, au-delà d'une œuvre prolifique, radieuse et parfois inquiétante, Friedler nous invite à modifier notre conscience d'être. L'art est source de révélation de soi, un lieu de partage et d'échange, une invitation au rêve, une quête du sens, une échappatoire aux médiocres réalités du quotidien, une voie vers l'inaccessible vérité de la vie. Une aventure métaphysique, «l'expression de l'indicible», dit Sonia Bresler[1]. «La force de Julien Friedler», précise-t-elle, «consiste à avoir ses gestes créatifs dans son espace et *Spirit of Boz* comme extension de ceux-ci dans l'espace monde.»[2]
C'est tout cela que pressent Friedler et à travers ses actions, ses performances, ses installations, ses peintures. Ses questionnements se font de plus en plus intenses et nécessitent une indispensable ouverture sur le monde. L'artiste, et plus souvent son double, sort de l'atelier et entre en scène. Nous en sommes les spectateurs et sommes invités à en devenir aussi les acteurs. Le monde du Boz commence à s'organiser. Jeanne Zeler arrive dans l'aventure afin d'en coordonner le développement. Début de l'écriture du *Livre du Boz*, qui accompagne la mise en place de la philosophie du *Boz*. Ce livre est une traque, une quête, une épopée, une œuvre méditative et épique, dont la rédaction occupe

les années suivantes et que Julien Friedler définit dans les *Fondamentaux* : «Trois clowns – Jack Balance, le Scribe et l'homme miroir – sont pris à leur propre piège : une vision qui se défile et leur glisse entre les doigts. À les voir évoluer on aura la sensation d'un rêve éveillé. Le récit est non linéaire, ouvert à tout va et savamment éclaté. Il se déroule sur plusieurs plans – simultanés – enchâssant les histoires les unes dans les autres comme dans un jeu de poupées russes. La temporalité est fluctuante, largement imprévisible. L'espace est indistinct. L'intrigue se dérobe…»

2003 : premières expositions. *L'infanzia dell'arte*, exposition personnelle à la Fondazione Mudima, Milan. Peintures de la série de la *Parole des Anges* et installation *Les Innocents* – commentaires sur Rai 3 de Philippe Daverio qui s'enthousiasme pour l'œuvre. Arturo Schwarz prend la parole lors du vernissage pour saluer la puissance du travail de Friedler et plus particulièrement des *Innocents*. Le catalogue de l'exposition reprend de nombreuses vues de l'atelier de Bruxelles.
Cette même année : deux participations à des foires, Art Brussels avec la Galerie Damasquine, et la Foire de Bâle avec la galerie Pailhas de Marseille. Réalisation des premières œuvres-installations mettant en scène ce personnage à la fois burlesque et dramatique qu'est Jack Balance, qui commence à conquérir son autonomie dans l'univers de Friedler : *BB Jack Balance, Jack Balance dans son transat*. Le monde du *Boz* se met en place et l'atelier, peu à peu, devient un lieu que l'artiste veut en expansion vers le monde extérieur.

2004, l'écriture est toujours présente, publication de *L'Œil d'Œdipe* aux PUF. Déconstruire le mythe pour en faire un fantasme, tel est l'objectif de Friedler, qui dénonce dans l'ouvrage l'hypertrophie de l'inconscient et invoque la nécessité de procéder en sens inverse : du fantasme vers le mythe, ce qui suppose l'élaboration de nouveaux «mythèmes». Nous reconnaissons là les préoccupations de l'artiste, bâtisseur d'une mythologie légendaire qu'il développe à travers un univers mythique qui s'ancre à la fois dans le réel et l'inconscient.
En 2004 deux expositions personnelles s'ajoutent à son parcours : *Paroles et Paraboles ou le Mythe en question* au Passage de Retz, Paris ; *Memories* chez David Di Maggio Gallery, Berlin. Friedler participe aussi à deux expositions collectives: *De leur Temps – Collections privées françaises*, Musée des Beaux-Arts, Tourcoing ; *Vanitas, Eitelkeit der Eitelkeiten*, IKOB, Eupen.

[1] In Sonia Bressler, *Julien Friedler. De la Métaphysique de l'errance*, Jacques Flament Éditions, Mariac, 2013, p. 75.
[2] *Ibidem*, p. 76.

2000-2009 : après *La Parole des Anges*, la peinture domine cette période. De la naissance de *Spirit of Boz* jaillit une force créatrice qui transcende l'œuvre picturale en une irruption spontanée et conquérante, imposant la peinture, comme source d'énergie à la fois introspective et jaillissante. *La Parole des Anges* contenait déjà tous les aspects de la méditation qui inspirera par la suite le travail de l'artiste. La complexité de son œuvre y est dessinée de manière prémonitoire, activant aussi toutes les facettes qui composent la diversité du personnage Julien Friedler : le psychanalyste, l'écrivain, le poète, l'artiste. Tous tendent vers un même but, celui de réactiver les mythes dans une société en équilibre instable, afin d'y trouver un sens. C'est dans cet esprit de recours aux grandes mythologies fondatrices que Friedler peint une série de figures emblématiques et légendaires, des géants fabuleux, envoûtants, personnifications imaginaires de nos peurs inconscientes : *Le Foudroyer* (2004), *Ecce Homo* (2009), *Le Cavalier de l'Apocalypse* (2009), *Le Clown androgyne, Le Guerrier* (2010) et d'abord *Le Shaman* (2000), figure puissante de l'univers friedlérien, particulièrement significative de l'œuvre de l'artiste. Cette représentation pourrait être son propre portrait. Le shaman est, en effet, dans la tradition, le poète, l'érudit, le sorcier qui délivre un message de l'au-delà pour les vivants.
Dans ces mêmes années, il produit trois œuvres importantes : *Les Demoiselles revisitées* (2005), installation de trois sculptures en résine, librement inspirées des *Demoiselles d'Avignon* de Picasso, qui seront exposées en 2007 à la Francis Naumann Gallery, New York. Il réalise aussi deux sculptures hyperréalistes : *Le Juif errant* (2004), image archétypale d'un personnage à la fois terrifiant et mélancolique, et enfin une représentation de *Arafat* (2004), qui est vendue chez Phillips de Pury & Company, à Londres en 2005. Ces œuvres témoignent d'un réalisme critique envers la société, rappelant que Friedler cherche à retranscrire des images frappantes et signifiantes.

2005 : *Les Innocents* sont présentés dans une mise en scène originale intitulée *La Fin des temps*, produite lors du Festival des Flandres 2005 et construite autour de la musique d'Olivier Messiaen (*Quatuor pour la fin des temps*) et des mots de Primo Levi. Ce moment émouvant invite le spectateur à revisiter la Seconde Guerre mondiale et à repenser le présent. Toujours en 2005, le cycle de peintures *La Parole des Anges* est montré à Galerie Philippe Cazeau - La Béraudière, Paris.
Enfin il ne faut pas oublier, en cette fin 2005, la naissance de la matrice mère de l'entière pensée de l'artiste qu'est *Spirit of Boz*, concept indispensable à l'élargissement du discours sur l'art à la totalité des êtres en quête d'eux-mêmes et des autres. *Spirit of Boz* est le creuset où s'analyse notre environnement et où s'élabore la prise de conscience des turbulences qui agitent notre monde, c'est aussi le lieu de l'action et de la pensée proliférante qui s'alimente aux rumeurs de nos sociétés pour que tous ensembles, nous les combattions, en défense d'une utopie fondatrice d'une société où l'art serait salvateur.

2006 : parallèlement à la peinture Julien Friedler poursuit et développe l'épopée légendaire du *Boz*. Création de l'association Spirit of Boz. En cherchant à projeter le champ de l'art dans le champ social (et non l'inverse), Julien Friedler a créé *Be Boz Be Art*. Un programme complet : artistique, humaniste et philosophique dont l'objectif principal consiste à générer des flux créatifs. Dans cet univers, à la fois imaginaire, mais aussi, bien réél, il construit une œuvre labyrinthique, hypertextuelle et multimédia qui met en connexion un réseau d'énergies destinées à débusquer des connivences secrètes entre les êtres les plus disparates et les plus éloignés géographiquement grâce à l'action qu'il mène à travers *Spirit of Boz*. Sonia Bresler en parle ainsi : « L'œuvre la plus complexe de Julien Friedler n'est pas celle qui se donne à voir… Son œuvre est un geste global, il y a un début, une impulsion, puis il y a son élan, son mécanisme, puis il y a sa spatialité et enfin son prolongement. Il aime à parler de travail en rhizome. L'œuvre de Julien Friedler est *Spirit of Boz*. »[3]

Le 2 décembre 2006 (http://rebelle.blogspirit.com/archive/2021/04/29/julien-friedler-dealer-d-utopies-3251717.html) a lieu *La Nuit du Boz*, qui se déroule au Canal à Bruxelles. Affichage dans les rues de Bruxelles, en happening, la soirée s'annonçait animée. Sonia Bressler raconte : « Tout le monde s'amuse, se joue des musiques, des bulles de Champagne, une douce ivresse poétique s'empare des danseurs d'une nuit sur fond de musiques électroniques. Projection de la vie qui passe ou allégorie contemporaine de la caverne ? Ici débute la *Forêt des âmes*. » L'évènement, moment disruptif dans la banalité quotidienne, introduit à l'ensemble des projets qui alimenteront la machine à penser le monde selon la logique de l'art, selon la logique d'un temps arrêté sur la méditation, sur l'autre rive de nos êtres, loin des contingences et des injonctions matérialistes de notre sociétés. Friedler invite chacun à être « Be Boz Be art ». *Be Boz Be Art* est un programme contemplatif, apolitique. Il s'agit d'un

[3] *Ibidem*, p. 79.

mouvement de chercheurs d'art. Les interventions permettent de faire naître l'expression artistique là où elle paraît manquer. Le programme se déploie selon trois axes de travail : *La Forêt des âmes*, *Le Clochard Céleste* et *Give up*. Cette part de l'œuvre de Friedler, pluridisciplinaire et collégiale, constitue une tentative de fusion entre diverses formes d'expression. L'art est ici le support d'échange et de communication, il incarne la fin des certitudes et le début d'une ère créative, invitant chacun à y participer…

De 2006 à 2009, mise en place des concepts fondateurs de *Spirit of Boz* (https://docplayer. fr/200236625-La-foret-des-ames-de-julien-friedler. html).
La Forêt des âmes - Le Tour du Boz en 80 ans est la première action qui mène à la construction de *Spirit of Boz*. Il s'agit d'un questionnaire, qui est distribué au cours des évènements happenings du *Boz*, et auquel chacun est invité à répondre. Six questions qui introduisent au cheminement de la pensée profonde, élan collectif et interrogation sur soi-même : 1. Dieu existe-t-il ? 2. Comment caractériser cette époque ? 3. Comment voyez-vous l'avenir ? 4. Êtes-vous heureux ? 5. La sexualité est-elle importante ? 6. Qui suis-je ? Le questionnaire est présenté pour la première fois au public le 2 décembre 2006. Dans l'intention de Friedler l'expérience se poursuivra pendant 80 ans, s'achèvera donc en 2086, «au-delà de nos vies» précise l'artiste comme une forme de vanité, le but étant de recueillir les réponses à ces six interrogations. Depuis 2007 et encore aujourd'hui, les acteurs de cette aventure ont parcouru des territoires innombrables pour recueillir, dans les endroits les plus insolites de la planète, les pensées réfléchies ou fugaces de milliers de participants qui ont accepté de répondre à ces six questions fondamentales invariables quelles que soient les sociétés. Du Togo à Santiago du Chili en passant par New York, Milan, Rome, Paris, Londres, Moscou, Katmandou, Lhassa, Pékin, la *Forêt des âmes* propose à chacun de s'arrêter.

2007 : les questionnaires arrivent du Rwanda et du Maroc, de Bulgarie, du Brésil. Des prisonniers, des malades, des élèves des écoles, des étudiants offrent par l'écriture, le dessin de partager ce moment d'éternité. Car il s'agit bien de cela. Les questionnaires ainsi recueillis seront scellés dans des colonnes dont la multiplicité créera cette *Forêt des âmes*. Septembre 2007, Carmen Ferreyra sillonne l'Amérique du Sud. Avec ses équipes, elle ramène des réponses de Buenos Aires, Córdoba, Rosario, Loncopué (province de Neuquén), Gualeguaychú, Santiago de Chili,

et Montevideo, des favelas de Belém au Brésil. Mise en place de *Give up* et premiers objets reçus en partage : *Give up* est un programme d'échange qui se développe sur 10 ans, c'est aussi une œuvre qui se construit autour du don, du « lâcher-prise ». Le don d'un objet quelconque, d'un objet du quotidien ou même d'une œuvre. Ce programme a d'abord été développé au Togo, en Argentine, puis en Indonésie, et en Europe… Une des actions les plus significatives de ce «voyage» *Give up*, fut menée à Loncopué, en Argentine où la population de cette petite ville de 6 000 habitants, complètement étrangère aux préoccupations artistiques, fut invitée à partager sa réalité quotidienne, par la réalisation de dessins, de peintures ou le don de quelque objet. Ils remplissent aussi le questionnaire de *La Forêt des âmes*. Un concours sélectionna vingt-cinq parmi la centaine d'œuvres recueillies, formant un corpus homogène de témoignages qui furent ensuite intégrés à la collection du *Boz* constituant la preuve la plus éloquente qui soit de l'impact d'une réflexion sur la création chez des individus dépourvus de toute référence dans le domaine. Remarquables sont les dessins exécutés par Ida Leandro.
Également en 2007, le programme de *Spirit of Boz* propose un principe d'échange et un dialogue avec les êtres les plus oubliés de notre société. Il s'agit du programme intitulé *Le Clochard Céleste* : «Des rues de Bruxelles, aux périphériques de Jakarta ou encore avec les enfants des rues au Rwanda, le programme *Clochard Céleste* consiste à donner les moyens de l'expression artistique à des personnes en situation de détresse ou de précarité. C'est l'expression artistique telle qu'elle peut naître partout.»
Exposition *In Quest*, à la galerie Philippe Seghers à Ostende (commissaire Michael Dewilde). Cette exposition est accompagnée d'une performance de Jack Balance sur la digue d'Ostende (https://www. paperblog.fr/209641/la-cabine-du-boz-performance-a-ostende/ – https://www.youtube.com/ watch?v=xshbcF0DZLI). «Vers 14heures, une armada de sosies de Jack Balance s'est déployée autour de la cabine. Bonnet noir, lunettes, faux nez, moustaches fournies, T-shirt rouge et questionnaire du *Tour du Boz* à la main, ils vont à la rencontre des badauds, à qui ils proposent de répondre aux six questions.»
Revenons à Julien Friedler qui mit en place cette machine du *Boz* dans une période où il s'interrogeait sur les fondamentaux de son action artistique. Alors qu'il peignait depuis déjà quelques années, il est allé puiser aux origines les plus éloignées de notre civilisation, aux sources les moins altérées par des idées préconçues, les réponses à son questionnement : « De quoi s'agit-il ? », interroge

Friedler. « En place d'une définition abstraite, toujours réductrice, nous nous efforcerons d'illustrer ici un lieu d'émergence : un conglomérat d'affects, de pensées et de sensations, nés d'un enchaînement d'actes interrogeant le statut de l'artiste. »[4] C'est ce statut qui l'intéresse, qui légitime sa propre œuvre et celle de tant d'autres.

Malgré toute l'effervescence produite par ce monde du *Boz*, Julien Friedler poursuit son œuvre personnelle. Peintures, sculptures et installations continuent d'envahir l'espace de l'atelier. Sa peinture issue des lettres et des signes continue de développer ses thématiques rituelles, proches d'expériences de transe et d'hypnose. L'artiste scrute, fouille la matière afin d'en extraire la sève vitale. La forme picturale est proche du graffiti. Ce sont des œuvres primitives à la matière magmatique et rugueuse.

2008, l'aventure de *Spirit of Boz* se poursuit. Des premiers éléments recueillis lors de cette quête menée aux quatre coins du monde, émergent des pépites qui confortent l'artiste dans sa conviction que l'art est ferment de nos vies, générateur d'une force de lumière et de vérité. 18 juin 2008, les œuvres réalisées à Loncopué, petit village perdu de Patagonie, sont présentées chez Sotheby's à Munich, lors d'une exposition où les dessins, peintures, sculptures et questionnaires sont montrés à des collectionneurs habitués aux œuvres cotées d'artistes confirmés. L'évènement provoque l'interrogation. Friedler répond qu'il s'agit là « d'aller chercher l'art, là où on ne l'attend pas. » Parallèlement à l'exposition présentée chez Sotheby's, une performance *Be Boz* se déroule à l'église Heilig-Kreuz de Munich. Durant la cérémonie religieuse, le prêtre invite chacun à réfléchir au questionnaire de *La Forêt des âmes*. Dans son homélie il souligne : « Les questions de l'être et du devenir, de l'apparence et de la vérité ne sont pas étrangères au projet *Be Boz*. Il s'agit d'un questionnement où la réponse importe peut-être moins que la question ». Les six questions sont inscrites au-dessus du chœur de l'église, alors que se déploie au plus haut de la nef l'installation *L'Envol* (2008) où s'enroulent des questionnaires dans un mouvement de spirale.

Un évènement *Give up* intitulé « Out There in the Middle of Nowhere » organisé à la Galerie der Künstler de Munich incite les visiteurs à offrir un objet symbolisant leur désire intime, dans un rond de cendre. La trilogie munichoise marque un moment important de l'histoire naissante de *Spirit of Boz*. Il existe une vidéo de cette aventure : https://www.dailymotion.com/video/x4pj56

2008 : Friedler crée l'installation, *La Forêt des âmes*. Neuf colonnes de bois surmontées de masques d'inspiration africaine, réalisés en résine transparente qu'une lumière led illumine de l'intérieur. L'effet est saisissant, la musique qui l'accompagne invite à la méditation. Cette installation est la préfiguration d'un ensemble de colonnes monumentales dans lesquelles seront scellés les questionnaires recueillis dans le monde.

En 2008 se poursuit l'action *Give up Togo*. Agnès Mukarubayiza, chargé du programme du *Boz* dans ce pays, récolte de nombreux objets symboliques dont la *Statuette des jumeaux* qui servira de point de départ à une performance d'artistes belges à l'atelier du *Boz* à Bruxelles en 2010.

2009 : année importante pour Jack Balance. La Christopher Henry Gallery de New York présente la première exposition personnelle de Julien Friedler dans sa galerie, *Who is Jack Balance ?*, avec pour commissaire Gabrielle Bryer. Le communiqué de presse précise : « Sur deux étages de la galerie l'exposition nous entraîne à la découverte de Jack Balance et du Monde du Boz. À travers ses écrits, ses peintures, ses sculptures et ses happenings le projet conceptuel de Friedler nous conduit dans l'aventure d'un monde parallèle où l'artiste nous amène à nous confronter aux questions non résolues qui hantent nos esprits… Il y a de la spiritualité dans le monde imparfait de Friedler : il nous aide à voir, comprendre et accepter l'inacceptable imperfection de notre condition humaine. Pour ce faire il invente une figure allégorique de lui-même, Jack Balance, dont les aventures permettent à l'artiste de distiller son message. »

Deux autres expositions se déroulent cette même année, l'une au MUBE (Museu Brasileiro da Escultura), São Paulo, Brésil, en octobre (https://www.julienfriedler.com/exposition/mube/). Cette vaste rétrospective met en scène le travail de Friedler. Imprégné de concepts philosophiques ou de références à l'histoire de l'art et au Pop Art, l'exposition met en lumière la coexistence de plusieurs mythologies. À la manière du terme *Boz*, construction sans véritable signification, tout le projet possède une dimension ludique et humoristique, mais aussi un aspect psychologique. L'exposition propose une trentaine d'œuvres, couvrant différents champs artistiques : peintures, sculptures, littérature, vidéos, photographies, installations et performances. La présence de Julien Friedler au Brésil est aussi l'occasion de performances de rues durant lesquelles chacun est invité à remplir un questionnaire, donner un objet, proposer un dessin. La collection du *Boz* s'enrichit.

[4] Julien Friedler, *Les Fondamentaux*, La Route de la Soie - Éditions, Paris, 2020, p. 7.

L'autre exposition de cette année 2009 se déroule à la National Gallery for Foreign Art à Sofia en Bulgarie, de mai à juin. L'exposition intitulée *Dialogues* (https://www.spiritofboz.com/julien-friedler/julien-friedler-artwork/sofia/) confronte les œuvres de Julien Friedler au projet *Be Boz Be Art*. Conçue comme une exposition conceptuelle, et atypique, Julien Friedler y fait dialoguer le singulier avec l'universel, le rêve et l'idéal avec la réalité, la modernité avec les traditions, l'écrit et le visuel, dans le dessein de faire réagir et participer les visiteurs, invités à répondre aux six questions du *Tour du Boz en 80 ans*.

2009 est aussi l'année où est exposée pour la première fois l'Installation *La Forêt des âmes*. Isolde Brielmaier la propose dans une exposition collective à la Jack Shainman Gallery de New York. L'exposition illustre le rôle significatif des artistes africains ou d'influence africaine sur la scène mondiale. Elle est présentée dans le cadre du projet *Spirit of Boz*. Malgré les déplacements incessants, Julien Friedler poursuit son œuvre picturale : *Ecce Homo* (2009), *Le Cavalier de l'Apocalypse* (2009) et bien d'autres œuvres significatives de la puissance introspective de l'artiste, naissent dans l'atelier de Bruxelles. Friedler affirme désormais son geste pictural. C'est un exemple remarquable de cette attitude, qui s'illustre dans un style ouvertement subjectif qui d'Appel, passe par De Kooning et arrive à Basquiat mais dont l'objet n'est plus le tourment du moi et l'extase de l'artiste (« tragedy, ecstasy and doom » proclamait la génération de l'Expressionnisme Abstrait) mais les formes fluides et errantes, les idoles et les totems, les constellations et les animaux, les abysses et les batailles.

2010 : exposition *Spirit of Boz, the Truth of the Labyrinth*, CW Gallery, New York, autour de la légende du *Boz* et de sa projection dans la réalité littéraire du *Livre du Boz*. Cet ouvrage à croissances multiples donne ici lieu à une interprétation sous forme de bande dessinée qui met en scène nos trois clowns en quête du divin. Il y a un peu de burlesque, un peu de tragique dans ces aventures qui de résonance en résonance, d'association en association, créent une trame transversale, oblique en deçà de l'intrigue qu'elle développe. Une trame propice à l'inconscient et au mythe qu'il sous-tend. Friedler développe son texte : *La Vérité du Labyrinthe* qui donnera par la suite lieu à des débat, et sera publié en 2017.

Rencontre 2010 : conférence-débat, Monaco, juillet 2010, sur la thématique *Spirit of Boz*.

Give up Togo continue son aventure. Après ses voyages au Rwanda, Agnès Mukarubayiza est de retour en Afrique dans le cadre du *Tour du Boz en 80 ans*. (https://www.spiritofboz.com/be-boz-be-art/the-program-around-the-world/togo/). Les habitants du canton de Tovegan proposent de rebaptiser un village : le village du *Boz*. Nombreux questionnaires et objets recueillis.

10 octobre 2010 : une importante performance se déroule à l'atelier du *Boz: Give up Togo/Bruxelles – La performance des Jumeaux*. Un groupe d'artistes bruxellois, inspirés par les objets ramenés du Togo, entre en dialogue artistique avec notamment la statuette des jumelles, petite sculpture symbolique togolaise et peint trois œuvres, dans une action qui participe du délire et de la transe (https://www.spiritofboz.com/be-boz-be-art/the-program-around-the-world/togo/).

2010 voit le retour de Julien Friedler à l'atelier. Sa production picturale s'intensifie, il peint *La Chute du Joker,* œuvre majeure qui signe une technique picturale proche d'une abstraction dramatique. L'écriture du *Livre du Boz* se poursuit.

Julien Friedler participe à une exposition collective à la Galerie Gourvennec Ogor de Marseille. Pour son inauguration la galerie réunit des artistes de générations différentes. Poétique et magique, et parfois troublante, elle propose de redécouvrir un panorama de choix esthétiques divers et de repenser des thèmes aussi différents que les relations humaines, le politique, le réel et ses métamorphoses mais aussi l'histoire de l'art, l'espace et l'illusion.

De 2011 à 2015 : les actions *Give up* et *La Forêt des âmes* se multiplient toujours au Togo, mais aussi à Bruxelles, à New York (2012). Sonia Bressler, philosophe et écrivaine, entame un périple à travers l'Asie dont elle ramène des œuvres peintes, des objets symboliques, et des questionnaires. Elle va d'abord en Indonésie à Jakarta en 2011, puis à Lhassa au Tibet en 2012. Elle est en Inde, à Bombay, à Katmandou au Népal en 2013, et toujours des papiers, des dessins, des collages, des objets singuliers viennent participer à la récolte du *Boz*. Elle se rend dans le Gānsù, en Chine, en 2015 et plus récemment chez les Ouïgour (2017). Ces périples alimentent son propre travail d'ethno-philosophe : « J'observe les métamorphoses de l'humanité », dit-elle, « pour mieux comprendre et transmettre ». Grace à son engagement, les échanges et les dialogues se sont diversifiés, l'art servant de vecteur de communication selon la théorie du *Boz*. Des interviews, des reportages jalonnent ce parcours en un programme d'écoute et de découverte des autres, et d'échanges aussi qu'elle appelle *The Wall of Humanity*. C'est une recherche spécifique à l'intérieur

de l'univers du *Boz* que la philosophe a mené aussi bien en France, qu'en Indonésie, qu'au Tibet, qu'en Chine, et qu'elle poursuit depuis 2012.
En ces années-là, deux livres consacrés à l'univers de Julien Friedler paraissent. En 2012, Norbert Hillaire publie *Double vue, 50 fragments pour Julien Friedler* aux Éditions Somogy, Paris. «Face à l'univers de Julien Friedler», écrit-il, «à la frontière du social, de l'esthétique et des sciences du rêve, nous avons voulu en partager l'enjeu.» En 1er septembre 2012 : exposition personnelle *Les Disparus* à la Galerie Gourvennec Ogor de Marseille (https://www.julienfriedler.com/exposition/les-disparus/). Confrontant le spectateur à une série de photographies prises au printemps 2012 dans son atelier bruxellois, l'artiste nous emmène aux confins intimes de son œuvre, dans le cercle privé de sa mémoire d'homme et d'artiste. En dévoilant les marques d'un processus créatif ardent, irradiant l'espace de matériaux et de pigments, de corps et de signes l'artiste nous dévoile son champ de bataille intérieur. Aucune peinture réelle n'apparaît sur les photographies. Seules des traces de leur existence sont visibles, tels les vestiges d'une œuvre dont on ne sait si elle est réellement achevée ou non encore terminée. Au milieu de l'exposition, la poupée avec l'étoile juive, témoin des atrocités et des êtres à jamais disparus, seule la mémoire les sauve. L'artiste non plus n'apparaît pas, il n'est présent que par sa propre absence.
Le soir du vernissage Julien Friedler, ou plutôt Jack Balance, exécute la *Performance des allumettes*, des allumettes, de l'alcool, une paire de ciseaux, une toile et un bol-réceptacle pour recueillir les morceaux découpés. La toile est débitée en petits bouts. Une allumette est craquée, puis une autre, la toile s'embrase, elle est réduite en cendre. Allégorie d'une disparition programmée, interrogation sur la vanité des choses. L'artiste continue son cheminement de passeur.

2013 : Publication chez Jacques Flament Éditions du *Livre du Boz*. Ainsi le définit Julien Friedler : «Le *Livre du Boz* n'est ni un livre, ni un poème, ni un conte, encore moins un drame ou un essai. Il n'est rien, hormis le style qui l'inspire et le hante. Ici point de repères. Aucune balise. On vogue au gré du vent. Les histoires se tissent, finissent, renaissent au fil de l'eau, avant qu'une tempête ne se lève pour nous emporter au loin, au seuil d'une nouvelle vision. Car tel est le livre du Boz, une œuvre hors normes, inclassable, créée par un errant pour d'autres errants.»
2013 : Sonia Bressler consacre un livre à l'œuvre de Julien Friedler : *Julien Friedler. De la Métaphysique de l'errance*, Jacques Flament Éditions: «Ni le temps, ni l'espace tels que nous les connaissons», écrit Sonia Bressler, «ne suffisent à saisir la forme, la matière de la pensée et de la création de Julien Friedler… Il faut avec lui accepter de poser l'art (au sens de créativité) au cœur de la vie, de la construction sociale et économique. Son travail c'est écouter la mesure du mouvement du monde, c'est définir une alternative.» Sonia Bressler se rend au Népal où elle organise un atelier chorégraphique, *La Forêt des âmes*, mis en scène par Marylin Alasset. Elle se rend aussi en Inde à Bombay (conférence + questionnaires - vidéo et rencontres avec des artistes).

2012-2015, la peinture : Friedler peint des œuvres importantes en cette période riche en événements «du dehors». Un repli s'impose, il faut travailler, peindre, inventer aussi dans l'atelier : toiles, plaques de métal, cartons, objets d'usage commun deviennent les contenants de microcosmes jaillissant de manière sporadique et inquiétante, capables de capter les sursauts, les rythmes syncopés, les états fiévreux et les opacités d'un univers métissé dans lequel s'animent des agrégations de petits esprits et de serpentins (*Saturnins*, 2012), des lémuriens et des paysages enchantés (*Le Parapet*, 2012), des couleurs sabrées et des cris étouffés (*La Chute du Joker*, 2010), des feux d'artifices et des cosmogonies (*Planète Alpha*, 2012), une bestialité suintante et un décorum raffiné (*Maou*, 2011). L'espace omniprésent de la peinture de Friedler met ainsi en scène un monde en ébullition dont les minuscules cellules, soumises à un mouvement ondoyant, sont engagées dans une danse de formes et de signes sinueux qui suggèrent les palpitations de la nature. C'est un monde proliférant, intense, dramatique mais aussi joyeux. Des paysages, de la lumière, des paillettes, le geste de Friedler libère une énergie créatrice qui explose en feux colorés sur la toile.
L'année 2012 annonce la période nomade de l'artiste. Entre 2012 et 2018 Julien Friedler abandonne une vie sédentaire et entame une circulation voyageuse qui l'amène à séjourner fréquemment dans des hôtels. En ces occasions, poursuivant sa méditation picturale, il produit en six années un ensemble de plus de 300 œuvres sur papier. Petits formats faciles à produire et transporter. Ils appartiennent à cette inspiration méditative et colorée qui oscille entre figuration et abstraction, où les fantômes errants habitent des univers incertains. Ces petites œuvres sont reliées aux grandes toiles de l'atelier de la même période ; elles véhiculent la même force, la même énergie, le même mystère.
2014 : exposition *Voyage*, Museo Civico Archeologico

Girolamo Rossi, Forte dell'Annunziata, Ventimiglia, Italie. À cette occasion Jacques Flament Éditions publient le catalogue de l'exposition. Sont exposées quelques grandes œuvres archétypales et primitives de la série des figures emblématiques des années 2008-2011, puis des œuvres de la série des paysages, planètes et univers enchantés (2010-2014), et enfin une série d'œuvres sur papier exécutées pendant les voyages de l'artiste. *Voyage* reflète les aspects d'une méditation intérieure, voyage intime que Friedler restitue dans une œuvre suggestive et poétique. Les peintures dialoguent avec les installations permanentes du Musée Archéologique, dans une évocation intemporelle qui remonte aux sources de l'art.

Les voyages se poursuivent, alternant avec des présences à l'atelier.

Des rencontres autour du texte de la *Vérité du Labyrinthe* sont organisées à Bruxelles.

En 2014 : performances de Carmen Ferreyra autour du thème de *La Vérité du Labyrinthe*, une à l'Armory Show de New York et l'autre à l'Untitled Art fair de Miami.

Dès 2014, de nouvelles œuvres voient le jour, exécutées selon une technique nouvelle que l'on pourrait qualifier de «Peinture liquide», expression empreintée au critique italien Gianluigi Colin qu'il utilisa dans un article de 2016, dans le *Corriere della Sera. Totems* (2014), *Le Patriarche* (2014), *Ecstasy* (2014), *Le Totem et les deux Chevaliers* (2014), *La Grotte aux résurrections* (2015) et de nombreuses autres œuvres sont autant de signes de l'activité ardente du peintre.

Depuis 2012 et jusqu'à 2015 des personnages fantomatiques, les *Schnarks*, peuplent l'atelier de l'artiste à Bruxelles ; bouffons dérisoires, ils sont la personnification difforme ou fantastique des songes les plus inquiétants, mais sont aussi les héros fabuleux, les êtres légendaires habitants de mondes inconnus. *L'Homme poubelle* (2014), *Démon* (2014), *Le Noir Chevalier* (2014) … ils sont élaborés à partir de chiffons et de matériaux récupérés, nés de l'objet, ils s'identifient dans une histoire ordinaire mais exceptionnelle aussi, que nous conte Julien Friedler, ils sont aussi les personnages de la légende que bâtit Julien Friedler qui sont exposés en même temps que les peintures.

2015 : trois expositions personnelles et trois participations à des expositions collectives marquent cette année 2015. *Amok & Kalinka* à la Riflemaker Gallery de Londres, solo show qui réunit des «peintures liquides», des peintures des années 2012-2014 et des installations *Schnarks.*

Une exposition personnelle, *Mania Boz*, à la Fondazione Mudima, Milan, accompagnée de la publication d'un catalogue avec un texte de Dominique Stella et Gianluca Ranzi. On y retrouve le travail de Julien Friedler, depuis *La Forêt de âmes* aux peintures les plus récentes, ainsi que les *Schnarks*. Un troisième événement se déroule cette même année. Trois œuvres de la série des paysages (2012-2014) et *La Chute du Joker* occupent la scène de l'ancienne église anglicane de Bordighera, alors que commentant ces œuvres Philippe Daverio et Julien Friedler dialoguent sur le thème de l'*artiste-shaman* (https://www.bordighera.tv/2016/06/spoleto-julien-friedler-%E2%80%9C-retro-boz%E2%80%9D/).

Toujours 2015, à Bologne, le récit de Friedler *La Vérité du Labyrinthe* sert de point d'appui à une exposition-dialogue entre Friedler et Maria Rebecca Ballestra à la galerie Spazio Testoni. Depuis 2010 Julien Friedler écrit *La Vérité du Labyrinthe.* «Les objectifs de *La Vérité du Labyrinthe* sont ceux de tout honnête homme en quête d'une spiritualité moderne» , écrit Friedler. «Au travers de mes expériences, de mes recherches, j'ai cherché à tisser un cheminement pour atteindre la paix et la sérénité. Pour nous sortir du chaos, nous devons, étape par étape, comprendre de quelle matière nous sommes tous faits. Au fil des textes, le bruit et la fureur s'éloignent.» À Venise, cette fois, *La Parole des Anges*, est exposée à l'occasion de la Biennale 2015 à Palazzo Molin. Cette exposition réunit de nouveau Julien Friedler et Maria Rebecca Ballestra, organisatrice de l'évènement, qui y dévoile son cycle de recherche *Journey into Fragility*. Le travail de Julien Friedler est aussi présent à la Bienal de las Fronteras Tamaulipas, à la frontière entre le Mexique et les États-Unis, première édition de ce festival d'art contemporain qui réunit 5 curateurs et 55 artistes de différentes parties du monde.

Sonia Bressler poursuit la production de documentaires autour de *Spirit of Boz*, cette fois à l'atelier de Bruxelles. Et les questionnaires continuent d'être proposés à la réflexion des participants aux performances.

2016 : l'exposition *Mania Boz* présentée à la Fondation Mudima à Milan poursuit son itinérance au Museo Civico di Villa Bassi à Abano Terme en Italie. Une scénographie plus «sépulcrale» présente uniquement les œuvres picturales et les *Schnarks*, dans les sous-sols voutés du musée. L'exposition très suggestive a parfois effrayé un public quelque peu dérouté.

Les œuvres prendront ensuite la route de Spoleto, où cet été 2016 le Museo Palazzo Collicola Arti Visive présente, sous le titre *Retro Boz*, une rétrospective complète du travail de Julien Friedler sous le commissariat de Gianluca Marziani. Mille cinq cent mètres carrés d'exposition déroulent les étapes successives de la production de l'artiste depuis les premières tableaux de 1998 jusqu'au dernier tableau *22 mars 2016* que l'artiste a peint le jour des attentats de l'aéroport de Zaventem, à Bruxelles. L'aspect sanglant du tableau, réalisé selon la technique des « coulures », communique cet effroi qui nous saisit tous, dans un monde en fureur. Ce monde, c'est ce que continue de peindre Julien Friedler. À l'occasion de cette exposition le supplément dominical du *Corriere della Sera* publie en pleine page de couverture l'œuvre *Totems* (2014).

La Forêt des âmes poursuit son chemin, les neuf colonnes sont présentées au Museoteatro della Commenda di Pré à Gênes à l'occasion d'une rencontre sur la paix. Et une conférence-exposition autour de quelques peintures, intitulée *La Forêt des âmes*, a lieu à l'Alliance française, Casino Venier, à Venise. « À travers son œuvre Julien Friedler dessine les fondements d'une mythologie contemporaine », annonce le communiqué, invitant chaque participant à remplir le questionnaire de *La Forêt des âmes*. Julien Friedler répond aux questions d'un public nombreux et curieux. Les participations à trois expositions collectives jalonnent cette année 2016 : International Art Project 2016, Cap d'Ail. Julien Friedler participe à la Foire de Bologne avec la galerie Spazio Testoni. À cette occasion la toile *Gilgamesh* est acquise par la Fondazione Casa della Divina Bellezza à Forza d'Agrò, en Sicile, et Julien Friedler est accueilli sur place à l'occasion de l'inauguration de la fondation où la toile est exposée.

La peinture occupe d'une manière prépondérante la vie de l'artiste. Il exécute dans une technique sauvage, entre graffiti et coulures, deux grands formats de 300 x 200 cm, exemples magistraux d'une technique désormais maîtrisée. *Le Phoenix* (2016), *Crucifixion* (2016) constituent le centre d'une production particulièrement intense.

2017 : l'installation *La Forêt des âmes* poursuit son périple, elle est présentée à Spoleto à la Chiesa Santi Giovanni e Paolo durant tout l'été, alors qu'au printemps elle figurait dans une exposition intitulée *Boz Legend* au Castello di Rivara-Museo d'Arte Contemporanea, Rivara (Turin). La rencontre avec Franz Paludetto, maître des lieux et personnage mythique du monde de l'art contemporain, fut l'occasion d'échanges nourris.

Performance et conférence à Gênes : l'évènement *Face to Face* est présenté au Museo Villa Croce de Gênes et à la galerie UniMediaModern. Au musée une performance *Give up* invite les spectateurs à donner un objet et une présentation de *Spirit of Boz* à partir de vidéos retrace l'aventure du *Boz*, alors qu'à la galerie UniMediaModern Julien Friedler rencontre le public et propose des questionnaires du *Tour du Boz en 80 ans*.

En septembre, à Knokke au « Manoir », siège de l'association *Spirit of Boz* en Belgique, Julien Friedler entame un cycle de conférence annuelle : « Les grandes conférences de *Spirit of Boz* ». Luc Ferry, ancien ministre français de la Culture, dialogue avec Julien Friedler sur le thème *Vices et faiblesses de nos démocraties*. Il s'agit ici d'interroger nos démocraties, de mesurer leur transformation et d'évoquer l'hypothèse d'un art de réenchantement ? Un accrochage des œuvres majeures de Julien Friedler accompagne ce moment, permettant d'y découvrir également la dernière production de l'artiste, *Le Maître des couleurs* (2017), tableau monumental tout en dripping et images furtives. Une série d'œuvres de cire de l'artiste italien Francesco Sena est présentée conjointement à l'évènement dans une des salles du « Manoir ».

2017 : sortie du livre *La Vérité du Labyrinthe* de Julien Friedler, chez Jacques Flament Éditions (série Philosophies). « Ce livre, affirme l'auteur, est une invitation au voyage intérieur, à la recherche de sérénité. Le monde autour de nous fuse, fusionne en tous sens. Il est donc plus qu'urgent de trouver un moyen pour renouer avec la paix intérieure et ainsi rétablir l'harmonie et l'équilibre du monde. Le livre sert de support à la pensée labyrinthique de l'artiste qui y puise aussi l'énergie de ses œuvres peintes.

2018 : est une année riche en expositions entre la Belgique et l'Italie. La première exposition, intitulée *Spirit of Boz paintings*, se déroule au Berlaymont Building, Commission Européenne de Bruxelles, sous le patronage de Carlos Moedas, Commissaire européen à la Recherche, Science et Innovation qui introduit le vernissage par un discours émouvant (https://www.julienfriedler.com/exposition/spirit-of-boz-paintings/). À cette occasion sont montrées une vingtaine de peintures de grands formats des années comprises entre 2012 à 2018. Julien Friedler présente son projet participatif du *Boz* avec l'ambition qu'il puisse s'intégrer dans un programme d'actions culturelles de l'Union Européenne.

Puis de février à mars, quelques œuvres de Julien Friedler accompagnent la présentation de la collection *Be Boz Be Art* (*Be Boz Be Art and Friedler's Paintings*), à la galerie Gliacrobati de Turin. Les objets, les dessins et peintures récoltés, au Togo, en Argentine, en Indonésie, en Chine… sont exposés afin d'illustrer les objectifs du projet du *Boz*, chaque participant au vernissage, chaque visiteur est invité à remplir le questionnaire de *La Forêt des âmes*. Conférence de Julien Friedler lors du vernissage – nombreuses participations.

Le cycle *La Parole des Anges* est montré à deux reprises cette année 2018. La première fois à la SRValverde Gallery à Bruxelles et la seconde fois, en mode muséal et donc avec des formats de plus grande dimension, à La Cité Miroir de Liège. La piscine qui occupait autrefois l'espace central de ce musée, offre aux œuvres monumentales de Friedler une scénographie spectaculaire qui se déploie sur le pourtour. Le communiqué rapporte : « Cet ensemble de tableaux développe, dans un langage crypté, toute une symbolique de signes dont émanent des œuvres que l'artiste charge d'une valeur méditative, véritable chemin conduisant à une paix intérieure qui se veut force de vie et de partage. »

L'installation *La Forêt des âmes* est montrée à Arezzo, Italie, dans l'exposition *Vibrations* qui se tient à la Chiesa della Madonna del Duomo Vecchio. En même temps que l'installation sont exposés, *All Over II – La Parole des Anges* (2002), *Ecce Homo* (2009), *Crucifixion* (2016) et *Le Maître des couleurs* (2017) démontrant que malgré leurs approches picturales assez éloignées, les tableaux de Friedler crée un harmonie et un équilibre qui souligne le sens de la pensée de l'artiste.

Dernière exposition personnelle de l'année : *Behind the world* qui a lieu au Complesso del Vittoriano à Rome. Cet espace d'exposition situé dans le Monument à Victor Emmanuel est au cœur de la cité romaine. Il offre une opportunité exceptionnelle à l'artiste de se confronter à deux maîtres du XXe siècle, présentés au même moment au musée. En effet au Vittoriano se déroulent alors une exposition dédiée à Andy Warhol et une autre à Jackson Pollock. *Behind the world* est l'occasion de montrer les derniers tableaux peints au cours de l'année 2018 : *Ode Satanique* (2018), *L'Autre* (2018) et *Corps et Artifices* (2018) sont trois tableaux de grand format. *Corps et Artifices* est peint selon la technique des coulées, alors que dans les deux autres tableaux le peintre adopte une matière plus âpre, plus écorchée, comme un retour aux techniques de la période des années 2010. Le parcours de l'exposition offre un vaste ensemble d'œuvres et en sa partie centrale sont installées les neuf colonnes de la *Forêt des âmes*. Plusieurs périodes de production picturale se côtoient ici démontrant l'obstination de Friedler dans la permanence de sa recherche. Il

ne s'arrête jamais à un style, il n'entretient aucune habitude picturale. Son art évolue sans cesse, son inspiration demeure intacte. Chaque tableau entre dans le corpus global de sa production dont l'unité est la référence à une philosophie de vie et de pensée que l'artiste résume dans le *Boz*. Pour toute la durée de l'exposition les questionnaires laissés à disposition des visiteurs ont été remplis, chacun laissant une trace de son passage. La récolte fut abondante. Des trois mille visiteurs environ, six cent soixante-douze ont répondu aux six questions de l'enquête du *Boz*.

Toujours en 2018 deux expositions collectives en Italie autour de *La Vérité du Labyrinthe* : *Labrys, The Truth of the Labyrinth*, Parco Basaglia et autres lieux de la ville de Gorizia, et *Labrys, The Truth of the Labyrinth*, Spazio Testoni, Bologne, toujours en collaboration avec Maria Rebecca Ballestra qui illustre dans son travail formel un labyrinthe tracé avec les lettres et phrases du livre de Friedler.

A Paris Julien Friedler participe à l'Outsider Art Fair avec la galerie Gliacrobati de Turin, proposant un mur d'œuvres sur papier de la série des *Voyages*.

En septembre nouvelle rencontre à Knokke pour « Les grandes conférences de *Spirit of Boz* », avec la participation de Pascal Bruckner et Eric Sadin sur le thème *Identité et Citoyenneté, avant et après Internet.* Documentée par une vidéo : https://vimeo.com/307944894.

Julien Friedler poursuit son travail pictural. Une importante modification s'opère dans les thématiques et aussi la stylistique des tableaux. 2018 marque le début d'un nouveau cycle de peintures que Friedler intitule *Mapping*. C'est aussi l'année où Julien Friedler rencontre Carlo Silvestrin qui sera le producteur de l'exposition *È finita la Commedia* à Venise, Chiesa San Samuele (2022), durant la période de la Biennale.

2019-2021 : l'artiste ne quitte plus l'atelier, retraite contrainte due aux conditions sanitaires. Ce lieu de réclusion porte à la méditation et l'influence. Il réalise l'installation *Les Pierrots*. Son art s'apaise tout en conservant cependant l'esprit du mystère et de la légende qu'il construit dans cette oscillation constante entre dramaturgie et explosion vitale. Dans la série *Mapping* l'expression visuelle suit un projet qui dépasse toute solution graphique ou esthétique, elle rejoint une recherche qui se rattache à des problématiques certes philosophiques et spirituelles mais surtout picturales. Le monde de Friedler est intuitif et son art, essentiellement lié à une attitude mentale, est la forme exprimée d'une contemplation intérieure et d'une expérience de vie, transfigurée par l'expérience de la peinture. Car il s'agit ici véritablement de peinture : une matière parfois âpre, parfois rayonnante, conductrice de flux visibles ou invisibles, d'énergies vives qui palpitent et naissent de la couleur. Lumières et couleurs émergent de la toile dans une sensation explosive ou pacifiée selon des contrastes qui figurent un souffle, une respiration tendue vers le mystère de la Vie. Il s'agit ici d'impressions abstraites.

Durant cette période particulière quelques projets d'expositions voient le jour.

En 2019 *Les Innocents* sont présentés au Forte Santa Tecla à San Remo. L'installation occupe la cour centrale de cette prison désaffectée, l'effet est saisissant. Le succès est au rendez-vous, plus de 3000 personnes visitent l'exposition au cours du mois de mai. Le cahier, mis à disposition du public, a permis de recueillir les réflexions émues des visiteurs.

2020 : *La Forêt des âmes* est présentée au Beffroi de l'église Saint-Germain-l'Auxerrois, Mairie du 1er Arrondissement, à Paris. Devant la Colonnade de Perrault du Louvre les portes du Beffroi s'ouvrent sur le déploiement des neuf colonnes. Les visiteurs sont invités à remplir le questionnaire de *La Forêt des âmes*. L'installation voyage depuis désormais plus de dix ans. Le nombre de questionnaires recueillis dans le monde au cours de ces années s'élève à plus de 75 000. Ces derniers, répertoriés et dupliqués, vont désormais pouvoir rejoindre la destination qui leur est réservée et constituer le cœur de colonnes monumentales érigées dans plusieurs points de la planète. Nous suggérons Venise comme point de départ de ce nouveau projet…

Deux expositions *Mapping* ont lieu, en pleine période de pandémie et de confinement : l'une à Palazzo Libera, Villa Lagarina (Rovereto) et l'autre à la Fondazione Sant'Elia, Loggiato di San Bartolomeo de Palerme. A Palerme le commissariat de l'exposition est aussi assuré par Gianluca Marziani. Ce-dernier écrit : « *Mapping* est un titre parfaitement adapté à la géographie "chromosomique" de Friedler. Des centaines de tableaux qui sont disposés comme des particules aléatoires sans centre de perspective, des acides nucléiques idéaux (les éléments qui composent la double hélice de l'ADN) qui créent de multiples noyaux à chaque fois inégaux, confirmant cette dimension inclusive du corpus, d'une œuvre unique gigantesque dont émerge l'énergie épiphanique de Babylone et la puissance cathartique de Shiva. » Dans la ville et même en Sicile, *Mapping* est la première exposition muséale organisée après le confinement. La foule des visiteurs s'y presse par petits groupes de quinze personnes, afin de suivre les explications enflammées de Marziani. La presse se fait l'écho enthousiaste de l'évènement. Le 18 septembre 2020 à Turin, au Palazzo Barolo, Julien

Friedler participe à l'hommage rendu à Maria Rebecca Ballestra décédée dans l'année. Il évoque leur amitié et leur complicité de travail, à cette occasion est projetée une vidéo *La guaritrice* à laquelle participe Friedler et dans laquelle à travers trois performances Maria Rebecca Ballestra évoque sa lutte contre la maladie, la souffrance. « Exister n'est pas seulement une chose facile à faire, mais c'est aussi une chose difficile à comprendre. Vous venez au monde sans l'avoir demandé, et vous êtes presque toujours obligé de le quitter contre votre volonté… », écrit-elle.

En 2021, à la Galleria Civica Cavour di Padova, pendant les deux mois d'été, *Legends-Mapping II*, propose une nouvelle sélection d'œuvres du cycle *Mapping* (https://www.7goldtelepadova.tv/2021/07/22/friedler-in-mostra/). L'artiste, contraint par la pandémie à l'enfermement, peint avec acharnement. Les tableaux *Mapping* sont l'expression d'une méditation qui se matérialise dans la couleur, celle-ci apparaissant comme l'âme génératrice, véritable matrice mère qui fusionne tout en un esprit vivant. La vie est pulsation, respiration, damnation, salvation. Telle est l'œuvre, « une conjonction des contraires, une écriture paradoxale, une inscription des flux qui traverse l'Esprit », écrit Friedler dans *La Vérité du Labyrinthe*.

Anthologie

Sonia Bressler
Julien Friedler, témoin du siècle (extraits)

Ma première rencontre avec Julien Friedler remonte
à février 2006. Une pièce immense, son atelier en
plein cœur de Bruxelles, j'allais et venais entre ses
installations *Les Innocents* et ses toiles se faisant.
Son œuvre immense, mouvante, changeante,
perpétuelle. Un parfait équilibre d'inexactitudes,
de coïncidences, de regards croisés sur l'histoire
le temps, le dépassement de soi et des autres.
Comprendre que l'art doit se faire malgré la pluie, les
guerres, les atrocités, les religions, les droits. Malgré
soi, malgré les autres. Humain, trop humain, l'art
se cache, se révolte, dénonce, théorise. L'œuvre de
Julien Friedler, j'ai la chance de la découvrir sur deux
années, de l'interroger. C'est cette rencontre que je
livre en quelques clichés.

Sommes-nous encore capables de parler d'innocence ?
Ce dimanche à Bruxelles. Février 2006. L'Histoire
n'aurait-elle pas de solution de continuité ? J'ai joué
sur les planches, dans l'atelier de Julien Friedler.
Couleurs, éclatements. À première vue, il faut se jouer
des codes, des imprévus. Puis pas à pas, l'emprise
de l'œuvre se fait plus grande. Plus monumentale.
Quelque chose de notre chimie y bouge. Mais quoi ?
Pas à pas, puis clichés après clichés, deux années
se sont écoulées au rythme de la création, au rythme
de la pensée. Une pensée se faisant, se nourrissant
d'un hier et dévorant un demain. Entre mysticisme et
passions (in)humaines. Les siècles passent avec leurs
monstruosités, les destructions… Nous errons d'une
fin de civilisation à une autre. Fin de l'hégémonie
américaine aujourd'hui, éclatement des blocs et
pourtant au milieu de notre errance, une voix pointe,
un œil s'incline, une main dessine et déchaîne. Julien
Friedler au milieu de l'humanité en pagaille. Il se joue
des codes, il invente, perpétue la réflexion, propage le
désordre, remue nos sensibilités. Une œuvre unique
parfois sombre, parfois lumineuse. Avec cette même
certitude : la lumière qui s'attarde devient l'ombre
d'une autre lumière. Nous sommes à Bruxelles dans
ses ateliers. Nous pourrions être ici, là, ou ailleurs.
Balancier fragile de l'espace et du temps. Je joue. Tu
joues. Vous jouez. Nous jouons. Mais eux, jouent-ils ?
Ceux privés de tout, ceux dont le rien fait un grand
tout. Eux dont le regard a été pris quelque part dans
un amas de poussière(s). Eux qui sont-ils ? C'est
vous, c'est moi si nous regardons au présent ? Mais si
nous regardons au passé, ce sont ceux exilés, tués,
abandonnés au coin d'une route pendant la guerre.

Laquelle ? La seconde guerre mondiale. Sans aucun
doute, si nous regardons l'installation des *Innocents*
de Julien Friedler. Photographie d'une famille.
Sourires éternels. Poussières d'exil. Vieux rêves
enfouis ? Le temps est distendu dans cet espace
barbelé.

La nécessité de témoigner
Nous sommes en quête de la lumière, de la vérité.
Mais est-elle une ? Multiple ? Valse incertaine des
choses, des petits bruits du quotidien. Les cris des
enfants dans la cour de récréation. Le souffle d'un
enfant endormi. Les piaillements des oiseaux au petit
matin. La première brume. Les premières pluies du
printemps. Une porte claque. Le sang se déploie.
Tâche de couleur. Fuite de la vie. Un cœur s'arrête.
Un monstre naît. Il faut qu'en ce début de XXIe siècle,
une personne témoigne, avec conviction, mais surtout
ses tripes, avec sa sensibilité, et, expose son vécu.
Julien Friedler dresse une œuvre bouleversante qui
voit le monde à travers sa lucidité, sa course à sa
perte, sa course à la destruction de soi et des autres.
Chaque toile, chaque installation, ici découvertes sont
un œil ouvert sur les yeux fermés. Œil fictif qui fouille
l'existant pour lui faire dire son être. Chaque création
de Julien Friedler est une attention témoignant,
chargée de l'inquisition qui voudrait aboutir à la
certitude de l'identité infaisable, œil braqué sur le
dedans, vers le dessous, mais aussi vers l'extérieur,
au fait de toute l'aventure. Trajet attentif vers soi,
les autres et le monde. Il faut risquer la distance de
l'ailleurs pour se rencontrer et témoigner avec force.

Gino Di Maggio
Julien Friedler et l'étincelle de vie

Combien de fois ai-je cité la réponse que Robert
Filliou fit à la question «Qu'est-ce que l'art» et la
réponse synthétique, paradoxale, géniale : «L'art est
la chose qui rend la vie plus intéressante que l'art
lui-même». C'est donc la vie même qui constitue le
cœur de la question, et c'est de la vie que l'on part
et à la vie que l'on retourne, l'art servant de facteur
vectoriel, tel un pont jeté entre deux rives pour les
relier et échanger émotions, espérances, révolte et
conscience, dialogue et tous les possibles. En tout
cela l'art devient une des composantes les plus
importantes de la vie, et donc cette chose ou cet
ensemble de choses et d'activités que l'on appelle
créatives dont nous nommons, par convention, le
résultat, art. Et ceci, par maints aspects, apparaît
comme une idée dérangeante, surtout pour l'artiste
que l'on imagine presque comme un démiurge tout

puissant, capable de créer de manière autonome, momifié dans sa tour d'ivoire et détaché des relations avec ses semblables et avec le monde.
Julien Friedler, avec son travail est au contraire la preuve vivante que l'artiste opère constamment en contact avec le monde et, bien que son point de vue soit individuel et résulte de sa propre capacité d'observation et de ses expériences vécues, son projet se diffuse au-delà de lui-même, dans une dynamique tournée vers l'autre, et se présente comme une expérience fondamentale de vie.
Après tout, l'artiste est authentiquement ainsi, non seulement parce qu'il se déclare et s'auto définit artiste, mais parce qu'il ressent l'urgence presque obsessionnelle de le faire, de créer constamment et toujours. Et ceci constitue presque une des caractéristiques principales de ce que j'ai appelé, me souvenant de Giacomo Leopardi, l'immensité de l'énergie qui sous des formes particulières investit l'existence et la rend diablement vivante et que je retrouve non seulement dans les installations et la peinture de Friedler mais surtout dans son projet visionnaire qui réussit à faire converger, se confronter et se rapprocher des mondes lointains et des vies parallèles. J'ai l'impression que tout ceci arrive parce que ceux qui se sentent et s'auto-définissent artistes comme ceux qui ressentent la prédisposition innée et se définissent comme scientifiques sont ceux-là mêmes qui mieux que les autres ont conservé la mémoire biologique de ce que nous sommes et de notre provenance originelle, une forme de mémoire biologique que, de manière évidente, la grande majorité d'entre nous a perdue mais qui grâce à l'art revient sous la forme d'une étincelle d'énergie qui se rend à nouveau visible.
(extrait du catalogue *Mania Boz*, Mudima, Milan, 2015)

Norbert Hillaire
Fragments

Modernité et Postmodernité : mise au point
Friedler est un homme du salut, mais de quoi ? Est-il moderne ou postmoderne ?
Ce qui est à l'œuvre ici, c'est une régression qui s'annonce comme telle : non pas une régression narcissique, mais l'épreuve d'une double déception, déception de la modernité et déception de la postmodernité. Évidemment Friedler est de prime abord un peintre postmoderne, tant sont nombreux les signes, les références, les techniques qui l'identifient *a priori* au territoire de la postmodernité : *bad painting*, graff, etc. Pourtant, même si ses emprunts à Basquiat, à Penk sont évidents (en

même temps que certains rappels de Cobra) et attestent de cette esthétique du « diversel » et non plus de l'universel qui fonde la postmodernité, c'est paradoxalement du côté de certains modernes que se trouverait plutôt la clé de cette œuvre (mais on a pu dire à juste titre que Basquiat était le dernier des modernes). Régression au sens de Paul Klee, par exemple vers une enfance qui vient questionner et l'histoire et son involution qui culmine dans le postmoderne. Mais qui n'est en aucune manière un infantilisme : « La fable de l'infantilisme de mon dessin doit avoir son origine dans les productions linéaires où j'essaye d'allier l'idée de l'objet – par exemple, un homme – à la pure représentation de l'élément ligne. Pour montrer l'homme tel qu'il est, il m'aurait fallu un tel fouillis de lignes parfaitement déroutant. Le résultat n'a été alors une représentation pure de l'élément, mais un brouillage tel qu'on ne s'y serait pas retrouvé. À part ça, il n'est certainement pas dans mes intentions de montrer l'homme tel qu'il est, mais tel qu'il pourrait être aussi. De cette manière, je peux parvenir à associer ma vision du monde au pur exercice de l'art. »
Les accents modernes de ces lignes n'ont rien de naïf, de régressif et témoignent au contraire d'une grande sophistication dans la recherche d'une épure quasi minimaliste de l'œuvre d'art (ils sont en ce sens, comme d'ailleurs les peluches, poupées, oursons utilisés par Friedler dans ses œuvres aux antipodes de l'usage fait de certains de ces mêmes accessoires par d'autres artistes contemporains, clairement postmodernes).

Postmoderne pourtant
Post moderne pourtant, au sens, à l'ordre binaire de l'opposition de l'autre et du moi, Friedler vient substituer (par exemple dans des peintures faites par d'autres et intégrées à l'œuvre) la complexité du rhizome qui tisse les différences et cette « altérité intime », comme l'appelle encore Marc Augé, rend proprement impensable l'idée même « d'individualité absolue ».
(in *Double Vue, 50 fragments pour Julien Friedler*, Somogy Éditions d'Art, Paris, 2012)

Gianluca Marziani
Retro Boz

Julien Friedler est un artiste qui échappe aux catégories et aux systèmes élémentaires. Lorsqu'en février dernier je suis entré dans son atelier à Bruxelles, j'en ai eu la confirmation : face à moi se tenait un *personnage nucléaire*, un de ces titans du flux quotidien, capable de gérer le chaos anthropique, de survoler le marasme du monde pour conférer un nouvel ordre aux choses, selon des méthodes théoriques, au développement musculaire certain. Friedler est un intellectuel d'excellence qui, à un certain moment, à l'accomplissement de la catharsis philosophique, a choisi le camp fangeux de la vie réelle et totale. Naturellement, l'approche imaginative reste prédominante, le travail se développant désormais à l'intérieur d'un *système organique*. Choisir son camp n'admettait pour lui aucun compromis : créer afin de mieux comprendre l'humanité et ses nécessités impérieuses, capter le potentiel des individus, leurs espaces de croissance et d'échange. Renoncer à l'olympe académique signifiait étendre le regard au-delà de l'écriture, du narcissisme de l'auteur, de l'individu et de l'œuvre en elle-même. Cela signifiait se connecter aux voix hétérogènes du monde, aux communautés isolées, aux cultures africaines, aux groupes minoritaires et capter les différences et les divergences d'opinion. Le sujet était finalement le monde réel, celui de la vie telle qu'elle est, vécue, supportée, partagée…

Quand je parle d'*organique*, il s'agit d'un processus créatif se rapprochant des activités essentielles du corps humain : manger, mastiquer, digérer, expulser et régénérer au sein du moteur continu du flux biologique. Le corps est une machine complexe qui impose un soutien alimentaire et relève d'un cycle régénérateur ; ainsi l'art de Friedler est un mécanisme révélateur, nécessitant un processus participatif et humanisé, d'où disparaît le principe d'ordre et de clarté, caractéristique du contrôle artificiel, laissant place aux effets fondamentaux du vrai. Le résultat implique un apparent marasme dans lequel objets et matières contribuent au bruissement du monde, se souillant des mêmes couleurs que nous retrouvons dans les tableaux, jusqu'à s'étendre au-delà de leur nature originelle, modifiant le sentiment d'espace, perturbant la perception même des vibrations des toiles. Le tableau et les objets participent d'un même dialogue soutenu, sans distinction, atteignant le point où l'échange devient acte générateur, où l'attraction entre peinture, couleurs et formes donne naissance à des énergies à émission prolongée. Dans ce sens, « organique » implique une germination continue, une production de sens (et contresens) qui élève la température figurative et laisse apparente la structure préparatoire, comme s'il n'existait pas d'épilogue, comme si toute fin était une pause momentanée dans le cycle du monde. Aux vues du magma palpitant des tableaux, de la densité intense des signes et des codes, du dispersement des couleurs par les fluides, j'appellerais cela le *métabolisme iconique*.

Une production qui recrée une esthétique vivante, définie et en même temps indéfinissable, simple et énigmatique, transformable et adaptable, directe mais métaphorique. Un métabolisme qui ressemble à un laboratoire chimique placé entre les mains d'un illuminé visionnaire au sein d'une montagne sacrée. Si je devais choisir un artiste pour parler du concept de *catharsis*, Julien Friedler excellerait à l'illustrer. Son art consiste en une purification systémique au cœur des remugles du monde globalisé, un acte générateur continu qui métabolise le chaos par un usage alchimique des matériaux, des couleurs, fragments, citations… Ce n'est pas par hasard qu'ayant été élève de Jacques Lacan, années après années, de symbiose académique et intellectuelle, notre ami finit un jour par refuser ce monde, consacrant l'art visuel comme approche privilégiée de sa recherche et de sa finalité jusqu'à en faire son nouveau principe de vie et de révélation.

Chaque tournant majeur de l'histoire de Friedler est cathartique mais aussi chacun des chemins empruntés par son travail. Chaque fois que l'on voit que le pathos augmente, le ton de la dramaturgique friedlérienne s'élève jusqu'au point d'implosion, ce moment qui définit la vraie nature d'une vision radicale. L'artiste belge utilise la détonation des sentiments, la passion immodérée pour la vie et la beauté, recherche l'équilibre à travers une fuite extrême qui ne prévoit aucune médiation. Il aspire à la plénitude de l'idée, à la circularité du dessin, engendrant une filiation complexe à transmettre aux autres, libérant la vision de la vie biologique de l'être, instillant des valeurs au patrimoine artistique en tant que bien commun à partager : au-delà de l'artiste lui-même, de l'œuvre, du cycle narratif en cours.
(extrait du catalogue *Retro Boz*, Mudima, Milan, 2016)

Gianluca Ranzi
Au pas de dance pour concevoir le futur

…La danse de Friedler le porte ainsi à naviguer alentour en un voyage dont le but ne semble plus être la destination finale mais le voyage lui-même, le menant au-delà des colonnes d'Hercule de sa propre existence. Parce que Friedler sait bien que l'attachement à soi-même augmente l'opacité de la vie et qu'à l'intérieur de soi-même on ne peut que perdre la vision de l'art. Pour cette raison, tout comme ses toiles qui voyagent au-delà d'elles-mêmes, grouillant de vitalité animiste exprimée en un signe ou une matière chromatique animée de sa propre vie jaillissant dans chaque coulure, Friedler lui aussi se dédouble, se multiplie dans une généalogie

de personnages, *Jack Balance*, *Le Boz*, *Le Scribe*, *L'Homme Miroir* qui rendent compte de son désir d'extraire de lui-même et de la singularité de son histoire pour retrouver dans une interdisciplinarité complexe un grand nombre de points de vue, d'apports, de références, de sollicitations, de contradictions, qui ont fait écrire à Norbert Hillaire : « *Le Boz* c'est une manière de faire des mondes ». Ce n'est pas par hasard que les mythes et les mystères habitent depuis toujours le travail de Friedler, qui de manière subtilement ambiguë demeure suspendu en équilibre entre récits alimentés par sa propre histoire confrontée à celles des autres et transcendance de l'Histoire qui se réalise dans le recours aux mythes dans lesquels l'aspect négatif du quotidien peut trouver un sens et une réhabilitation culturelle ou comme dirait Friedler, produire un supplément d'âme là où règne la mésaventure. Le travail de Friedler, tant du point de vue pictural qu'installation, élabore ainsi des seuils à franchir dans un balancement d'aller et de retour comme s'il voulait affirmer que les barrières n'existent que pour être dépassées devenant ainsi des points de contact, des ponts, des barques, des chaînes de vie. Ces travaux, qui dans certains cas sont des projets développés à grande échelle, se basent sur des collaborations et l'intégration d'expériences extérieures (comme dans le projet du *Clochard Céleste* qui recueille les dessins de groupes sociaux en difficulté), sur des dédoublements et des superpositions (dans *Give up*, les assemblages naissent du dialogue qui l'artiste établit avec certaines communautés de référence comme le village de Tevogan au Togo ou encore avec de jeunes artistes belges) ; ils se basent aussi sur des sollicitations dirigées vers l'extérieur et qui comme un boomerang reviennent ensuite à leur base (c'est le cas du projet déjà cité de la *Forêt des âmes*). Tous ces seuils ne sont plus des barrières ou des obstacles, mais un espace de transition dans lequel, comme dit Benjamin, « sont compris mutation, passage, mers, sens ».
(extrait du catalogue *Mania Boz*, Mudima, Milan, 2015)

Erno Vroonen
Le Monde du Boz

Qu'est-ce que l'art et à quoi sert-il dans notre société ? La discussion n'est pas nouvelle et elle a été argumentée de manière récurrente de bien nombreuses fois. C'est, sans aucun doute, le privilège de nos sociétés démocratiques, mais aussi celui de l'art lui-même, que de pouvoir se dresser

contre une doctrine qui se veut absolue ou un point de vue restrictif. Friedler, en tant qu'auteur et écrivain puis en tant que clown, affirme dans son *Livre du Boz* que l'art, plus que toute autre discipline, possède la capacité de comprendre la vraie nature des choses et par conséquent l'essence même de la vie. Cette déclaration peut être considérée comme étant trop restrictive, ou trop définitive, notamment dans le domaine de l'art. Friedler, cependant, ne se considère pas comme faisant partie du débat. Il se sent comme une sorte d'outsider dont l'ambition est de mettre en évidence les excès du système dans lequel le prix de marché d'une œuvre d'art est devenu plus important que la valeur intrinsèque de l'œuvre elle-même. L'Art peut-il se réduire à n'être qu'un symbole de puissance financière ? Ou l'art peut-il avoir une autre signification ? Friedler essaie de déterminer la pleine valeur de l'art à travers son travail. Il élargit ses critères d'action et, ce faisant, il rend l'art accessible à un public de non « initiés ». Cela explique pourquoi il présente des œuvres là où elles sont le moins attendues, dans des lieux insolites, ou expose un type d'art totalement en décalage par rapport aux doctrines généralement admises. Qui détermine quel est le bon – ou le mauvais – contexte pour l'art après tout ? L'artiste laisse la question ouverte. Cependant, Friedler exige plus de l'art et donc de lui-même. Pour que l'art ait une plus grande signification culturelle qu'il n'en a actuellement, il doit agir au-delà des limitations restrictives actuellement établies, relever les défis qui s'offrent à lui et développer de nouveaux signifiants qui pourraient avoir un sens nouveau pour une société future. La réalisation de cette ambition est indissociable de la prise de conscience qu'un grand vide s'est installé au cœur de la société actuelle qui aspire à trouver un nouveau sens à sa raison d'être. L'œuvre de Julien Friedler invite à la contemplation et à la méditation. Il peint des figures chamaniques, des civilisations primitives ou anciennes, et des signes familiers aussi bien qu'extraterrestres, afin de sonder de nouveaux cheminements de conscience.
(extrait de *Julien Friedler Be Boz, Part III*, éditions du Chaman, 2008)